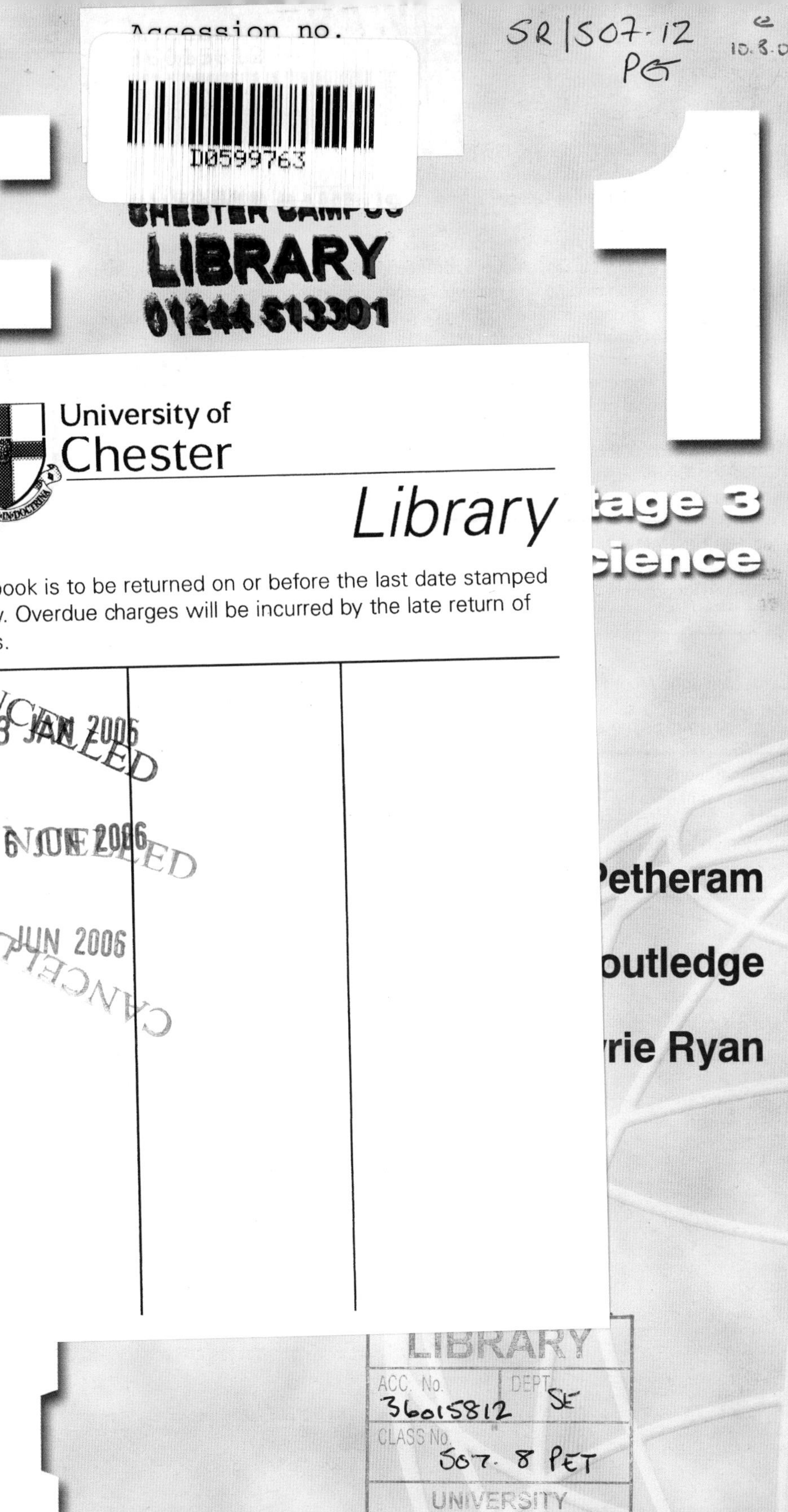
Key Stage 3
Science
Petheram
Routledge
Ryan

Published in 2002 by:
Nelson Thornes Ltd
Delta Place
27 Bath Road
CHELTENHAM
GL53 7TH
United Kingdom

02 03 04 05 06 / 10 9 8 7 6 5 4 3 2 1

A catalogue record for this book is available from the British Library

ISBN 0 7487 6792 4

Illustrations by Lisa Berkshire, Ian West and Ian Foulis & Associates
Page make-up by Tech Set Ltd

Printed and bound in Italy by Canale

Contents

Biology

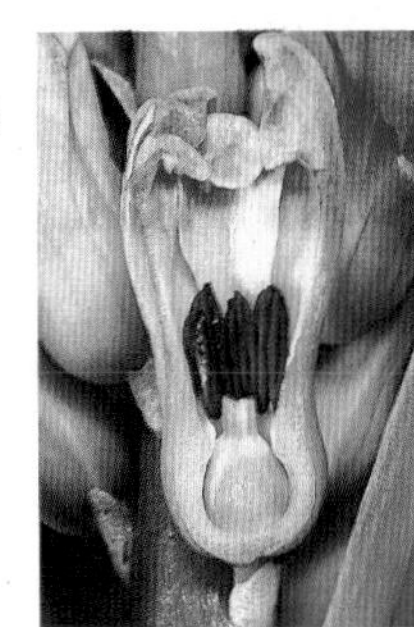

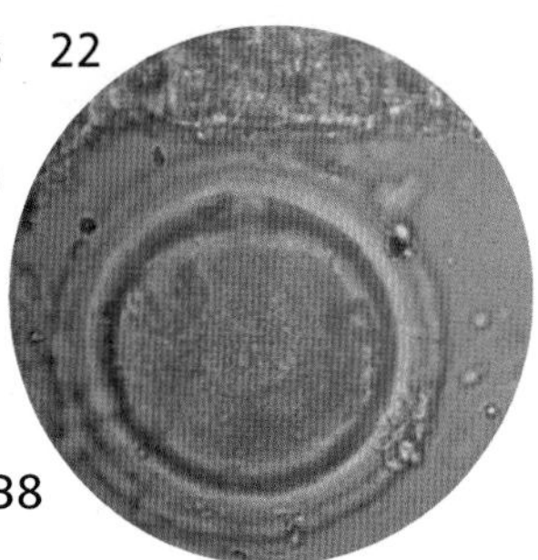

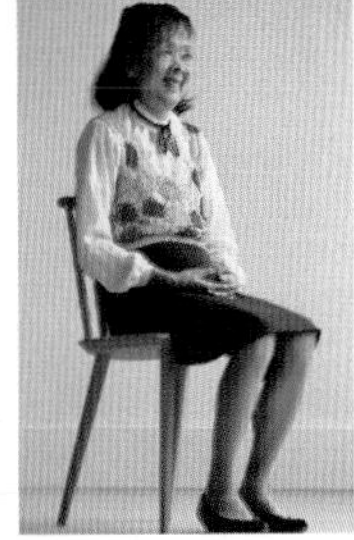

Chemistry

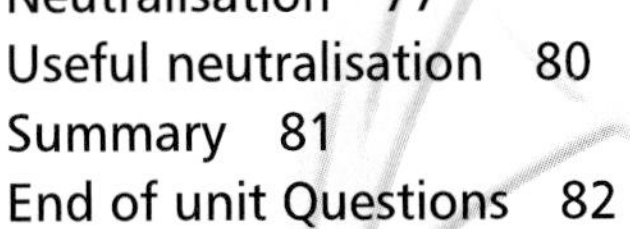

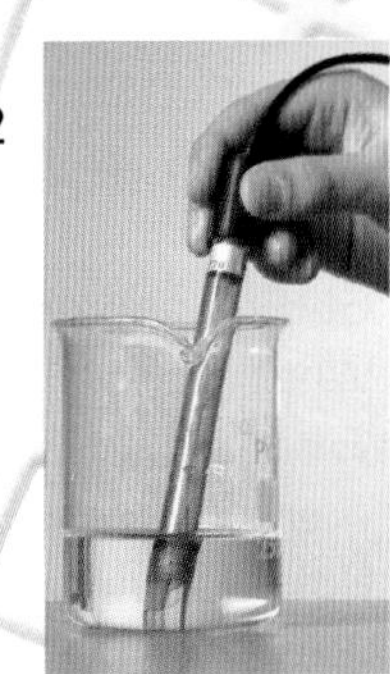

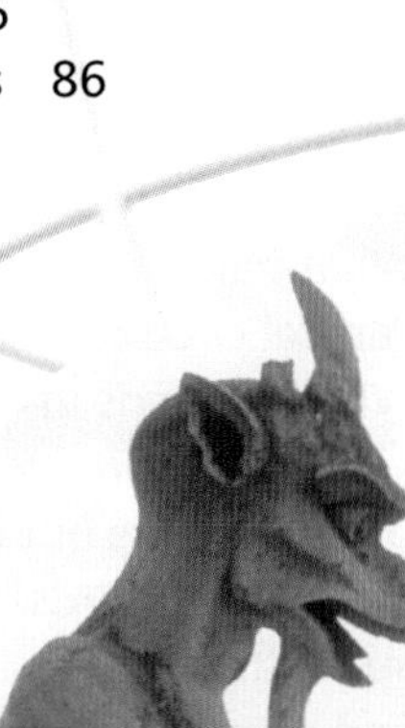

7G Particles 97

7H Solutions 107

Physics

7I Energy resources 123

7J Electrical circuits 139

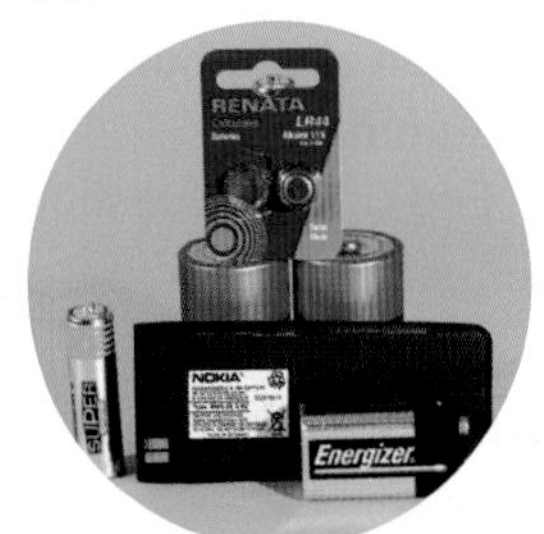

7K Forces and their effects 153

7L The solar system and beyond 169

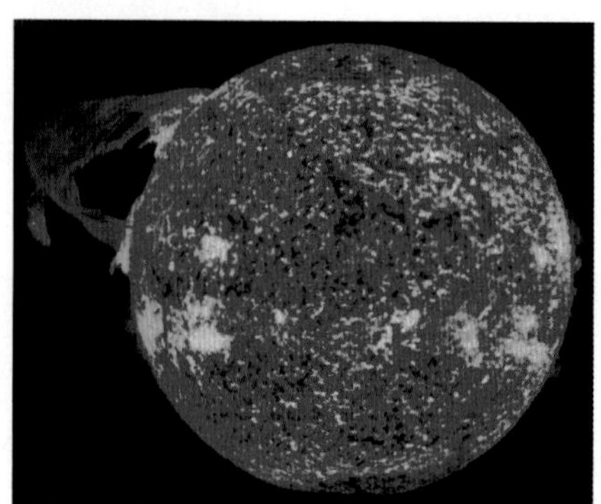

7A Cells

Introduction

Almost all living things, including animals and plants, are made of cells. Some, like humans, are made of billions of cells. In this unit you will find out a lot more about cells and what they do. You will find out how new cells form and how they make up organisms.

You already know

- the names and functions of many of the organs of animals and plants

In this topic you will learn

- that cells are the basic units of life
- that cells are organised into tissues from which organs are made
- about cell structure and the differences between plant and animal cells
- about the functions of some cells

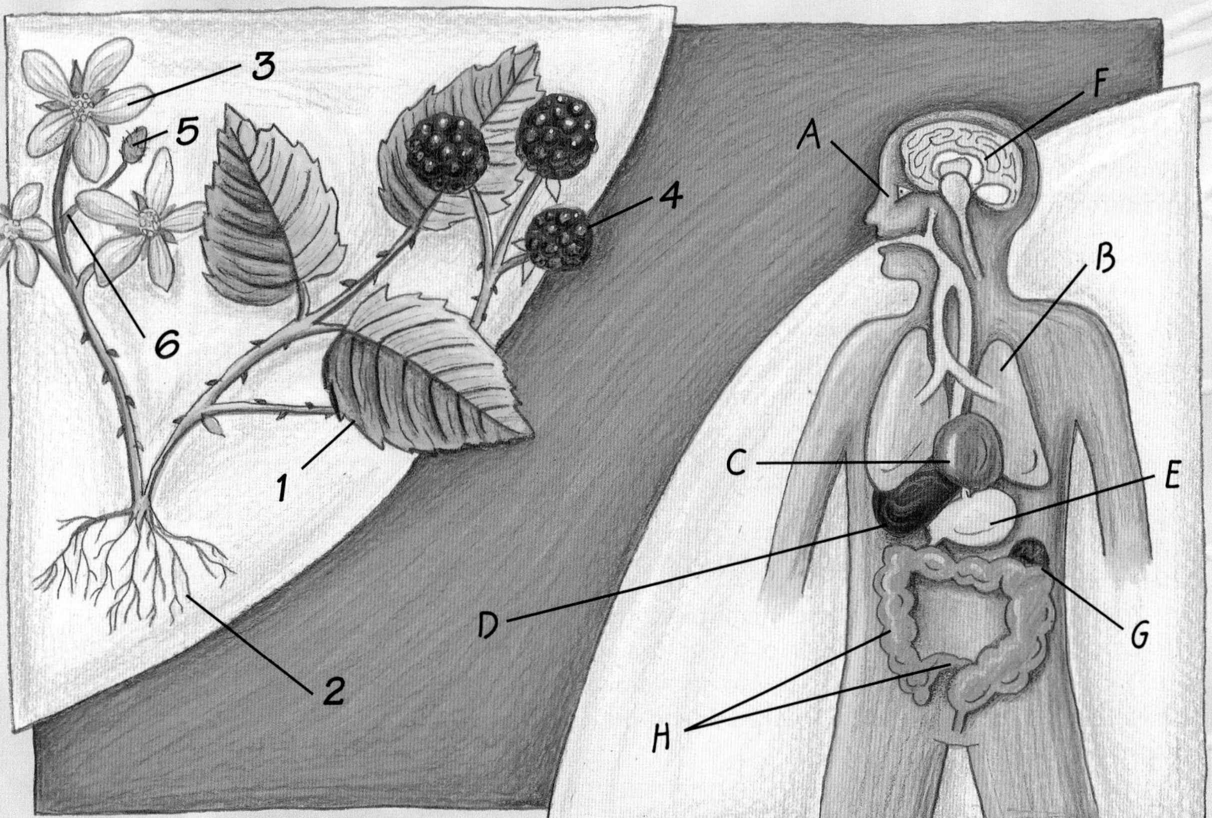

1 What can you remember?

Look at the two diagrams above. Write down the name of each labelled organ and its function. You could make a table of your information or you could try to display it in a way that would help others to learn about animal and plant organs.

A1 Having a closer look

YOU WILL LEARN!

- how to use a microscope properly
- how to make your own slides and observe them using a microscope
- how to make accurate drawings of what you see through a microscope
- how animal and plant cells are different

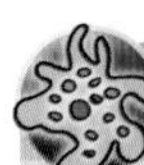

1 Using a magnifying glass

Use a magnifying glass or a hand lens to look at some objects around you. The skin on the back of your hand, the tip of a pencil or the surface of your desk are all good places to start but find some more. Try to draw some of the things you can see.

A magnifying glass helps you to see things that are already visible to the naked eye. To see really small things you need to use a microscope. All microscopes have the same basic parts although there are lots of different types. Yours may look different from the one in the diagram.

A microscope needs to shine a bright light onto the **specimen** you are looking at. Some microscopes have a light built in. Others have a mirror to reflect light onto the specimen.

Your teacher will show you how to set up and focus the microscope so that you can look at your specimen. You will also have to make a slide of your specimen before you can look at it.

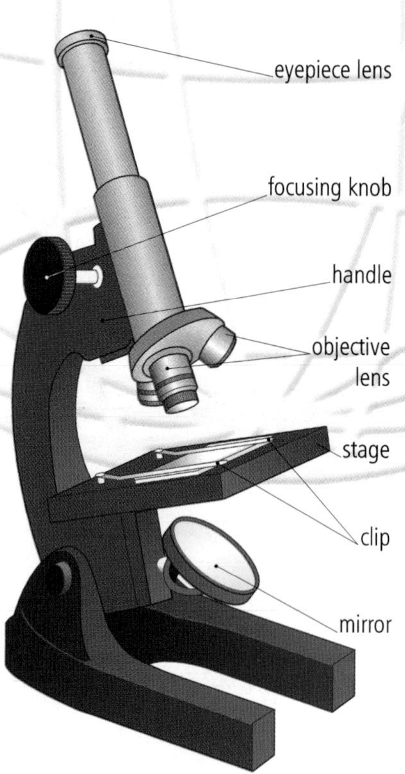

Parts of a microscope

Magnification

It is important for a scientist to know how much bigger a specimen looks through a microscope. This is called the **magnification**.

To work out the magnification, look at the eyepiece lens. It will tell you how much it magnifies (×5, ×10, etc.). Now look at the objective lens, making sure you look at the one you are actually using. It will also tell you the magnification. Multiply the magnification of the eyepiece by the magnification of the objective lens. This tells you how much bigger the specimen looks through the microscope.

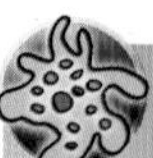

2 Looking through a microscope

Try making slides of some of these: 1 cm^2 piece of newspaper, a grain of salt or sugar, or a hair. Draw what you see. Try different magnifications. Next to each drawing you do write a label saying what you looked at and the magnification you used.

How big is it?

Put the edge of a clear ruler on the microscope stage. Look at it through the microscope. How many millimetres is it across the **field of view**? Try to use this information to estimate the size of the objects you have drawn.

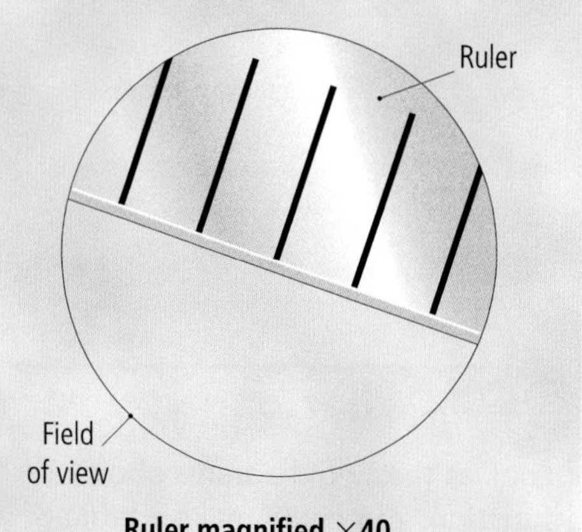

Ruler magnified ×40

Looking at cells

Robert Hooke was born in 1635 on the Isle of Wight. In 1665 he made himself a microscope. He cut very thin slices from a piece of cork and looked at them through his microscope. He noticed that there were lots of spaces in the cork, each one surrounded by a wall. He thought they looked like the cells where monks lived in a monastery. He drew what he saw and published his drawings in a book called *Micrographia*.

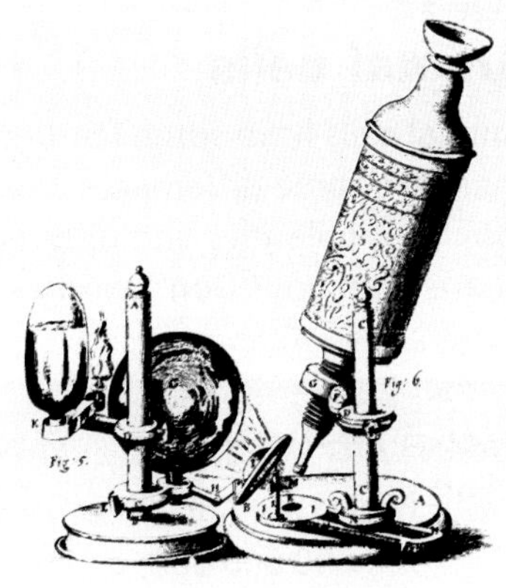

Robert Hooke's microscope

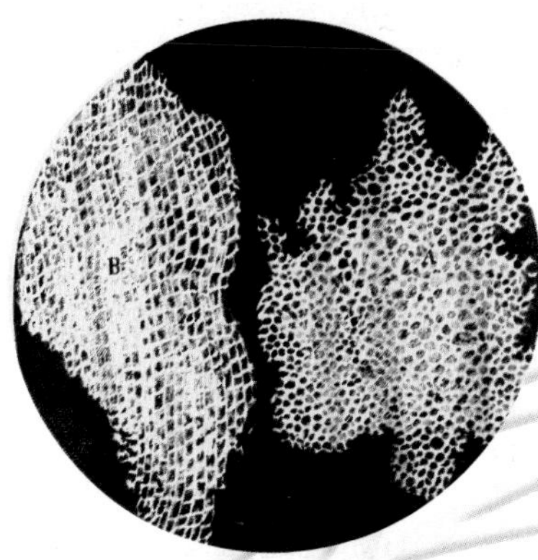

How Robert Hooke drew cork cells

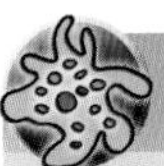

3 Robert Hooke

Find out more about Robert Hooke. Get information from books, CD-ROMS and the Internet. Use the information you find to write about his life and what he did, especially what he found out about cells. You could present your work as a cartoon, a newspaper article, a poster or a computer presentation. Perhaps you could put Robert Hooke in a class book about famous scientists.

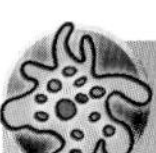

4 Make your own plant cell slide

1. Peel away the layers of an onion. You will find that there is a very thin layer that you can peel away. This is the **epidermis layer**; it is only one cell thick.
2. Cut a 1 cm square from this epidermis layer.
   Take care if using a scalpel.
3. Lay it as flat as you can on a microscope slide.
4. Put a couple of drops of iodine solution on the onion epidermis. This stains the cells so you can see them more easily.
   Iodine: avoid skin contact.
5. Put a cover slip on top. Try to do this carefully to avoid getting any air bubbles under the cover slip.
6. Look at the cells under low and then high magnification.
   - **a** Draw what you see. Work out the magnification for each drawing and label each one.
   - **b** Pick out just one cell and draw that. Try to estimate the size of your cell.

     Try making slides of some other plant cells. Remember that you need to get a very thin layer of cells so that light can pass through easily. Some examples you could try are moss, leaf surface, petals, potato scrapings, tomato. Draw what you see and label your diagrams. Remember to add the magnification and an estimate of size. Can you see **chloroplasts** in any of your cells? Find out what they are for.

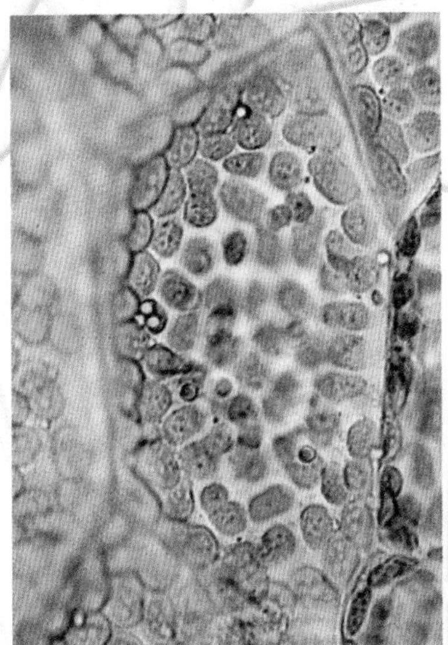

Plant cell

Animal cells

Animal cells have some features in common with plant cells but there are some differences as well. We can use a microscope to look for similarities and differences. The easiest animal cells to look at are from you! Don't worry – you can get some painlessly!

Did you know

Your body contains about a million million cells. That's a trillion, or 1 000 000 000 000, or 10^{12}.

5 Looking at animal cells

1 Get a clean cotton bud and wipe it on the inside of your cheek.
2 Smear the cotton bud on your slide. **(Dispose of your cotton bud and any contaminated glassware safely – your teacher will tell you what to do with them.)**
3 Add a couple of drops of methylene blue stain to the smear on your slide.
4 Carefully put a cover slip on top.
   a Draw what you see.
   b Think about how the cheek cells are different from the plant cells you have looked at.
   c Summarise the differences between animal and plant cells.

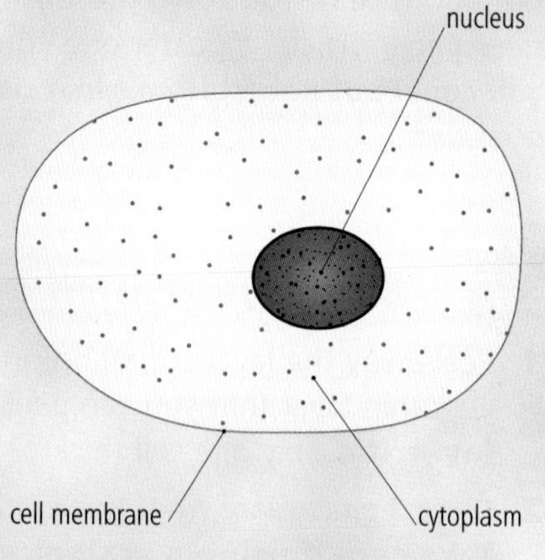

Typical animal cell

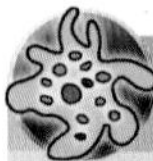

6 Make a model cell

You should have found out a lot about the structure of cells and the functions of the different parts. So far, however, you have only drawn cells in two dimensions. You can try making a model of an animal or plant cell. This will help you to understand what they are really like in three dimensions and how the different parts fit together.

A polythene bag could represent the cell membrane. Wallpaper paste or jelly could be used as the cytoplasm. What about the other parts? Use your imagination!

When you've made your model you need to label the different parts and say what they do. Each group could present its model to the rest of the class and explain what each part is.

Scientific models are not always completely accurate. What are the **limitations** of your model? Discuss this with the rest of the class.

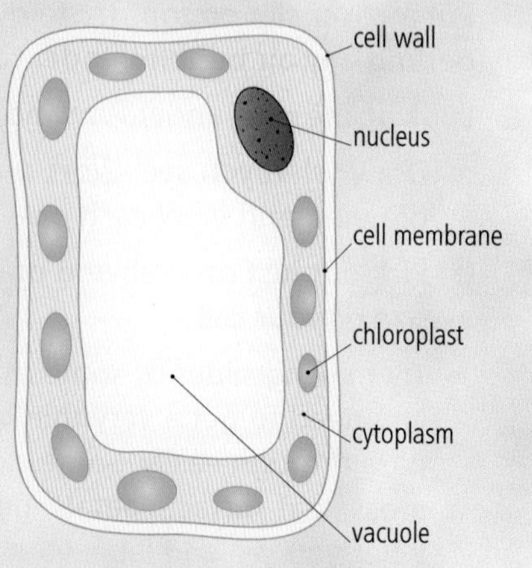

Typical plant cell

A2 Different cells, different jobs

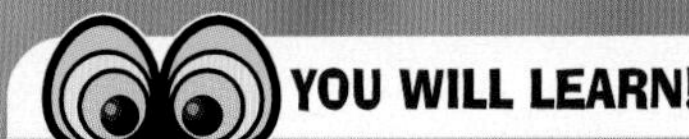

- how to use **secondary sources** to find information
- that there are many different types of cell
- a cell's structure helps it to carry out a certain function

So far, most of the cells you have looked at have been quite simple. All cells have the same basic parts found in animal or plant cells. There are thousands of variations of these basic types, all with specialised functions. The appearance of the cell depends on its function, as different jobs require different cell structures.

1 Identifying cells

Look at the diagrams of cells below.

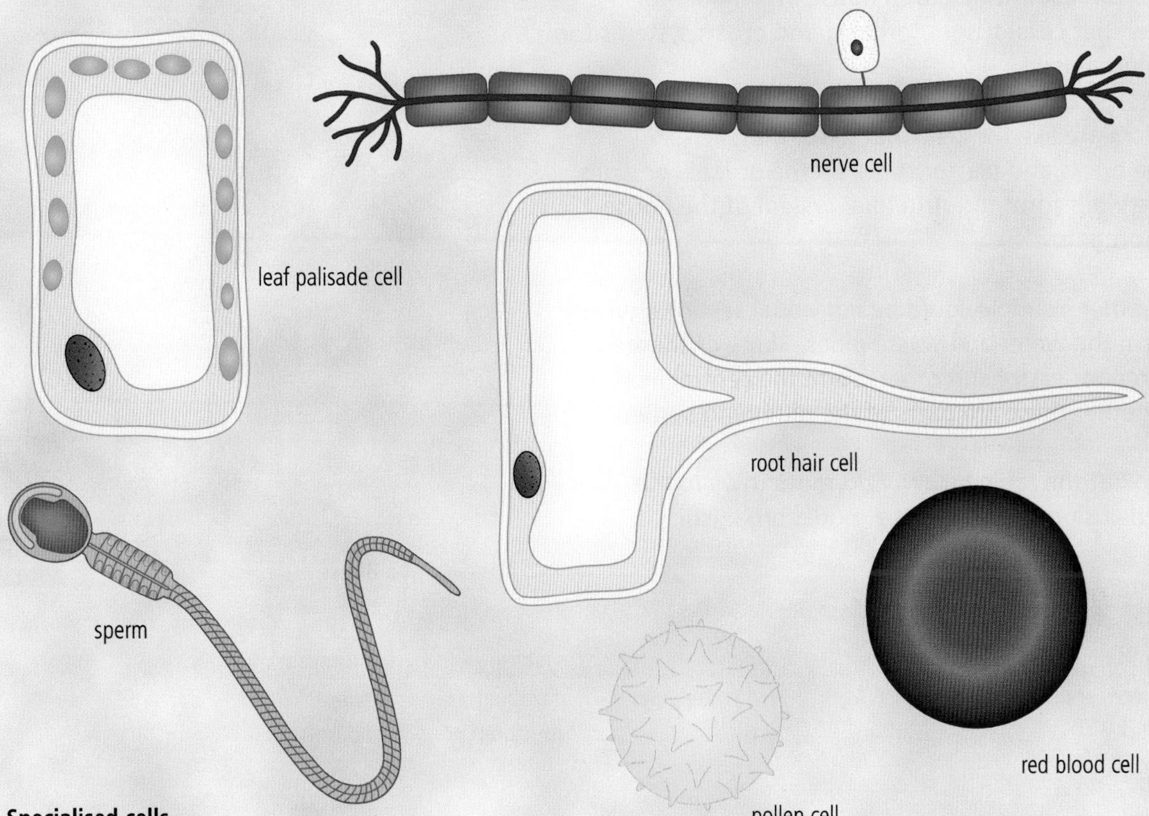

leaf palisade cell
nerve cell
root hair cell
sperm
pollen cell
red blood cell

Specialised cells

Find out more about cells using books, the Internet and CD-ROMS. Find out about the cells and explain how the structure of each one helps it to carry out its specialised function.

Did you know

Viruses are not cells. They grow by taking over animal or plant cells and 'telling' them to make new viruses. Scientists can't decide if viruses are alive or not.

Cells, tissues and organs

YOU WILL LEARN!

- cells form tissues and tissues form organs
- the names of some tissues in plants and animals
- how tissues are organised

Although cells have specialised functions, they usually need to work together in groups to carry out these functions. A group of cells of the same type is called a **tissue**. Different types of tissue work together in **organs**. A plant leaf and a human heart are both organs. Organs work together to form **organ systems**. A group of different organ systems make up an **organism**.

1 Using a house as a model organism

You can use the idea of a house as a model for the way that cells, tissues, organs, and organ systems form an organism!

Bricks are like the cells that make a tissue.
The bricks and plaster make up the organs, or walls.
The walls form the structural system of the house or organism.

Another example could be individual sections, which form the water and waste pipes. Some of these carry hot water and others form the central heating. Together these are parts of the plumbing system.

Look at the table below. Add more rows to the table using the house as a model organism.

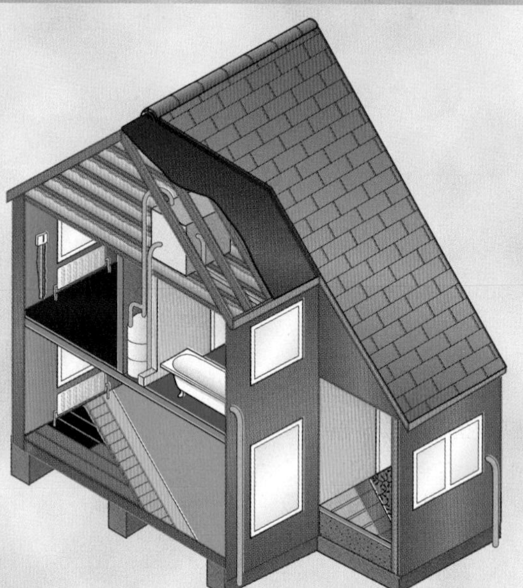

'Tissues' of a house

cells	tissues	organs	system	organism
pieces of pipe	pipes	hot water pipes	plumbing	house
bricks	wall	walls	structural	house

What are the limitations of this model?
Could you improve it?

Now try to make a similar table for the human body. Include the *skeletal, muscular, nervous, digestive, circulatory, and reproductive* systems. Find out about the cells, tissues and organs that make up these systems. The words in *italics* will be helpful for finding the information you need. Think of an interesting way to present what you find out.

Looking at tissues

Now you can look at some real tissues. Some can easily be seen with the naked eye, while others need a microscope.

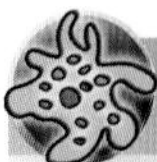

2 Some animal tissues

The rat in the photograph has been cut open to show some different tissues.

Make a list of the tissues you can see. For each tissue, write about its functions.

(You could dissect a chicken leg and identify the tissues you see. **If you do this, you must wash your hands afterwards and disinfect the bench you used.***)*

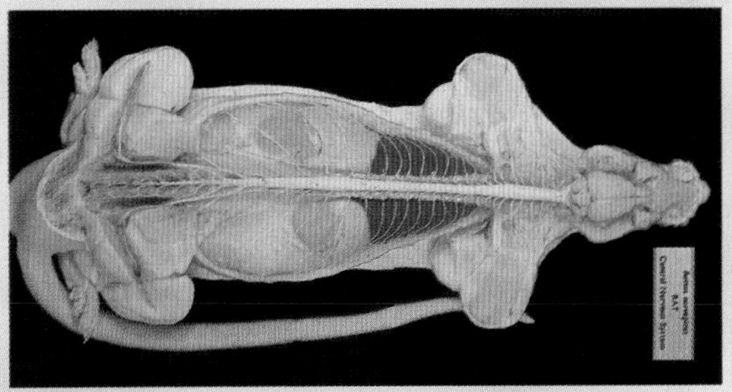

Dissected rat showing different tissues

3 A plant leaf

Look at the diagram of a section through a privet leaf, as seen through a microscope.

Some tissues are labelled. Find out the function of each one. Identify the cells that make up each tissue. Explain how the cells are adapted to carry out their function.

Put the information you find in a table.

Name of tissue	Function of tissue	Name of cells	Adaptation
upper epidermis			
palisade layer			
spongy layer			
lower epidermis			
vascular tissue			

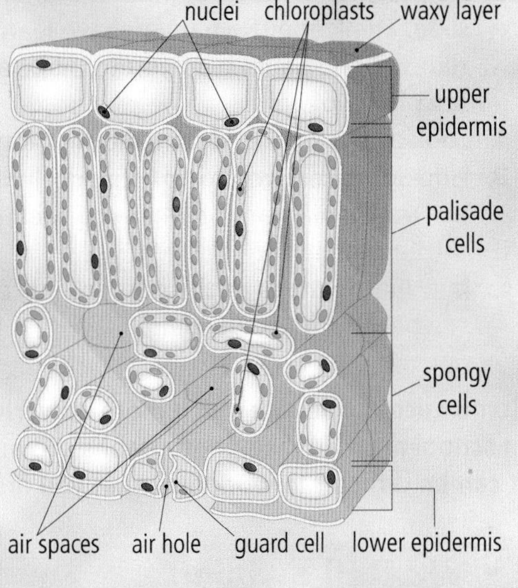

Section through a leaf

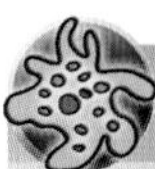

4 Repairing tissues

If someone is seriously burnt they may need a skin graft. This is where skin from one part of the body is placed on the damaged part to repair it. Find out about skin grafts and present your findings to the rest of the class.

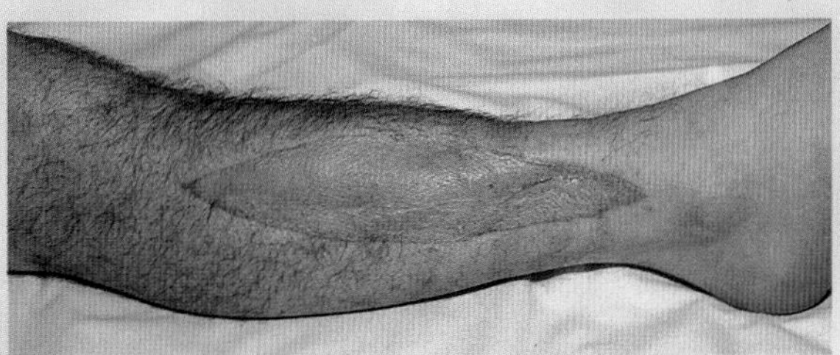

Skin grafts can be used to repair damaged tissue

A4 Making new cells

YOU WILL LEARN!

- cells can make new cells by dividing
- organisms grow when new cells are made and increase in size
- cell division starts with the nucleus dividing

You have looked at a lot of different cells. We will now see some cells dividing and find out how they do this.

Points to discuss

We will look at cells dividing in some plant cells.

1. Which parts of a plant might be best to look for dividing cells? Remember that cells divide so that the plant can grow.
2. Which parts of a plant are actually growing?
3. How will you be able to tell which cells have just divided?

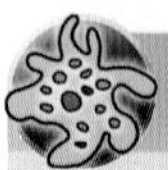

1 Looking at dividing cells

You will be given some plant material that has dividing cells. Green filamentous algae from a pond or aquarium, yeast cells in a 0.5 % solution of glucose, or the tip of the root from a broad bean will probably show you some cells that are dividing.

1. Take a small amount of plant material and make a microscope slide. Think about what you have learned about making slides. That should help you to make a slide where you can see plenty of cells.
2. Look at the slide under medium or low magnification.
3. Find some cells where you think cell division is occurring.
   - **a** Draw a diagram of what you see. Remember to label your diagram.
   - **b** What features of the cells you have drawn made you think that they were dividing?

Did you know

The most powerful microscopes are called **electron microscopes**. The most powerful can magnify about 500 000 times!

Some microscopes are much more powerful than the ones you use in school and can take photographs showing great detail (although it can be difficult to work out what you are looking at!).

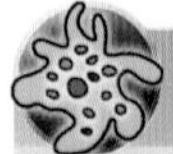

2 Cell division

Look at the photographs below. They have been taken through a microscope and show the nucleus during the stages of cell division. The photographs are jumbled up. Try to work out the order in which they were taken.

Explain why you put the photographs in the order you did.

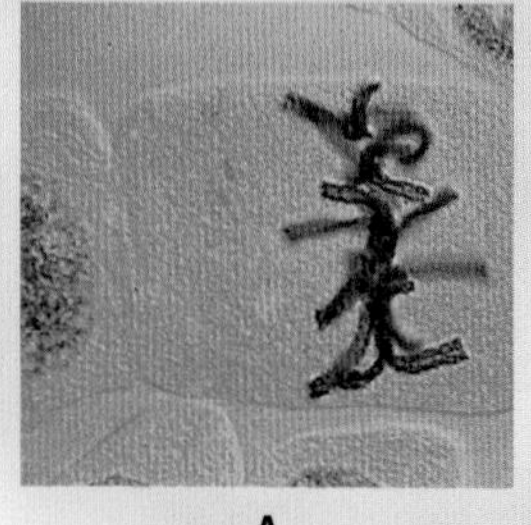

A

B

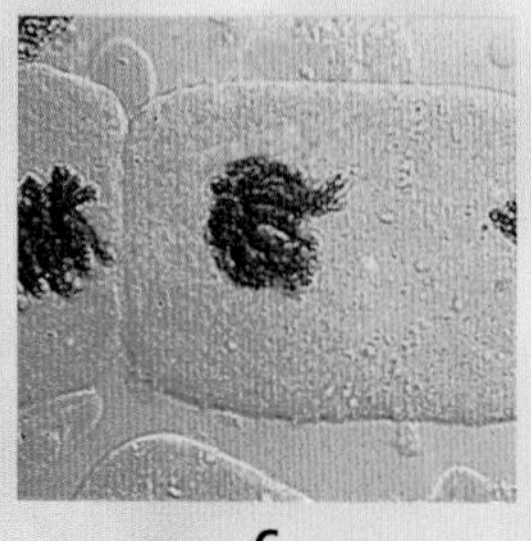

C

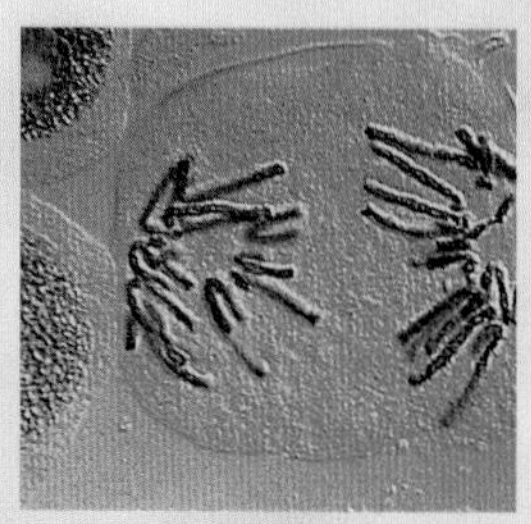

D

Cells and fertilisation

YOU WILL LEARN!

- cells have a nucleus containing all the information that is passed on from one generation to the next
- in plants, pollen and ovules contain specialised cells that allow information to be passed on
- the pollen nucleus joins with the nucleus of the female gamete inside the ovule to make a new and unique cell

You already know that in flowering plants pollen is passed from the male to the female parts of flowers and that this can happen in a number of different ways. In this lesson we will look at some ovules and some pollen.

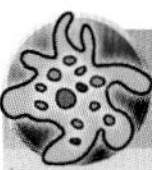

1 Looking at ovules

You can see ovules using a hand lens or magnifying glass. Your teacher will give you a flower.

1. Find the ovary.
2. Slice along the ovary with a scalpel and carefully open it.
3. You will see ovules arranged inside. Draw what you see. Label your diagram.

Take care when using a scalpel.

Section through a flower

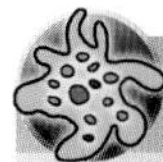

2 Looking at pollen

Pollen grains are a lot smaller than ovules and you will need a microscope to see them. Your teacher will give you a flower.

1. Find the stamen.
2. Tap the stamen on a microscope slide. You will see some of the yellow pollen fall onto the slide.
3. Add a drop of water and cover it with a cover slip.
4. View your slide under medium or low magnification. Draw some of the pollen grains you see.
5. Now make another slide but replace the water with 10 % sugar solution.

Wait a few minutes then see if you can see **pollen tubes** growing from the pollen grain. Draw what you see.

In flowers these pollen tubes carry the nucleus from the pollen grain right into the middle of the ovule.

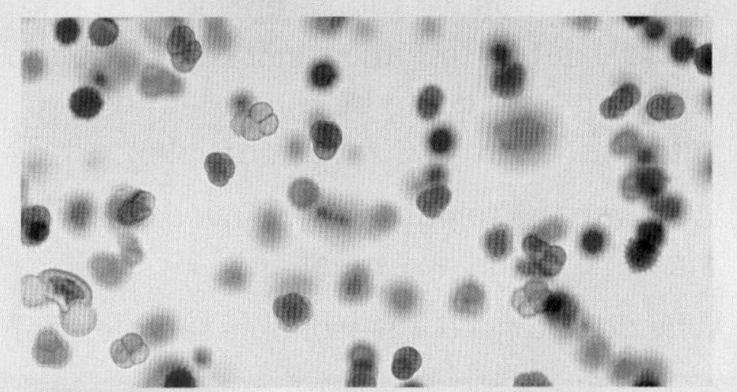

Pollen grains come in lots of shapes

Did you know ?

All plants have their own different shapes and patterns of pollen cells. Forensic scientists have proved that a person has been in a particular country by finding pollen on their clothes and identifying it as being from a plant found only in that country.

A company was fined a few years ago for selling expensive Scottish heather honey that contained pollen from a plant found in Mexico!

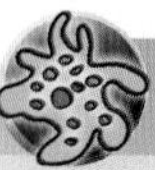

3 Investigating pollen tube growth

You have already seen pollen tubes growing. These were grown in 10 % sugar solution. But do they grow best at this concentration? Would they grow better in a more concentrated solution or would they be better in a less concentrated solution? Your task in this activity is to find the sugar concentration that is best for pollen tube growth.

Your investigation needs to be a fair test and you need to get reliable results. When you get your results you need to be confident that your conclusion is correct. When you do experiments with living things you need to be careful about your results. All living things are different — one or two pollen grains might have died or they might not have the important gene that makes them grow. To get round this you need to look at quite a few pollen grains — 20 is probably a good number. Less than this could mean that any differences in your results are due to the quality of the pollen rather than the effect of the sugar concentration. More than 20 would take too long to observe and to collect your results. You can choose your own **sample size** but make it a sensible one.

Points to discuss

In an investigation we should only look at one **variable** – in this case the sugar concentration – everything else should be controlled to keep conditions the same (as far as possible).

- What are the things that you need to keep the same in this investigation?
- Why do you need a reasonable sample size?

You will be given a flower with mature pollen, a range of different concentrations of sugar solution (0 %, 5 %, 10 %, 15 % and 20 %), some microscope slides and cover slips, and a microscope. Can you think of anything else you might need?

It is impossible to count out 20 pollen grains onto your slide, as they are far too small. Instead you should shake some pollen onto a slide, add a drop of sugar solution (say 20 %) then give the pollen grains some time to grow. Observe the slide under the microscope. You need to look at 20 grains and see how many have grown. But you need to look at 20 grains at **random** — it's not a fair test if you pick out those with pollen tubes and look at them. So how can you look at a typical selection of 20 grains?
When you've done this you need to repeat your experiment with another sugar concentration. What are you going to keep the same?

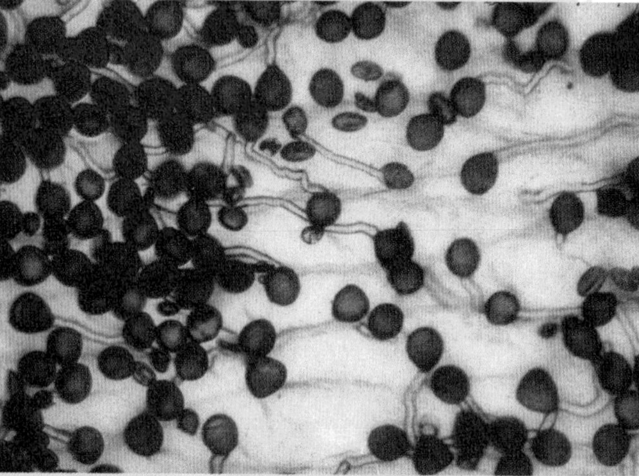

Pollen grains – some of them have pollen tubes

Once you've collected your results you need to present them in a table. What is your table going to look like?

Results are often easier to understand if they are presented visually in a graph or bar chart. You need to think about the best way of doing this. (Remember that the variable you are changing should go along the *x*-axis.)

Write a report for your investigation. Explain very carefully what you did. Another scientist should be able to repeat the experiment exactly as you did it. Explain what you did to make it a fair test and why it is important. Explain why you needed to observe a large sample of pollen grains. What conclusions can you make from your experiment? How do your results help you to reach this conclusion? Do you think your experiment was accurate and reliable? How do you know?

A6 Cells and growth

YOU WILL LEARN!

- cells can grow to form new organisms

Once the male and female nucleus join together, cells start to divide and grow. As more cells are formed they start to **specialise**, forming the different tissues and organs of the new organism.

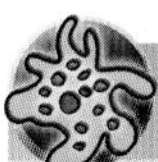

1 New lives

Look at the pictures below. They show the development of a human embryo from a single fertilised cell. Try to describe what you can see happening in each photograph. Think about the different tissues and organs that are being formed.

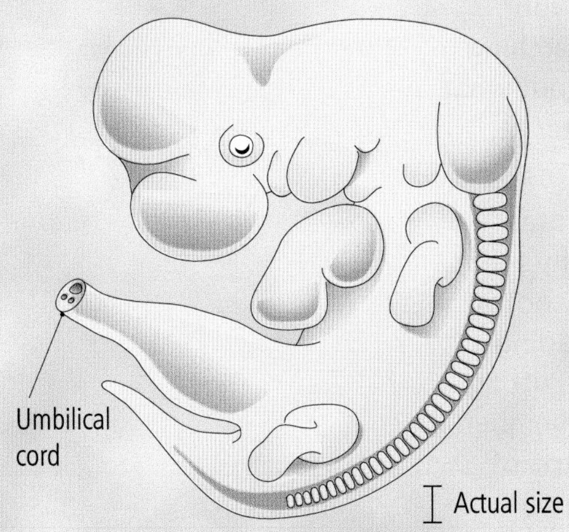

4 week fetus

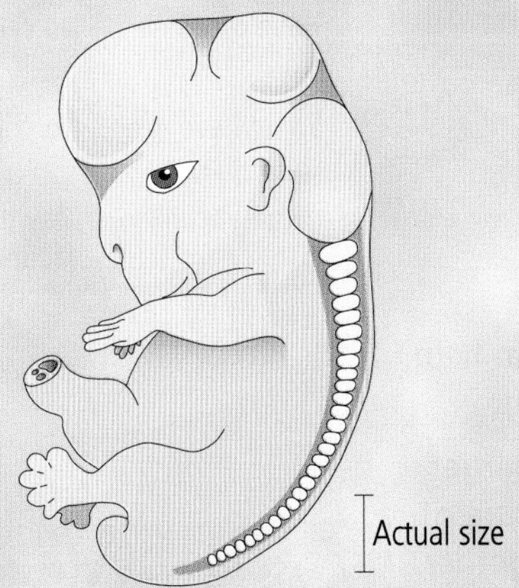

6 week fetus

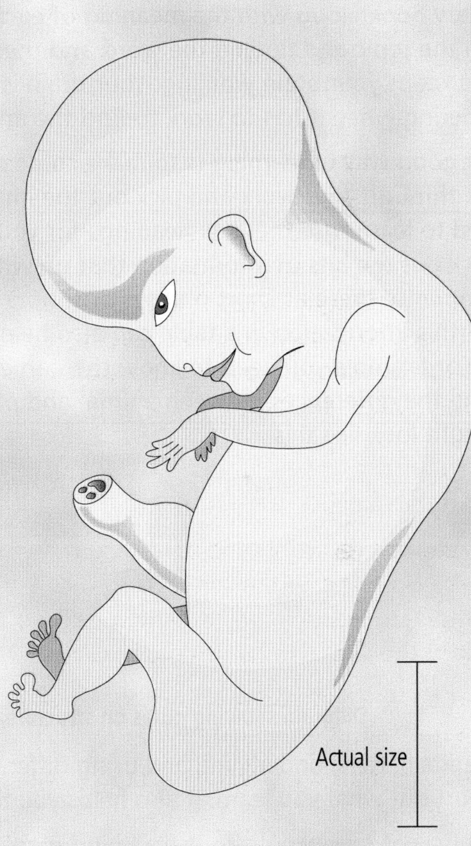

8 week fetus

Did you know

The blue whale grows from a single cell weighing less than a milligram at fertilisation to 26 tonnes by the time it is 1 year old! This means it increases in size 30 000 000 000 times!

A7 Learning how to learn

- some methods of helping you to remember the work you have done

You have now completed this first unit. The knowledge and ideas you have gained in this unit will be used in later units to further develop your knowledge and understanding of science. It is a good idea to review what you have learnt. If you do this at the end of each unit, it makes it much easier to learn what you have done. You might also have a test about this unit!

Some people try to learn by reading work they have done over and over. This takes quite a lot of time and is **not** an effective way of learning. It is much easier to learn if you have to think about the information and actually use it.

Another useful hint is to make a science vocabulary book. At the end of each unit there is a list of key words. Write these in your vocabulary book along with the meaning of each word. Searching through the topic and finding the word and then working out what it means keeps your brain working. Your brain is much better at remembering when it has to work to find the answer.

Another good way of learning is to make some summary notes. Go back through your work and pick out the important points that you need to learn. Use these as headings for your summary notes. Then pick out the bits of information that go with each heading and summarise these as short phrases or simple diagrams. Putting some of this information in a table can also help you to remember things. For example you need to know the names of the parts of a cell and the differences between animal and plant cells. Your work might look like this:

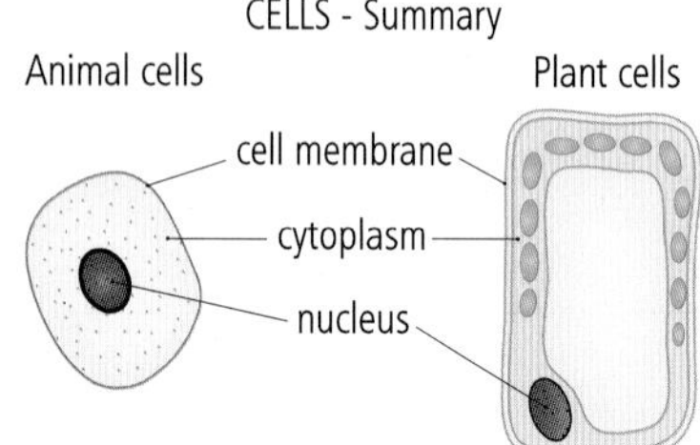

Diagram showing notes on structure of a cell

Plant cells	Animal cells
Have a cell wall	No cell wall
Some have chloroplasts	No chloroplasts
Large vacuole	May have small vacuoles

Using capital letters, underlining and using different colours can help you to sort out what you learn. It also helps you to remember it.

Another way of reviewing is to use a 'mind map'. You need a large sheet of plain paper (at least A3). You can then build up a picture of the things you have learnt and you can see how they all fit together.

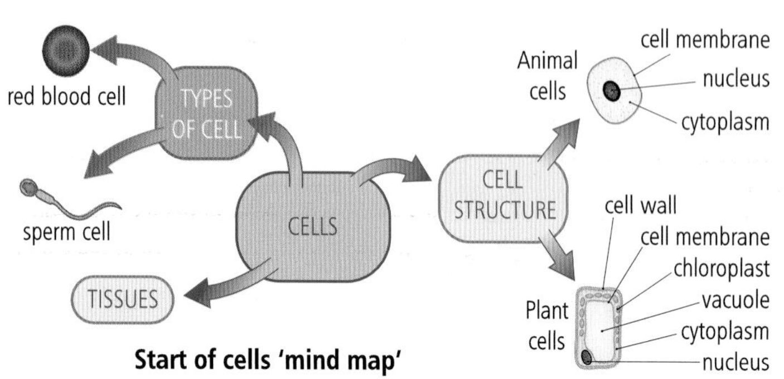

Start of cells 'mind map'

1 Review

Use one of the methods described on this page to produce a review of the work you have done in this unit.

Try different methods at the end of each unit and find out which is best for you.

Summary

Living things are made of cells. Most organisms are **multi-cellular** – they are made of millions of cells.

All cells have a **membrane**, **cytoplasm** and a **nucleus**. Plant cells also have a **cell wall**, **a vacuole** and often have green **chloroplasts**.

Although cells have these same basic parts, they have different structures so that they can carry out specialised functions.

A group of cells of the same type is called a **tissue**. A group of tissues that work together is called an **organ**.

Organisms grow by cells dividing into two new cells that each then gets bigger before dividing again.

The nucleus of a cell contains **genes** that carry information about how to make new cells, tissues and organs. **Fertilisation** is when genes from a male and a female organism join together to make a new set of information for a new organism.

Key words

cell wall
chloroplast
cytoplasm
fertilisation
gene
membrane
multi-cellular
nucleus
organ
tissue
vacuole

Summary Questions

1 a Draw a diagram of a simple animal cell. Label the main features and write a description of what each part does.

b Draw a diagram of a plant cell. Label the main parts and write a description of what each part does.

2 You are using a microscope with a ×6 eyepiece lens. What is the magnification when you use an objective lens of
a ×5 **b** ×20 **c** ×40 magnification?

3 Look at the diagram of a microscope field of view. The ruler is marked in millimetres. Estimate the size of the cheek cells you can see.

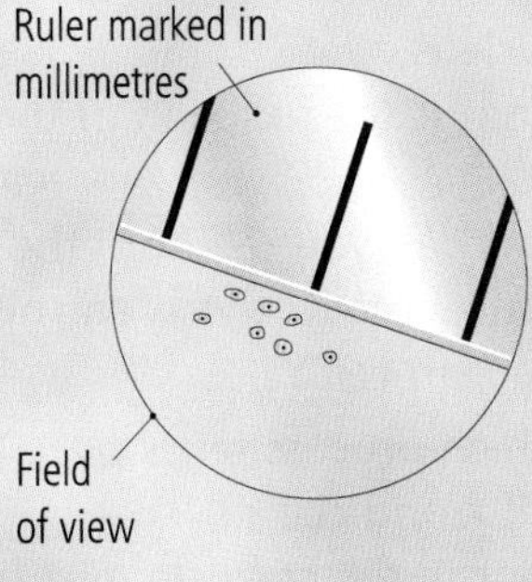

4 Imagine you are Robert Hooke in 1665. Write a report about your discovery of cells.
Draw a diagram to illustrate your report.

5 Some primary school pupils are coming to your school to learn about cells and you are going to help them. Make a worksheet to help them make an onion cell slide. Remember that drawings will help them to understand what they have to do.

6 a Put these words in the correct order, starting with the smallest unit:
system organism organ cell tissue

b Think of an example of each that link together in
i a human,
ii a plant.

End of unit Questions

1 The diagram shows a plant cell.

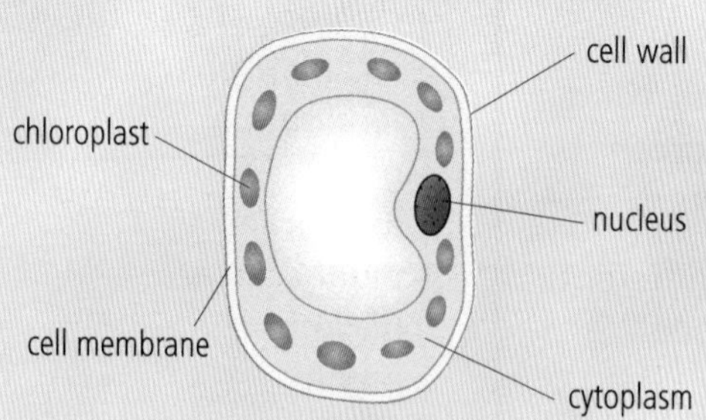

a **i** The cell is from a leaf. Give the name of the part which is present in this leaf cell but not present in root cells. *1 mark*

ii Give **two** parts labelled on the diagram which are not present in animal cells. *2 marks*

b Name the parts of the cell i–iv below.

function	part of the cell
a place where many chemical reactions take place	cytoplasm
photosynthesis takes place here	i
it controls the cell's activities	ii
it helps to keep the shape of the cell	iii
it controls substances entering and leaving the cell	iv

4 marks

2 The diagram below shows a cell from the inside of a human cheek. Name the parts A, B and C shown on the diagram below. *3 marks*

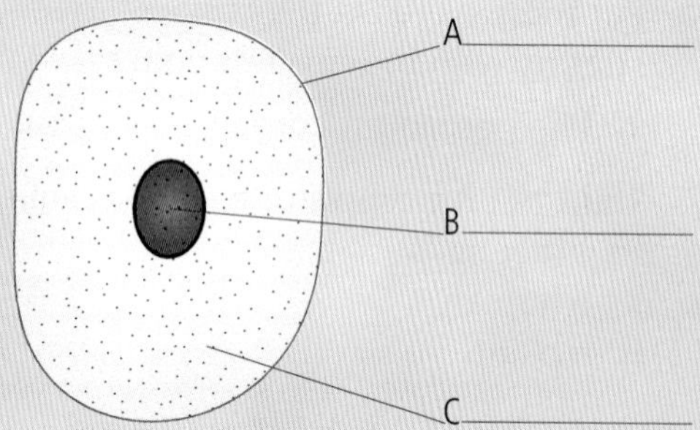

3 The following drawings show some plant and animal cells. Each cell has a different function.

a Name each cell: A, B, C, D and E. *5 marks*

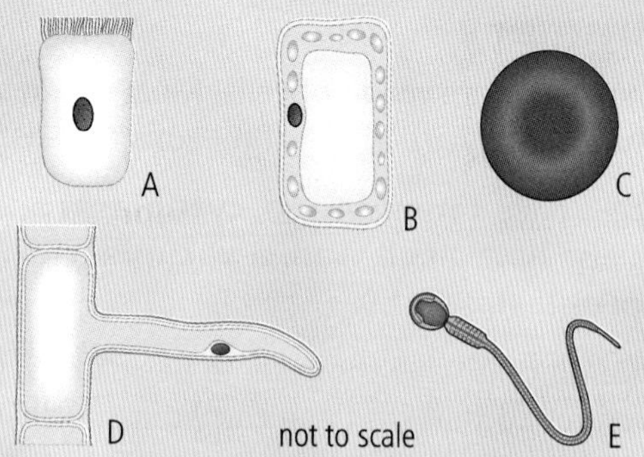

b The main functions of three of the cells are listed below. Write the letter of the correct cell next to each function.

i Photosynthesis

ii Movement of mucus

iii Carrying oxygen *3 marks*

c Give the name of the organ where cell E is produced. *1 mark*

4 The diagrams show two plant cells.

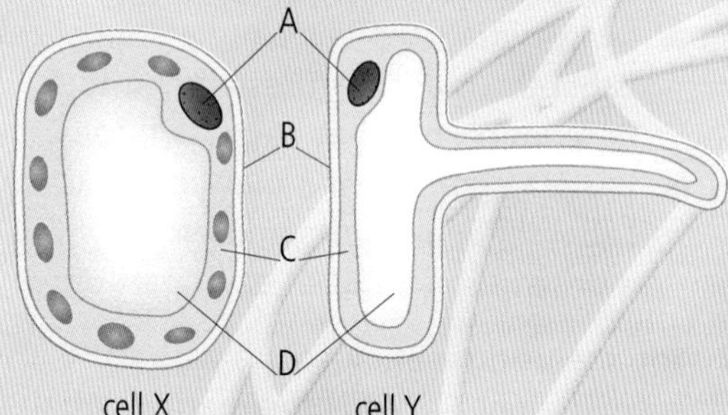

a In which part of a plant would these cells be found?

cell X *1 mark*

cell Y *1 mark*

b Give the name of part B. *1 mark*

c **i** Give the letter which labels the nucleus. *1 mark*

ii What is the function of the nucleus? *1 mark*

d **i** How can you tell from the diagram that photosynthesis **cannot** take place in cell Y? *1 mark*

ii Which process takes place in **both** cell X and cell Y? Choose the correct word from the following list:

egestion, fertilisation, pollination, respiration *1 mark*

7B Reproduction

Introduction

In this unit you will learn about reproduction in animals and plants. You will develop your knowledge and understanding of cells from Unit 7A. You will also find useful information from various sources and decide on the most helpful ways to present it.

You already know

- about the main stages of the human life cycle
- about the parts of a flower
- about pollination, fertilisation, seed dispersal and germination

In this topic you will learn

- more about reproduction in humans and how they protect and care for their offspring
- how reproduction in other animals is similar to and different from humans
- about how your body changes during adolescence

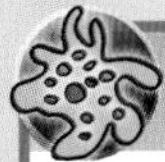

1 Parents and offspring

Look at the pictures above. Make lists of the parents you can see and their offspring. Try to draw diagrams showing how these fit into the life cycle of each organism.

B1 How new lives start

YOU WILL LEARN!

- different animals reproduce and develop in different ways

A new animal life starts when a sperm fertilises an egg cell (or **ovum**). This joins together genes from a male and a female to make a new individual. There are many different ways in which this happens. In some animals it happens inside the female's body but in others it happens outside. Some animals have internal fertilisation but then lay eggs, so the offspring develop outside the mother. Some animals normally fertilise one ovum at a time while others fertilise millions.

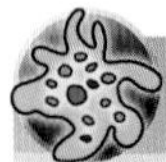

1 Different types of fertilisation

Look at the pictures below.

Find out about fertilisation in mammals, birds, reptiles, amphibians and fish. Make a poster to present what you find out. You should include information about whether fertilisation is internal or external, whether development is internal or external, how many ova are produced and how many of the offspring survive. See if you can find out any other interesting facts or any exceptions to the general rules.

Did you know

The Ocean Sunfish can produce 300 000 000 ova at a time, more than any other animal.

The spiny anteater and duck billed platypus are the only mammals to lay ova.

Points to discuss

1. You will have found out that animals with external fertilisation and development make most ova. Why do you think this is?
2. In mammals the fetus develops inside the mother. What are the advantages of this? Can you think of any disadvantages?
3. A few reptile and fish species do carry the fetus inside the body. Why do you think this doesn't happen in any species of birds?

Caring for the young

Even after they have been born, young animals have different levels of care from their parents. Many, like frogs, which hatch out as tadpoles, get on with no help at all from their parents. Most tadpoles die. Of the hundreds of fertilised eggs produced by one pair of frogs, probably only one or two will survive long enough to reproduce. The rest will be eaten by predators, starve, dehydrate, fail to find shelter or be killed by adverse weather conditions. Birds continue to feed their young until they can fly and look after themselves. Mammals produce milk to feed their young and look after them for a long time, sometimes for years. One of the reasons that mammals look after their young is to protect them from predators.

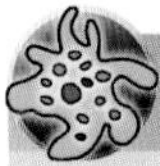

2 Looking after the young

Look at the pictures of some newly born mammals. Even though some look much more developed than others, they are all 1 day old.

a Why do you think these newborn animals are so different?

b Think about the ways they, and their parents, would live in the wild. Write about what you think it would be like to be one of these animals.

New born foal

New born kittens

New born rabbits

Humans spend longer with their parents than any other animal. Newborn babies are totally helpless at first. They need to be sheltered and kept warm. They need to be protected from predators. They are fed with milk from their mothers and even when they move on to solid food, they need to have it prepared and fed to them. Children need to learn how to behave as part of society. It takes many years for human children to learn how to survive independently. Although ways of raising children are different around the world and in different societies, they all have these basic needs. Becoming a parent means taking on a huge amount of work and is a massive responsibility.

Points to discuss

1. What are the needs of human children that make them different from most other animals? Do you think some animals have similar emotional needs?
2. Apart from parents, who else is responsible for a child developing into an independent adult?
3. Why do people choose to have children?

B2 Reproduction in humans

- the main parts of the male and female reproductive systems
- fertilisation is the fusion of an ovum and a sperm

Reproductive organs

The diagrams below show the reproductive organs of adult humans. They are designed to help a sperm to meet up and fuse with an ovum (**fertilisation**). Then the female needs to provide a safe place where the ovum can be provided with food and protected until the baby is ready to be born.

Did you know

When a baby girl is born, all the ova she will ever make are already in her ovaries. When she reaches puberty, one ovum will mature and be released from her ovaries every month for about the next 40 years. Boys don't start to make sperm until they reach puberty. Once they start they don't stop; they make millions of sperms every day.

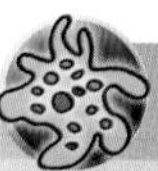

1 Human reproductive organs

Look at the diagrams of mature male and female reproductive organs. On your own diagrams, label the following parts: *ovaries, oviduct, uterus, cervix, vagina, penis, testis, sperm duct, glands*. For each part you label you should write about its function.

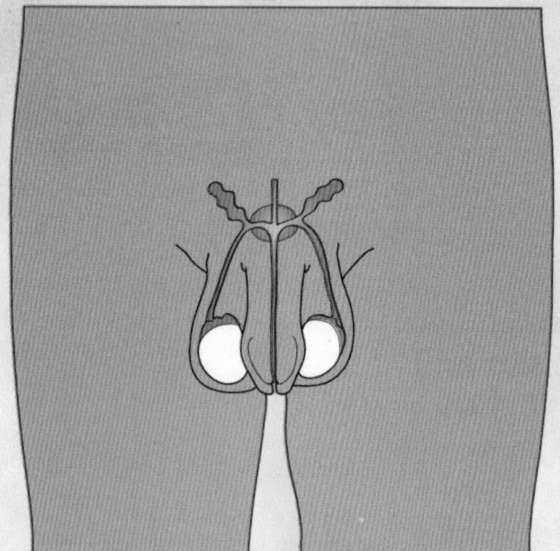

Male reproductive system

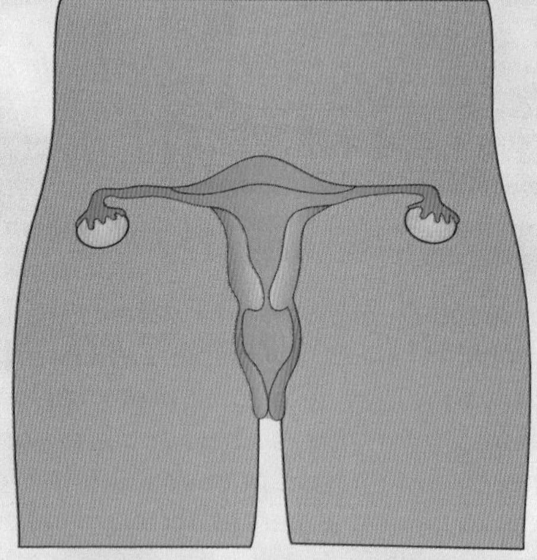

Female reproductive system

Points to discuss

Some people find it very difficult or even impossible to have children naturally. The three main reasons are:

- the man has a low sperm count
- the woman doesn't **ovulate** (release an ovum)
- the woman's oviducts are blocked.

Couples with these problems can often be helped to have a baby. What can be done to help them? Do you think that some of the solutions might cause people further difficulties or worries?

Sexual intercourse

Fertilising an ovum is not the only reason that people have sex. Men and women have sex as a way of showing their love for each other – that's why it's called 'making love'. It makes them feel very close to each other and gives them a lot of pleasure. If two people want to make love without a sperm fertilising an ovum, then they need to use **contraception**. Some people think it is wrong to make love just for pleasure and don't believe in the use of contraceptives.

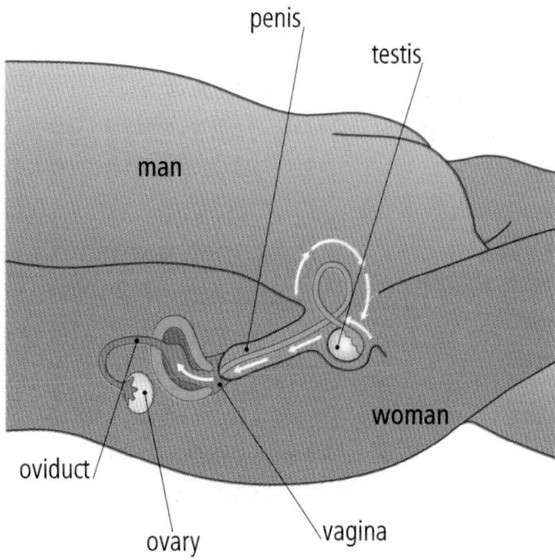

When a man is ready to make love (have **sexual intercourse**) he will feel excited and extra blood will flow into his penis. This makes it bigger and it becomes stiff. When a woman is ready and feels excited her vagina gets wider and makes extra fluid. This lubricates the vagina so that the penis can slide in more easily. The couple will move together so that the penis moves backwards and forwards in the vagina. This gives the man and the woman lots of feelings of pleasure. Eventually special muscles contract and pump sperm from the testes. These mix with fluid from the glands and make a liquid called **semen**. Semen is pumped into the vagina. This is called **ejaculation** or **orgasm**. Once they are in the vagina the sperms start to swim towards the uterus. Meanwhile the extra blood leaves the penis and it becomes limp again.

Did you know ?

A man ejaculates only about a teaspoonful of semen but this contains about 300 000 000 (3×10^8) sperms.

Points to discuss

Having sex with someone is a major responsibility. People need to be very sure that they are ready to take on that responsibility before they start having sex. Discuss points 1 to 6 below.

1. What is meant by the age of consent?
2. Lots of people tell lies and say they've had sex when they haven't really.
3. People should only have sex if they are married.
4. People should only have sex if they want to have a baby.
5. Different families have different beliefs about sex, often following the teachings of their religion.
6. Using contraceptives will definitely stop a woman getting pregnant.

2 Learning about sex

Imagine you are the parent of a girl or boy of your age.
How would you tell them about sex?
What would you tell them about?

Fertilisation

Of the 300 000 000 sperms that are ejaculated into the vagina, about 1 000 000 actually get through the cervix into the uterus. If an ovum has recently been released, a few thousand will find it in the oviduct and surround it. One sperm might manage to penetrate the ovum. It does this by making a special chemical that breaks down the ovum membrane. The sperm leaves its tail behind. The sperm nucleus enters the ovum and **fuses** with the ovum nucleus. This is **fertilisation**. As soon as this happens, the ovum membrane changes and stops any more sperms from entering. All the other sperms die. Sperms can live for 3 or 4 days in the oviducts, so if an ovum is released in this time it can be fertilised. An ovum can survive for about 3 days. During this time it can be fertilised.

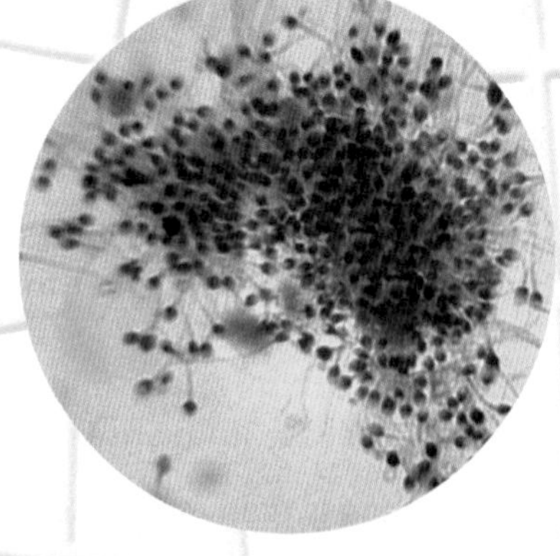

Sperm seen through a microscope

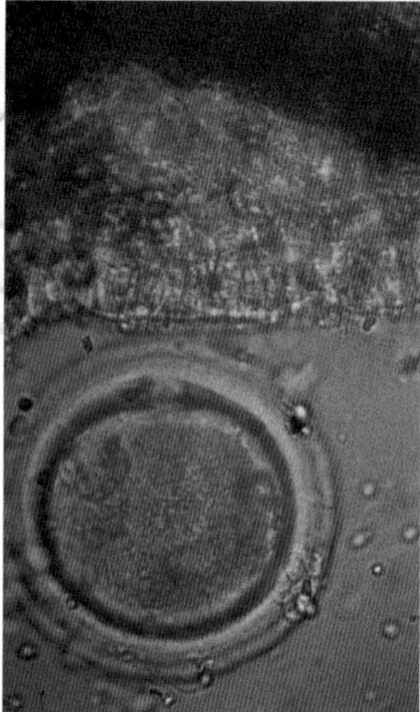

Ovum seen through a microscope

3 Fertilisation

Read the paragraph, look at the pictures above and look back at the diagram of the female reproductive organs.

a Imagine you are a sperm! Write a story about your journey from one of the testes to an ovum, which you fertilise!
b On how many days in a month is it possible for an ovum to be fertilised?
c The ovum and sperm are cells that are well adapted to carry out their functions. Describe the ways in which they are adapted. Illustrate your answers with diagrams.

Once an ovum has been fertilised it is a new cell called a **zygote**. It now carries information from both the mother and father and is the start of a new life. It continues to move down the oviduct. As it moves it divides into two cells, then four, then eight cells, until it is a ball of cells. It is now called an **embryo**. The embryo feeds on the yolk of the ovum. There is only a small amount of yolk in a mammal's ovum and only enough food for a few days. The embryo moves into the uterus. Here it sinks into the soft, spongy lining of the uterus, which is full of blood vessels. This is called **implantation**. The embryo gets food and oxygen from the blood vessels and continues to grow.

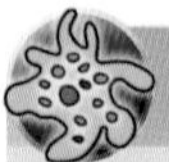

4 How embryos grow

a Read the paragraph above. Draw diagrams to show what happens to the zygote as it changes into an embryo and implants in the lining of the uterus.
b The ovum of a mammal has only a small amount of yolk. Why do birds and reptiles need much more yolk?

Genes and twins

The nucleus of every cell contains a set of genes. These genes contain all the information needed to make an individual organism. An ovum and a sperm only contain half a set of genes. Fertilisation is when the ovum and sperm fuse to make a new, complete set of genes. Each ovum and each sperm is different so every person has a totally unique set of genes. The only exception is identical twins. Identical twins occur when a zygote separates into two cells, which multiply into two embryos and so they have identical genes. Some twins are non-identical. They occur when two ova are fertilised by two sperms. They can be two boys, two girls or a boy and a girl. They don't have exactly the same set of genes. They have quite a lot of genes in common, just like any other brothers or sisters, except they are born together.

Although women normally release only one ovum each month, sometimes two or even more are released.

Identical twins

Non-identical twins

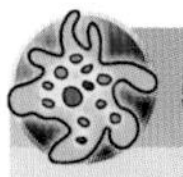

5 Twins

Read the information above. Think carefully about how cells divide and what happens in fertilisation.

a Try to work out how identical and non-identical twins happen. Draw a diagram to explain your answer.

b Can you work out how triplets can be born where two are identical and one is non-identical?

Did you know

The most children born to one mother is 69 to a woman in Russia. She had 16 pairs of twins, seven sets of triplets and four sets of quadruplets (four babies at once). We don't know how many were identical.

The most babies in one birth were nine to an Australian woman in 1971. All the babies died.

In November 1997 Bobbi McCaughey of Iowa, USA, gave birth to septuplets. The babies were named Kenneth, Nathaniel, Brandon, Joel, Kelsey, Natalie and Alexis. Their mother was taking a fertility drug to encourage her ovaries to produce ova.

The biggest multiple birth in the UK was sextuplets. The Walton sextuplets were born in 1983.

Most very large multiple births occur when the mother has taken fertility drugs.

The Walton family

B3 Pregnancy

YOU WILL LEARN!

- the fetus develops inside a membranous sac of fluid
- the fetus gets nutrients and oxygen from the placenta
- the fetus gets rid of carbon dioxide and other waste through the placenta
- the umbilical cord connects the fetus to the placenta
- harmful substances can pass from the mother to the fetus

When the embryo has implanted in the uterus it carries on growing. At first it absorbs nutrients and oxygen from the blood vessels in the uterus lining. It gets rid of carbon dioxide and other waste into these blood vessels. Soon these blood vessels cannot cope with the needs of the growing embryo. After about 3 weeks, **villi** (tiny finger-shaped projections) begin to grow from the embryo into the uterus lining. These develop into an organ shaped like a plate. This is called the placenta and it is connected to the embryo by the **umbilical cord**.

By about 8 weeks after fertilisation the embryo has developed most of the main organs of a human. It is now called a **fetus**. The blood of the mother and the blood of the embryo flow close together in the placenta but they do not mix. Food and oxygen go from the mother's blood to the fetus. Carbon dioxide and other waste go from the fetus's blood to the mother's blood. These substances move by **diffusion**.

The fetus develops in a bag called the **amniotic sac**. This bag is filled with a liquid called **amniotic fluid**. This sac protects the fetus from being damaged by bumps and knocks.

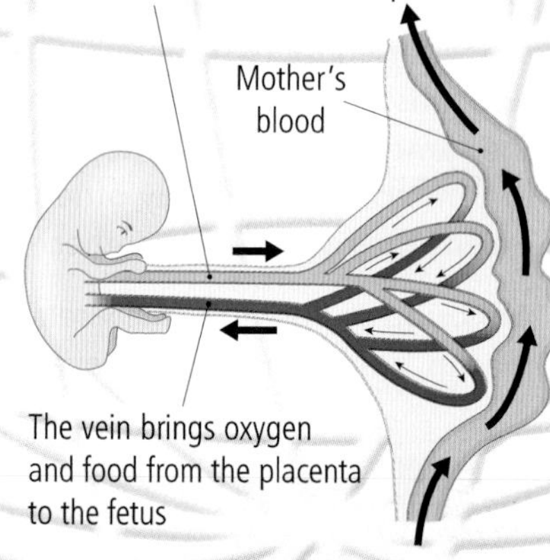
The artery carries carbon dioxide and other wastes from the fetus to the placenta
Mother's blood
The vein brings oxygen and food from the placenta to the fetus
oxygenated blood
deoxygenated blood
direction of blood flow

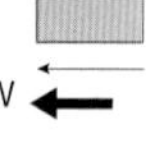

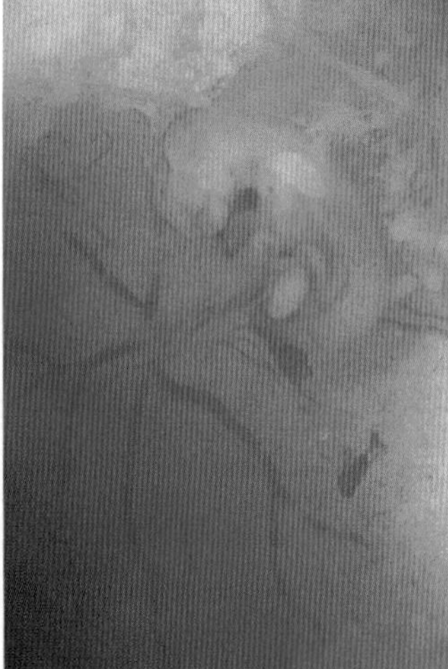

Fetus at 4 weeks

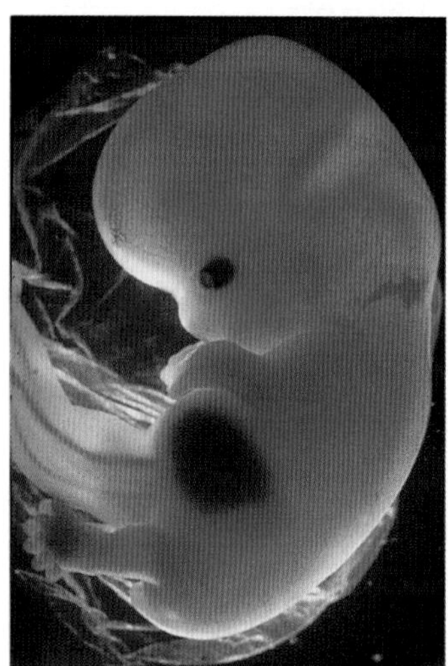

Fetus at 7 weeks

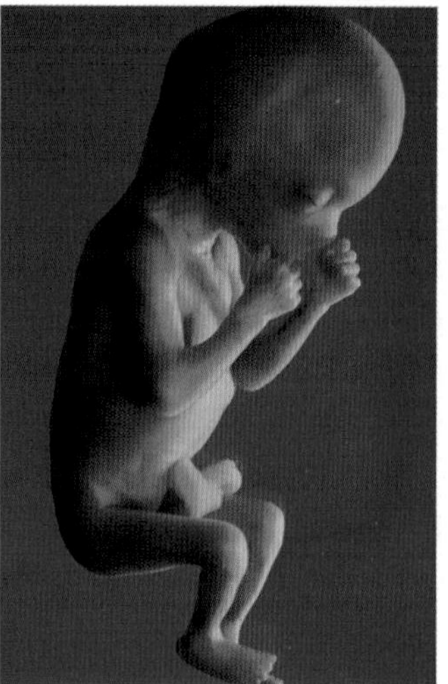

Fetus at 14 weeks

Did you know

In some books you will see the word foetus instead of fetus. Scientists around the world now agree that it should be spelt **fetus**.

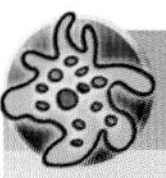

1 The developing fetus

a On a diagram of the fetus, umbilical cord and placenta, use colours to show that the blood of the fetus and the mother are separate. Use arrows to show the movement of nutrients, oxygen and carbon dioxide between the mother and the fetus. Make sure you add a key.

b Explain the difference between an embryo and a fetus.

c Draw a timeline to show the stages of development from conception to a baby ready to be born.
Write about the changes to be seen, how the fetus grows and show what it looks like.

Use books, CD-ROMS and the Internet to find your information.

Antibodies can pass from the mother to the fetus through the placenta. Antibodies are chemicals that protect us from diseases. Antibodies from the mother can protect a baby for about 6 months after it is born.

Dangerous things can also pass from mother to baby:

- viruses like ***rubella*** can damage the fetus
- carbon dioxide and nicotine from cigarette smoking
- alcohol
- other drugs.

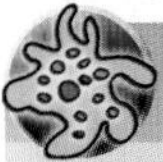

2 Caring for the unborn baby

Work in groups of three or four. Each group should work on one of the tasks below. Present your work to the rest of your class.

a Find out about what a woman should do to help the fetus to develop into a healthy baby. Find out about smoking, alcohol and drugs. Find out about what a pregnant woman should eat and about exercise. You'll find information in all the usual places but health leaflets will also be useful. You can get these from a doctor's surgery, health centre or clinic.
Design a poster to explain about caring for the unborn baby. You could include a wide range of information or just concentrate on one thing. You should say ***what*** to do and ***why*** it is important.

b Find out about thalidomide. Write an article about it for a scientific magazine aimed at young people.

c Find out why 12-year-old girls have a rubella vaccination but boys don't. Find out about other diseases that can pass from mother to fetus. Write about them.

Antenatal care

During pregnancy the woman will visit an **antenatal** clinic regularly. She will see a doctor and a midwife. She will be weighed and have her blood pressure measured. Blood and urine might be taken for testing.

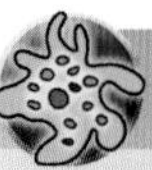

3 Antenatal care

Find out about the tests carried out at an antenatal clinic.
For each one find out why it is done.
Put the information you find in a table.

At about 16 weeks into her pregnancy the mother will probably have an **ultrasound scan**. This uses high frequency sound waves to show how the fetus is developing. Ultrasound is much safer than X-rays for looking at the fetus. X-rays can cause serious damage to cells, especially when they are dividing. An ultrasound scan also shows moving pictures.

Hospital staff need to be specially trained to **interpret** ultrasound scans. To the non-expert it can be difficult to work out exactly what the pictures actually show!

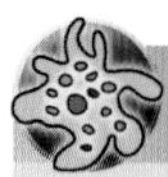

4 Looking at ultrasound scans

Look at the scans below.

- **a** What can you see? Draw a sketch of each scan and label the parts you can identify.
- **b** Why do you think it is easier to interpret the scans when you can see moving pictures?
- **c** Find out what hospital staff are looking for when they do a scan. If you get the chance, ask someone who has had a scan.

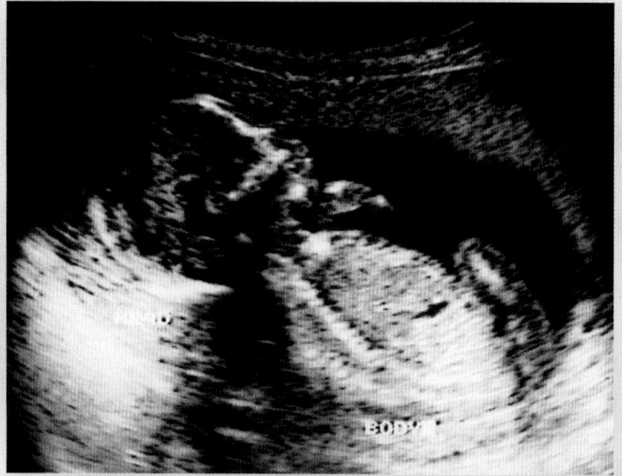

Ultrasound lets doctors look at the fetus

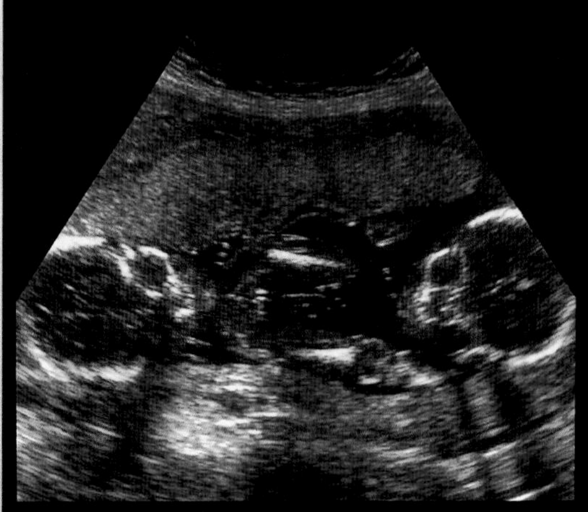

What does this ultrasound show?

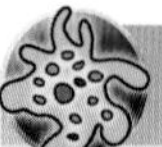

5 Internal or external development

- **a** Look back at the differences between internal and external fertilisation. In humans only one ovum is normally produced at a time. Why are so many more produced in animals that fertilise their ova externally?
- **b** What will normally be the first sign that a woman is pregnant?
- **c** Why does the uterus lining continue to thicken if a zygote implants?

Gestation

Not all animals are able to conceive all year round. Many only produce ova at a certain time in the year. This is often in the late summer or autumn.

The time that the fetus is developing inside the uterus is called **gestation**. In humans gestation is about 40 weeks or 9 months. The longest gestation of all mammals is about 20 months in an Asiatic elephant. The shortest is 12 days in the yapok, a water possum from South America.

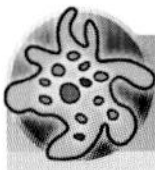

6 Gestation

The length of gestation varies widely in mammals. The table shows some examples of length of gestation and average mass of the female.

a What pattern can you see in the results?
b Plot a **scatter graph** of the data. Find more information about gestation time and mass of female. Add it to your scatter graph. You could put the information in a spreadsheet and use that to produce a scatter graph.
c Can you see any anomalous results that don't fit the pattern in your scatter graph?
d What other information would help you to make conclusions about the relationship between gestation time and mass of female?

Animal	Length of gestation (days)	Average mass of female (kg)
mouse	19	0.02
rat	22	0.3
rabbit	32	2
cat	60	5
coyote	60	15
chimpanzee	200	70
red deer	235	150
donkey	335	400
elephant	600	3000

YES, BUT I'M BIG FOR A MOUSE!

Did you know

The female red kangaroo has a mass of about 30 kg. Its gestation time is only 30 days. The baby is not very developed when it is born and spends the first 8 months of its life in its mother's pouch.

B4 The menstrual cycle

- ova are released from the ovaries about once a month
- this is part of the monthly menstrual cycle
- the menstrual cycle stops when a woman is pregnant
- the menstrual cycle is controlled by a woman's hormones

When a girl reaches puberty she starts to have **periods**. This is when the lining of her uterus breaks down. A small amount of blood comes out of her vagina. This is called **menstruation**. Menstrual bleeding normally lasts for about 5 days. The girl will use a tampon or sanitary pad to soak up the blood. At first, menstruation can be irregular but after a while it will happen about once a month. Menstruation is part of the **menstrual cycle**. Other things are happening inside her body during the rest of the cycle.

Remember that when a girl is born she has thousands of immature ova in each ovary. As soon as she has finished her period a new ovum starts to mature inside one of her ovaries. About 14 days after she started her period the ovum will be released from the ovary. This is called **ovulation**. While the ovum is maturing, the lining of her uterus starts to thicken again. This is to make sure that if an ovum is fertilised there is a good supply of blood vessels for the zygote to implant in. If an ovum doesn't get fertilised, then the uterus lining will break down and the cycle starts again. Special chemicals called **hormones** control this cycle.

1 The menstrual cycle

Draw a timeline to show the changes that happen during the menstrual cycle. Show the changes that happen to the lining of the uterus. Show when menstruation and ovulation occur. You could try to draw a circular timeline to show that it is a cycle. Mark the days when fertilisation is most likely to occur.

If an ovum is fertilised and the zygote implants, then the uterus lining will not break down. Instead it continues to thicken. When a woman is about 45–55 her periods stop. This is called the **menopause**. After the menopause a woman no longer produces ova.

Did you know

The oldest mother to give birth was an Italian woman called Rosanna Dalla Corta in 1994. She was 63. She had been given special fertility treatment. What are your views? How old will she be when her child is your age?

The oldest woman to give birth without fertility treatment was Ruth Kistler. She gave birth to a daughter in 1956, when she was 57 years old.

B5 Birth

- the fetus is pushed out of the uterus through the vagina
- the placenta is pushed out of the uterus through the vagina
- both are pushed by muscles in the wall of the uterus
- babies feed on milk from their mother's mammary glands
- milk contains nutrients and protects babies from disease

When the fetus is fully developed, after about 40 weeks, it is ready to be born. By this time it will have turned so that its head is just above the cervix. Hormones carry messages to the muscles in the wall of the uterus. These muscles start to contract. At first the contractions are about 20 minutes apart but they come quicker and quicker. At the same time the muscles around the cervix relax. The cervix opens up.

After a while the amniotic sac bursts.
The amniotic fluid comes out through the vagina.
This is when the **waters break**.
After many hours the baby comes out. It is still connected to the placenta by the umbilical cord.
The doctor will cut the umbilical cord.
This doesn't hurt, as it has no nerves.

A few minutes later the placenta is pushed out.
This is called the **afterbirth**.

1 Birth

- **a** Explain what happens at each stage in the birth of a baby.
- **b** Imagine what it is like to be a baby during birth. Write what happens.
- **c** Sometimes babies are born before 40 weeks. If they are born much too early, they are called premature. Find out about the problems faced by **premature** babies and about the special care needed by them.

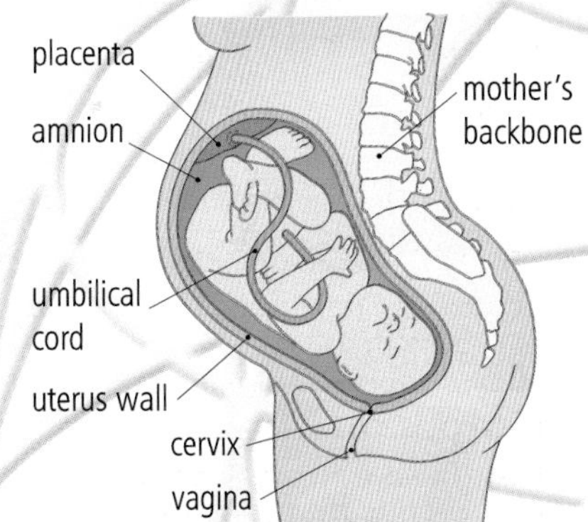

Ready to be born

After birth

Newborn babies are tired and at first they sleep a lot. Soon they get hungry however! The best food for a baby is milk from its mother. This contains all the nutrients it needs. It also contains antibodies that help to protect the baby against diseases. Babies can also be fed on formula milk. This is made from dried cow's milk with added nutrients to make it similar to human milk.
Babies need to feed a lot. They need a feed every 3 or 4 hours and they don't know (or care) if it's the middle of the night!

2 Feeding babies

Find out about formula milk. What are the advantages of breast-feeding over bottle-feeding? Can you think of any advantages of bottle-feeding?

Did you know

In 1938, Marion Chapman was born in South Shields. She weighed only 283 g and was only 31 cm long.

B6 Bringing up baby

YOU WILL LEARN!

- children grow as they become adults
- at some stages of life they grow faster than at other stages
- how to draw graphs to show growth

Humans look after their children for longer than any other animal. During that time they grow and develop through babyhood, childhood and adolescence until they become adults.
As they grow they have various needs. Some are **physical** needs such as being fed. Others are **emotional** needs like being loved.

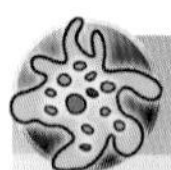

1 What a child needs

Think about all of a child's needs. The pictures will help you to start. Decide if they are physical or emotional needs.
Draw a table showing your ideas.

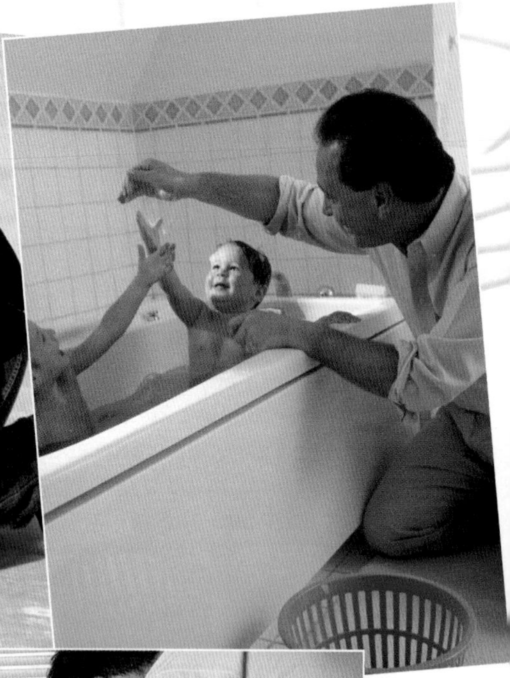

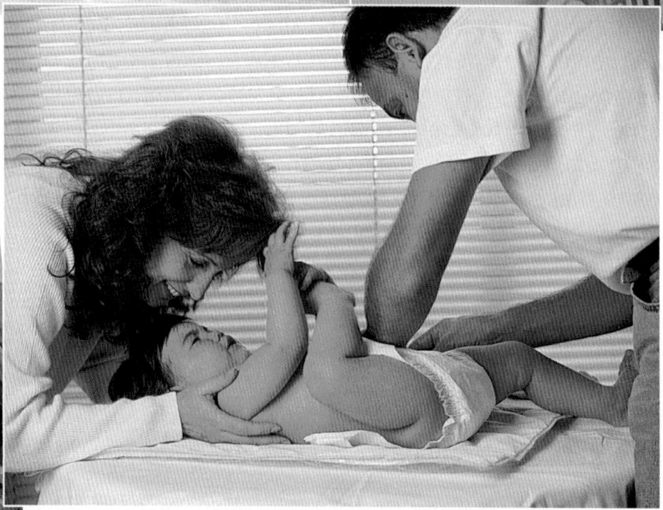

Points to discuss

Jordan is eight. He is about to get a new brother or sister. How could you explain to Jordan the changes that are happening to his mother? What is happening to the fetus growing inside her uterus? What will happen when the baby is born? How will Jordan's family life be affected? What could you do to make sure that Jordan doesn't feel left out?

Do you know anyone who has a very young brother or sister? Ask them what it is like.

2 Looking after baby

Imagine you are in charge of a playgroup for 12 children aged three and four. You have two helpers.

- **a** What are the needs of the children? How will you meet their needs?
- **b** Write out a timetable of activities for the children.
- **c** What needs will they have that don't fit into your timetable?

Growth

A human baby weighs about 3.5 kg but will grow into a much bigger adult! A human will reach his or her full height by about 20 years old. Different factors affect the **rate** at which we grow. The main ones are the height of our parents and the sort of diet we have. We don't grow at the same rate all the time.

Individual people will grow at different rates and will end up being different heights when they are adults. It's one of the things that make us all different.

Did you know

Robert Wadlow was 272 cm tall when he died, aged 22, in 1940. He was still growing when he died!

Pauline Musters was only 59 cm tall when she died, aged 19, in 1895.

Robert Wadlow and friend

3 Measuring growth rate

Look at the table below.

Age (years)	Height (cm)
0	50
1	70
2	86
3	96
4	104
5	111
6	116
7	121
8	126
9	131
10	136
11	141
12	145
13	155
14	165
15	172
16	174
17	176
18	177

It shows the height of James from birth to 18 years old.

a Produce a graph to show how James's height changes. You could enter the data in a **spreadsheet**. Then you could use the spreadsheet to draw a graph for you.

b At what ages was James growing fastest?

c Explain the differences in growth rate at different ages.

d What height was James when he was your age? Are you the same height?

e What is the problem with trying to compare your own height with James's?

f You might want to compare the growth rate of different children. This is difficult if you are just using height in centimetres. It would be better if you worked out the percentage increase each year. Do this and draw a table to show what you find. Or better still, try to set up your spreadsheet to work it out for you.

g Apart from height, what other ways are there of measuring growth? Try to find data and use it to produce other types of growth curve.

h Measure the height of all the students in your class. Display the information in tables and charts.
If you can, use a spreadsheet.

i Calculate the average height in your class.
Calculate the average height for boys only.
Calculate the average height for girls only.
Can you explain any differences?
How would this be different if you were 3 years younger or 3 years older?

j Find out about the average height of people your age. How many people in your class are exactly this height? Average height only gives a rough guide to how tall we might expect a person to be. It is more useful to see what **range** of height is expected for a particular age. Find information about expected height ranges. How many of your class fit into the expected range of height? Might you get a different result if you found the average for your whole year group? Remember your work from Unit 7A on **sample size**.

Points to discuss

How do we grow? Think back to the topic 'Cells'. Do adults have many more cells than a baby does? Do adults have the same number of much bigger cells than a baby? How could you find out?

B7 Adolescence

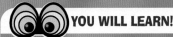

YOU WILL LEARN!

- adolescence is the time when we change from a child to an adult
- the first stage of adolescence is called puberty
- during puberty we develop secondary sexual characteristics
- puberty is a time of emotional changes
- puberty is due to the body producing higher concentrations of sex hormones

Adolescence is a time of changes in your life. You change from a child to an adult. You usually have a **growth spurt**. That means your rate of growth increases for a year or two. You go through emotional changes during adolescence.

The first stage of adolescence is called **puberty**. This is when your body changes as you develop **secondary sexual characteristics**. Puberty normally occurs in girls at about 10–13 years and in boys at about 12–14 years. Some people start earlier and some start later. Puberty can be a difficult time for young people **and** for their families!

Puberty starts when a child's body starts to produce higher concentrations of **sex hormones**. These are:

- in girls **oestrogen** produced in the ovaries
- in boys **testosterone** produced in the testes

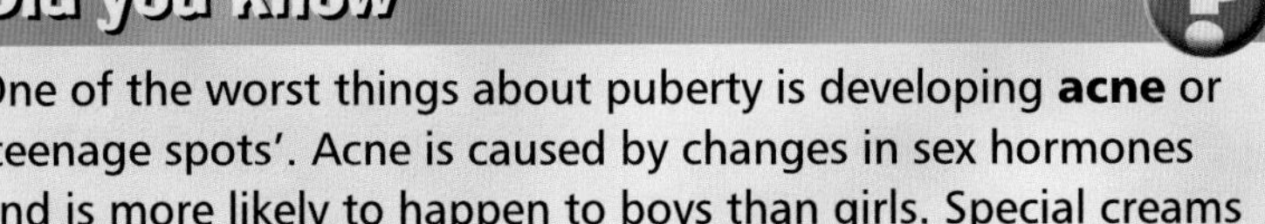

Did you know

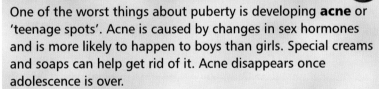

One of the worst things about puberty is developing **acne** or 'teenage spots'. Acne is caused by changes in sex hormones and is more likely to happen to boys than girls. Special creams and soaps can help get rid of it. Acne disappears once adolescence is over.

Your body's natural smells become stronger at puberty and personal hygiene becomes much more important.

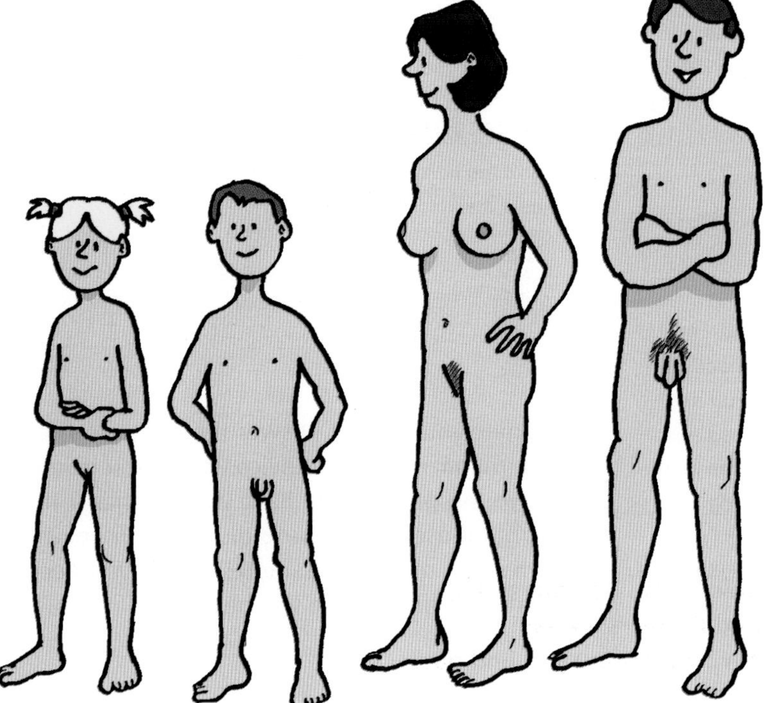

Child to adult

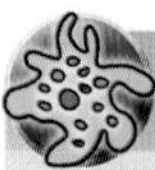

1 Secondary sexual characteristics

In the pictures on the previous page you can see some of the changes that happen during puberty. There are other changes that you cannot see. Draw a table to show changes that happen to girls and changes that happen to boys. You could add a column to show changes that happen to both boys and girls.

Points to discuss

Young people start puberty much younger than they did 50 years ago. In the 1950s it was quite common for girls to start having periods at the age of 16 or even older. Can you think of any reasons to explain this?

Emotional changes

Puberty is a time when young people's bodies are maturing. Their emotions mature as well but not always at the same rate. This can cause a lot of problems between young people and their parents. It can also be a cause of disagreements between young people and their friends.

2 Solving problems

Read the letters below. They are from a magazine for young people.

Dear Deirdre,
I am a 12-year-old girl. I am in my first year at High School. There is a boy in year 9 that I really fancy. I know he likes me as well because he told one of my friends that he would like to ask me to go to the cinema with him. My problem is that I think my mum and dad would say no because they always treat me like a little kid. I could tell them I am going to go with a girl in my class but they might find out. What should I do?

Susan

Dear Denise,
My parents think I am just a little kid but I'm not. I'm 12 years old and I'm at High School. All of my friends are allowed to wear make-up and jewellery but my parents won't let me because they say I'm too young. And they make me wear the same sort of clothes as my 9-year-old sister. How can I make them realise that I'm growing up and need to be treated more like an adult?

Lucinda

Dear Dave,
I am a boy aged 13. Some of the boys in my class have already started puberty but I haven't any signs at all yet. I'm getting really worried that there might be something wrong with me. I can't ask any of my classmates as they would laugh at me and I'm too shy to ask my mum or dad. Do you think I should go to see the doctor? I've heard that this is something to do with hormones. I thought the doctor might be able to give me hormone tablets or something. Can you help me?

Tom

Imagine you have to answer these letters in a teen magazine. What advice would you give to the young people who have written them? It might be useful for you to discuss your answers with some of your classmates before you decide what your final advice will be.

Summary

Fertilisation is where a sperm nucleus fuses with an ovum nucleus. Some animals reproduce using **internal fertilisation**. Other animals reproduce using **external fertilisation**. Once fertilised, some animals' eggs develop internally while others have eggs that develop externally. In humans, fertilisation and development are both internal.

The reproductive organs of a human are designed to give the best chance of fertilisation and development. The **fetus** develops in the **uterus**. The fluid in the **amniotic sac** protects the fetus. The fetus gets nutrients and oxygen from its mother via the **placenta**. It removes carbon dioxide and other waste through the placenta. The **umbilical cord** connects the fetus to the placenta. Harmful substances from the mother can reach the fetus through the placenta.

Ova are released from the **ovary** once every month in a woman. Every month the lining of the uterus thickens to get ready for a fertilised ovum. If an ovum is not fertilised, then the uterus lining breaks down. It comes out of the vagina as a **period**. These are stages of the **menstrual cycle**.

When the fetus is ready to be born the muscles of the uterus wall push it out through the vagina. When babies are born they feed on milk, which contains nutrients and provides protection against disease.

Animals grow by **cell division** followed by cell growth. In humans, growth is rapid at first then slows down. There is a **growth spurt** around the time of puberty. **Adolescence** is when children change into adults. This includes puberty when **secondary sexual characteristics** develop. Hormones control puberty.

Key words

adolescence
amniotic sac
cell division
fertilisation
fetus
menstrual cycle
ovary
placenta
puberty
secondary sexual characteristics
umbilical cord
uterus

Summary Questions

1 Explain these observations:
- **a** Most species of fish produce thousands or even millions of ova at a time.
- **b** Humans usually produce only one ovum at a time.
- **c** A baby zebra is able to walk the day it is born.

2 Draw and label diagrams of:
- **i** the female reproductive system, and
- **ii** the male reproductive system.

Explain the function of each part.

3 Draw a diagram to show how a fetus is protected inside its mother's uterus.

4 Explain with the help of a diagram how a fetus gets oxygen and nutrients and how it gets rid of carbon dioxide and other waste.

5 What harmful substances can pass from the mother to the fetus?

6 Summarise the stages of the menstrual cycle as a diagram. Mark on it:
- **i** when menstrual bleeding occurs,
- **ii** when ovulation occurs,
- **iii** when the uterus lining builds up,
- **iv** the days when fertilisation could occur.

How is the menstrual cycle controlled?

End of unit Questions

1 The drawing shows a flower.
Six parts are labelled, P, Q, R, S, T and U.

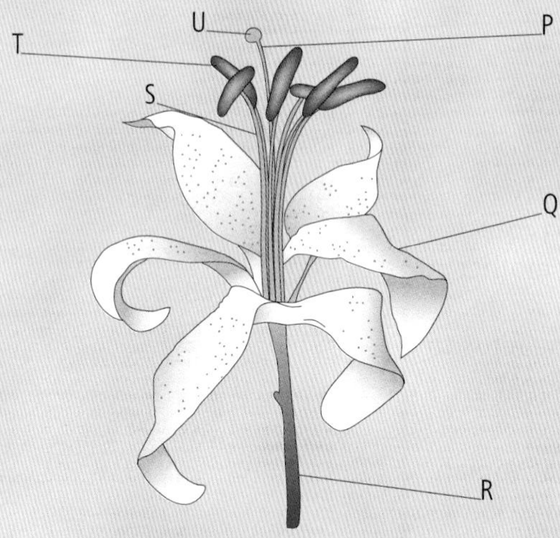

a The names of three of these parts are given in the table.
Copy the table and write in the correct letters for each part. *3 marks*

name of part	letter of part
anther	
style	
stigma	

b Which two letters on the drawing show parts of the stamen?
.... and ....
1 mark

2 The diagram shows a baby developing inside its mother's body.

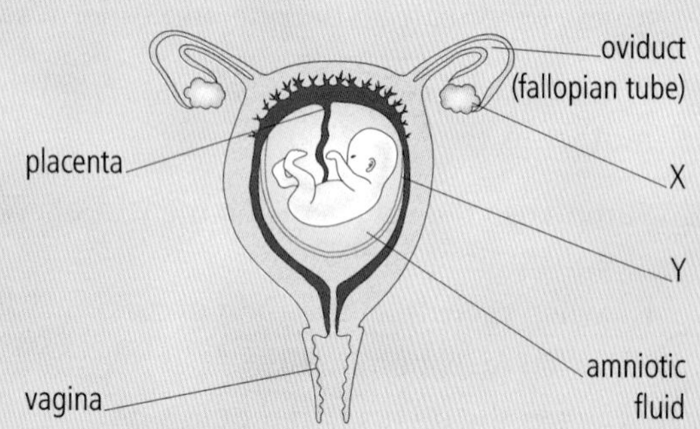

a Eggs are produced in organ X.
What is the name of organ X. *1 mark*

b The baby grows in a bag of amniotic fluid which is inside organ Y.
What is the name of organ Y? *1 mark*

c **i** Through which part, labelled in the diagram, is food passed from the mother to the baby? *1 mark*

ii Name **one** useful substance, other than food, which passes from the mother to the unborn baby. *1 mark*

d The diagram shows an organ system of the mother's body.
What is the name of this organ system?
1 mark

maximum 5 marks

3 **a** This question is about the menstrual cycle. Choose words from the list to complete the sentences. *4 marks*

a daily
the middle
a weekly
a monthly
the vagina
the uterus
an ovary
the beginning
the end

Menstruation is part of .... cycle.
The cycle begins when the lining of .... breaks away.
An ovum (egg) is released from .... at about .... of each cycle.

b During adolescence, boys' bodies change. Describe two of the changes.
2 marks

7C Environment and feeding relationships

Introduction

In this unit you will investigate habitats and the animals and plants that live in them. You will make environmental measurements in the habitats you study. You will survey the animals and plants in habitats and find out what they eat. You will learn how food chains can be linked together to make food webs.

You already know

- what we mean by a habitat and how animals and plants are suited to their habitat
- about consumers and producers and how they make up food chains
- what we mean by predators and prey

In this topic you will learn

- to identify differences between habitats and how they affect the animals and plants that live in them
- how animals and plants are adapted to live in a particular habitat
- how animals and plants are adapted to changes in their environment
- how animals are adapted to feed on particular foods
- how related food chains are part of food webs
- how energy is passed through food chains
- why it is important that there are different types of habitat

1 What can you remember?

a List all the food chains you can see in the picture above.
b List all the producers.
c Make a table listing predators and their prey.

Adaptations in a habitat

YOU WILL LEARN!

- different habitats have different features and different animals and plants live in them
- things like light, temperature, water and nutrients are environmental factors
- where animals and plants live within a habitat depends on environmental factors
- animals and plants are adapted to live in their habitat

Habitats

There are thousands of different **habitats** in the world. There are probably quite a few different habitats even in your school grounds and the area around it. The animals and plants that live in a habitat are called its **community**. A habitat and its community make an **ecosystem**. The animals and plants that live in a habitat will depend on its **physical features** and on its **environmental factors**. Physical features include things like whether it is rocky, sandy or soil-based. Environmental factors include things like light intensity, oxygen availability, carbon dioxide availability, temperature, the amount of nutrients and water.

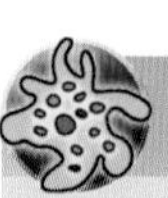

1 Describing habitats

Look at the photographs of some habitats.

a Describe the physical features of each habitat.

b Which environmental factors of each habitat will affect the type of animals and plants that form its community?

Animals and plants are **adapted** to survive in their habitat. This can include **physical** characteristics like the shape of the organism, the colour of the organism and how much fur it has. It can also include the organism's **behaviour**. Penguins huddle together in groups to keep warm. Woodlice mostly stay in dark, damp places to avoid dehydrating.

2 Adaptations

Look at the photographs of animals and plants.

For each animal or plant

a describe the habitat in which it lives,

b describe how it is adapted to live in that habitat,

c for each adaptation, say if it is physical or behavioural.

Working in a group, choose another habitat. You might find some information on the Internet. Make a list of some of the animal and plant species that form the community of that habitat. Find out how the different species are adapted for that habitat. Present what you find to the rest of your class. You will have to make sure that they understand what you are telling them. Use pictures to illustrate what you have to say. Make sure that what you write or say is organised logically.

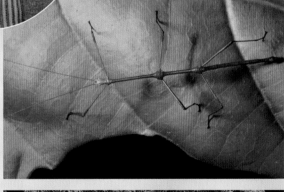

C2 Changing habitats

YOU WILL LEARN!

- environmental factors in habitats change daily, especially between day and night
- how to measure daily changes in environmental factors
- how animals are adapted to cope with daily changes in their habitat
- how to find patterns linking environmental changes to animal behaviour

Daily changes

Even within a habitat there will be changes in environmental factors every day. Some of these changes are caused by changes in the weather. Others can be caused by the activities of people.

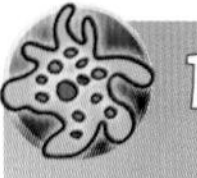

1 Measuring environmental changes

Think about the changes that take place around your school grounds over a 24-hour period.

a What sorts of things will change?

b How will these changes affect the animals that live in or visit the school grounds?

You will be able to observe some changes yourself while you are at school. Some are less easy to observe. Other changes will take place outside school hours. It will be useful for you to have accurate measurements of changing environmental factors over a period of 24 hours.

You can use datalogging equipment to measure some of these changes. Datalogging uses different **sensors** to measure data. It takes measurements automatically, even when you are not there! You can then use a computer to display what you have found out.

c Find out what sensors are available to you. Think about how you can use these to measure the environmental changes that happen over 24 hours.

d Which factors can't you measure by datalogging? Are there other ways you could find the information that you need?

e Use all your sources of information to show how a habitat within your school grounds changes over a 24-hour period.

f How would the population of animals change over the same 24-hour period? You will probably have seen some animals that live around your school, e.g. insects and birds. You can try a bit of guesswork by finding out about the sorts of animals that might live in the area. Foxes, squirrels and cats may visit. Can you think of any ways of checking if they actually do come into the school grounds? A video camera could help.

Present a display of the animals that are found in your school grounds. Use information about environmental changes to try to explain why they appear when they do.

There can be lots of different changes in environmental factors all happening at the same time. This can make it difficult to decide which is the most important. For example, slugs are more likely to come out at night. Is this because it is dark so they are safer from predators? Or is it because it is cooler and they are less likely to **dehydrate**? Do they prefer more humid conditions? How can we find out? Scientists like to do controlled experiments to reach valid conclusions.

Snails need a cool, damp place

Woodlouse

Did you know

In August 1936 in Hertfordshire the temperature rose from 1.1 °C to 29.0 °C in just nine hours!

OH, I THOUGHT YOU SAID WE NEED SHADES!

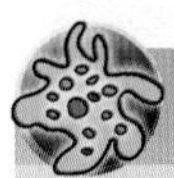

2 Factors affecting behaviour of invertebrates

Choose a common invertebrate found in your school grounds. Woodlice, slugs and snails are good examples.

a Where is it usually found
 i during the day, **ii** at night?

b Which environmental factors attract it to the place where it is normally found?

You will investigate the effect of one of these factors on the animal's behaviour.

c Decide what you are going to investigate. Write down exactly what you are going to investigate. Now write down what you expect will happen. This is your **prediction**.

d Now you need to plan exactly how you will do your investigation. It is important that your sample size is big enough to get reliable results.
How will you give the animal a choice of environmental conditions?
What variables do you need to try to control?
How will you make sure your investigation is a fair test?
What size sample will you use? Why did you choose this size?
How will you carry out observations to test your prediction?
How will you record your results?
Write out a plan of your investigation. Check it with your teacher. A diagram might help to explain what you are going to do.

e What do your results tell you?

f Were there any factors you could not control?

g Do your results prove that your prediction was correct?

h Are you confident that your results are reliable? Explain your answer.

Make sure you wash your hands after handling any animals.
Return any animals you use to the place you got them from.

Seasonal changes

YOU WILL LEARN!

- some animals and plants are adapted to avoid the problems caused by the changing seasons

Habitats change throughout the year. The temperature, rainfall and amount of food available all change with the seasons. Animals and plants are adapted to survive these changes in many different ways.

Did you know

In Siberia the temperature can vary from −70 °C in winter to +37 °C in summer!

How animals survive the winter

Many animals, especially birds, avoid winter by **migrating**. Others **hibernate**, like hedgehogs, squirrels and frogs. Animals that hibernate eat a lot of food in the summer and autumn. They use this food to build up thick layers of fat. They find somewhere safe to hide then go into a very deep sleep. While they are asleep they use their fat to keep them alive. Hibernation is a special kind of sleep. The body temperature drops and all non-essential body functions shut down.

Spring

Summer

Autumn

Winter

Other animals, especially insects, survive the winter by forming **dormant structures**. **Aphids** lay special eggs at the end of the summer. These eggs have an extra thick coat. Instead of hatching in the autumn they stay dormant throughout the winter and hatch the following spring.

All butterflies hatch as caterpillars. The caterpillars grow, and then form a **pupa**. The pupa changes into a butterfly. If a caterpillar pupates at the end of the summer, the pupa can survive the winter and emerges as a butterfly the following spring.

Did you know 

A hamster's body temperature can fall as low as 4 °C during hibernation. Its body will go quite stiff. Sadly many owners think their pet hamster has died. A lot of hamsters are buried alive while hibernating! Putting it in a warm place will often appear to bring a pet hamster back to life.

 1 Avoiding the winter

a Make a list of the problems that animals might face in the winter.
b Find out how the temperature, rainfall and hours of daylight change in your area.

Work in a group to investigate one of the items below. Present your findings briefly to the rest of your class.

c Find out about a British bird that migrates. What is its main food? Where does it migrate to? How far does it travel? At what time of year does it migrate? Why are there more species of migratory birds than other animals?
d Find out about an animal, other than a bird, that migrates. What is its main food? Where does it migrate to? How far does it travel? At what time of year does it migrate?
e Find out about an animal that hibernates. What is its main food? How does it prepare for hibernation? What problems will it face if there is unusually warm weather during the winter? How does it get food when it first comes out of hibernation?

Swallows

Canada geese

Grey whale

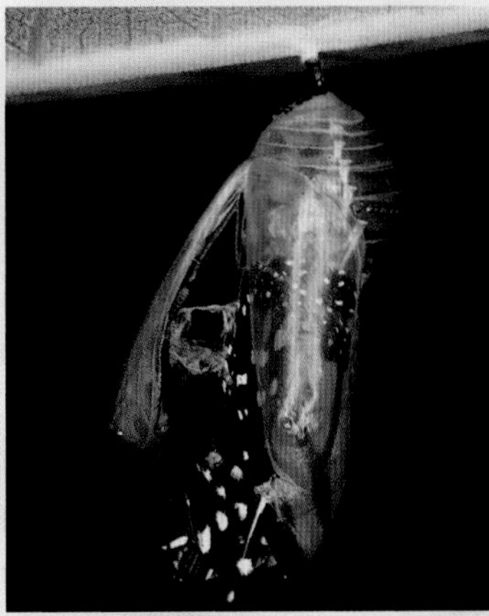

Butterfly pupa (chrysalis)

Frog

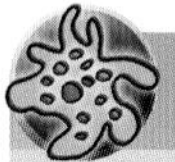

1 continued

f In the spring, dog owners often complain about the extra hairs they find on the furniture and carpets.
Explain why this happens.
How do animals that don't hibernate survive the winter in Britain?

g Find out about how a species of insect survives the winter.

Listen to all your classmates. Draw up a table to summarise the different ways of surviving the winter.

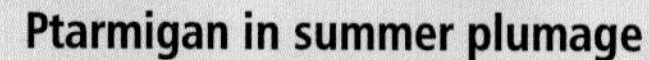

Ptarmigan in summer plumage

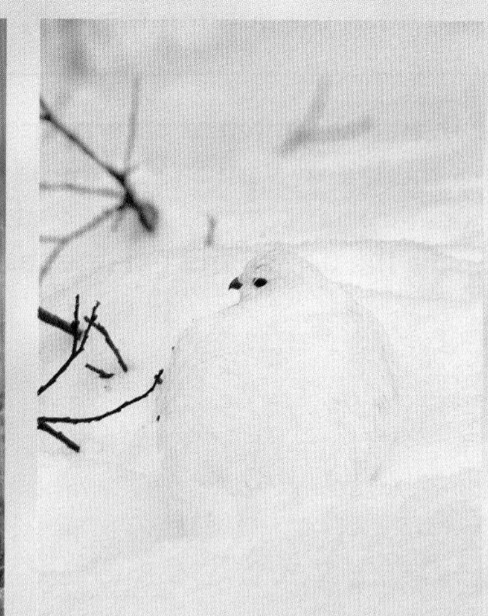

Ptarmigan in winter plumage

Red squirrel

How plants survive the winter

Plants face some difficult problems in the winter:

- If the ground is frozen they can't get water.
- Ice crystals form inside cells. These break the membrane and destroy the cell.
- Tree branches can snap if snow builds up on them.

Plants have many different adaptations to enable them to survive the winter. They often involve a **dormant** stage when the plant stops growing and there isn't any activity in the cells.

Some plants produce seeds in the autumn. The whole plant then dies, leaving the seeds to lie dormant in the soil. The seeds **germinate** in the spring. Plants with this type of life cycle are called **annuals**.

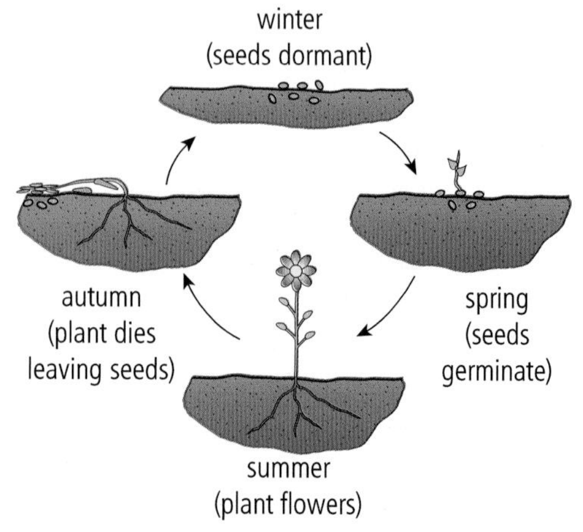

Life cycle of an annual

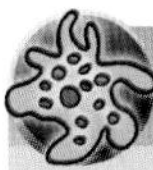

2 Germinating seeds

Seeds are a dormant stage in the life cycle of a plant.
Seeds contain very little water.

a Why will this help them to survive the winter?
b Design an investigation to find out if seeds are still **viable** (will still germinate) after being kept at freezing temperatures.

Some plants live for many years. They are called **perennials**. Many species of perennial appear to die each autumn. In fact they are still alive. Only the parts above the ground die. During the summer the plant sends food to a **storage organ** under ground. This survives the winter and starts new growth the following spring. Examples of perennials like this are daffodils, potatoes, onions, yams and garlic.

3 Storage organs

Your teacher will give you some storage organs to look at.

a Draw a diagram to show the life cycle of a perennial plant.
b Look at one of the storage organs. Cut it open. Draw a diagram to show how new growth comes from a storage organ. **Take care when using a scalpel.**
c Why are a lot of storage organs things that we eat?
d Storage organs contain water. Why don't they freeze?
e Daffodils are woodland plants. Why do they flower in spring?

Deciduous trees lose their leaves in winter. They remain dormant through the winter then start to grow again in spring.

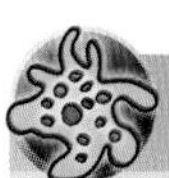

4 Winter twigs

Examine a twig from a deciduous tree in winter.

Take care when using a scalpel.

a Cut away a section of bark.
b How can you tell that it is alive?
c Cut a section through one of the buds. Draw what you observe.
d How is it adapted to protect it from freezing?
e How are evergreen trees, like firs, adapted to survive the winter? Think about the shape of the tree and the structure of the needles.

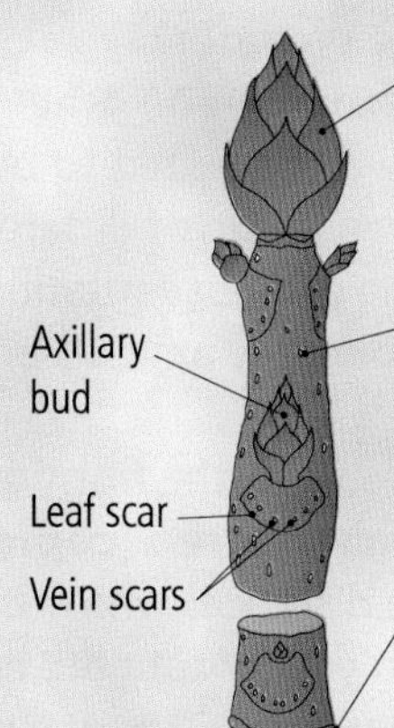

Winter twig from a horse chestnut tree

Predators and prey

YOU WILL LEARN!

- some animals have adaptations that protect them against predators
- some animals have adaptations that help them catch prey

A **predator** is an animal that kills another animal for food. The animal that gets eaten is called the **prey**. Predators are adapted to find, catch, kill and eat their prey. Prey animals are adapted to sense predators and hide from them.

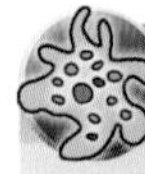

1 Predator or prey?

Look at the photographs:

Eagle

Tiger

Rabbit

Spider

Snail

Snake

- **a** Make a list of the predators.
- **b** What features of each are adaptations that help it to be an effective predator?
- **c** Using other sources of information, add other predators to your list. Describe how these are adapted to be predators. Try to find animals that show a range of different adaptations. Draw diagrams to show some of the adaptations.
- **d** Make similar lists to show how prey animals are able to avoid being killed.
- **e** Predators usually have their eyes at the front of their head. Both eyes work together to give **stereoscopic** vision. This makes it easier to judge distance, which is very important for catching prey. How could you investigate if this is true?
- **f** Many prey species are camouflaged. This makes it difficult for predators to see them. You can make 'animals' in different colours by colouring pieces of dough. Investigate the colours least likely to be seen by predators. Which colours are most likely to be seen by predators?

Did you know ?

Some animals protect themselves by having poisonous stings or bites. Others produce poison in their skins. These animals are often brightly coloured to warn predators to stay away. Some animals avoid being eaten by **'mimicking'** these animals. Hoverflies, for example, have no sting. They have a yellow and black striped body to mimic bees and wasps.

C5 Chains and webs

YOU WILL LEARN!

- how to find out what animals eat by making observations
- how to link animals in a food web
- that some plants are adapted to stop animals from eating them
- how to use different sources to find the information you need
- how changing the number of organisms in one part of a food web can affect other parts of the web

Food chains are a way of showing how energy passes from one organism to another. This happens when animals eat other organisms. The arrows show the flow of energy in a food chain.

lettuce → caterpillar → blackbird → sparrow-hawk

This tells us that a kestrel gets energy from a blackbird, the blackbird gets energy from a caterpillar and the caterpillar gets energy from a lettuce. The lettuce gets its energy from sunlight. It uses light energy to convert carbon dioxide and water to glucose. This is called **photosynthesis**. Oxygen is a waste product of photosynthesis.

Blackbirds eat more than just caterpillars. Many other animals eat caterpillars. This means that many different food chains are linked together. These make up **food webs**. We can work out the food webs in a habitat if we know what lives there and what they eat.

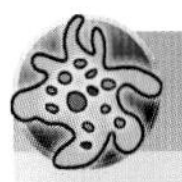

1 Evidence for food webs

Choose a habitat in your school grounds. The habitat you choose will depend on the type of area where your school is situated. It could be as small as a flowerbed.

a Your first task is to identify the different species that live in or visit the habitat. There are many ways of doing this:

- observation
- using pooters
- setting pitfall traps
- tree beating.

Find out how to carry out these methods. Decide which will be best in the habitat you have chosen. Now go out and identify as many species of plants and animals as possible in your habitat. You may find that **keys** are helpful for identifying what you find.

b Find out what the different animals eat. If you find an animal on a plant, there is a good chance it eats that plant. You may observe other evidence that tells you what animals eat. You can also look in secondary sources such as books, CD-ROMS and the Internet.

c Set up a database to record all the information you have collected.

Did you know

Owls eat small animals that they swallow whole, including the bones. Then they regurgitate these as **owl pellets**. Scientists collect these pellets. They can find out what the owl has eaten by identifying the bones in the pellets!

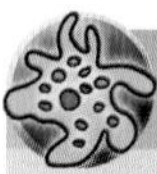

2 Making a food web

Use the evidence that you have stored on your database to create a food web for your habitat. You could do this as a wall display. Use pieces of wool to link the different organisms together. Remember that the links should show the direction in which energy flows through the food web.

Changes in one part of a food web can affect other parts of the web. Here is an example of a simple food web in a pond:

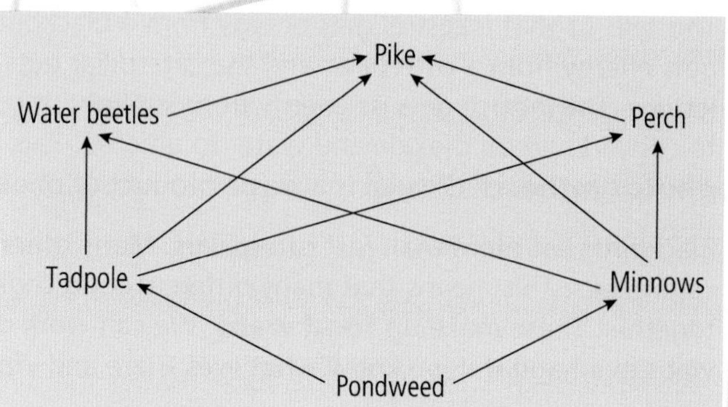

Plants are called **producers** because they photosynthesise to produce food. They use carbon dioxide and water, and energy from the Sun. Animals that eat plants are called **herbivores**. Animals that eat other animals are called **carnivores**.

Points to discuss

1. Pick out five different food chains from the pond food web above.
2. For each food chain, identify the producer, the herbivores and the carnivores.
3. In the summer the tadpoles will change into frogs and leave the pond. What will be the effect of this on:
   a the perch, **b** the minnows? Give reasons for your answers.

3 Changes in a food web

Look at the food web you made in Activity 2.

- **a** Identify any organisms that might be seasonal visitors.
- **b** Identify any organisms that might be killed in other ways, e.g. a gardener using **pesticides**.
- **c** What effects could these changes have in other parts of the food web?

Protecting plants

All food chains start with a green plant but, of course, plants don't set out to be eaten. Many have adaptations to deter animals from eating them. The spikes found on many cactus plants are an example of this kind of adaptation.

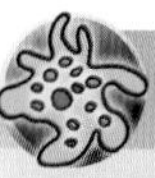

4 Protecting plants

Examine different species of plants. Identify adaptations that will deter animals from eating them. Use secondary sources to find other examples.

Summary

A **habitat** is any place where animals and plants live.
The animals and plants that live there are called a **community**.
The habitat and its community are called an **ecosystem**.
The community of a particular habitat will depend on the **physical features** and **environmental factors** of the habitat.

Animals and plants are **adapted** to live in their habitat.
Organisms can show **physical** and/or **behavioural** adaptations.

Environmental factors of habitats can vary throughout the year. They can also vary within a day. We can measure changes in environmental factors. Datalogging is often a helpful way of doing this. Animals and plants need to be adapted to survive changes in their habitats.

Predators are animals that kill other animals to feed.
The animals they eat are called **prey**. Predators are adapted to make them good at catching and killing their prey.
Prey animals are adapted to help them avoid being killed and eaten.
Plants often have adaptations that deter animals from eating them.

Animals and plants can be linked together in **food chains**.
A food chain shows how energy flows from **producers** (plants) to **consumers**. All the food chains in a habitat can be linked together to form a **food web**.

Key words

adaptation
community
consumer
ecosystem
environmental factors
food chain
food web
habitat
physical features
predator
prey
producer

Summary Questions

1 **a** Give examples of some physical features that would affect the animals and plants living in a habitat.
b Give examples of some environmental factors that would affect the animals and plants living in a habitat.

2 Explain the structural and/or behavioural adaptations that help the following organisms to survive in their habitat:
a swallow,
b limpet,
c giraffe,
d snail,
e monkey.

3 Make a list of some animals and plants that are adapted to survive the winter. For each one, say how it is adapted.

4 Look at the food web below:

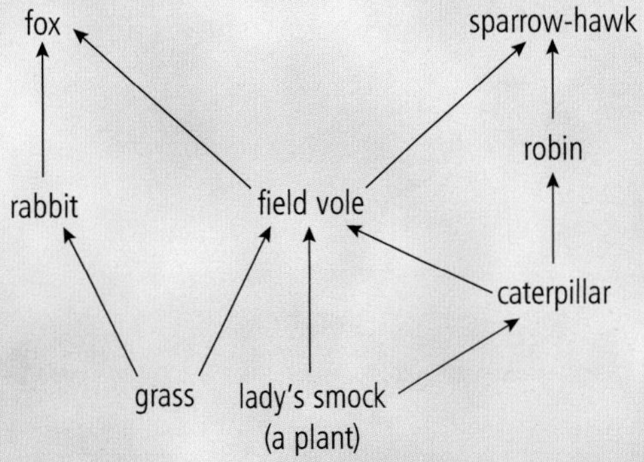

a Name **i** the producers, **ii** the consumers, **iii** the herbivores, **iv** the carnivores, **v** the prey, **vi** the predators.
b If the field voles died due to a disease, what would happen to
i the caterpillars, **ii** the robins,
iii the sparrow-hawks?

End of unit Questions

1 The five main groups of vertebrate animals are:

fish amphibians reptiles birds mammals

a Which sentence is true? *1 mark*

All vertebrates breathe with lungs.

All vertebrates have four legs.

All vertebrates have a backbone.

All vertebrates live on land.

b Megatherium was a large mammal. It is now extinct.
The drawing shows what scientists think Megatherium looked like.

i How can you tell, from the drawing, that Megatherium was a mammal? *1 mark*

ii Give **one** other way that mammals are different from other vertebrate animals. *1 mark*

c The drawing below shows a frog.

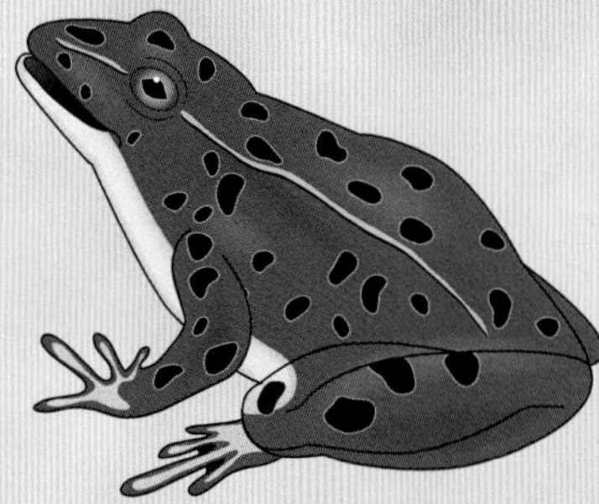

i To which group of vertebrates does the frog belong? *1 mark*

ii Give **one** way the frog is adapted for jumping. *1 mark*

iii Give **one** way the frog is adapted for moving about in water. *1 mark*

d The drawing below shows some frog's eggs. The female frog lays her eggs in water.

Give **one** reason why the eggs must be laid in water. *1 mark*

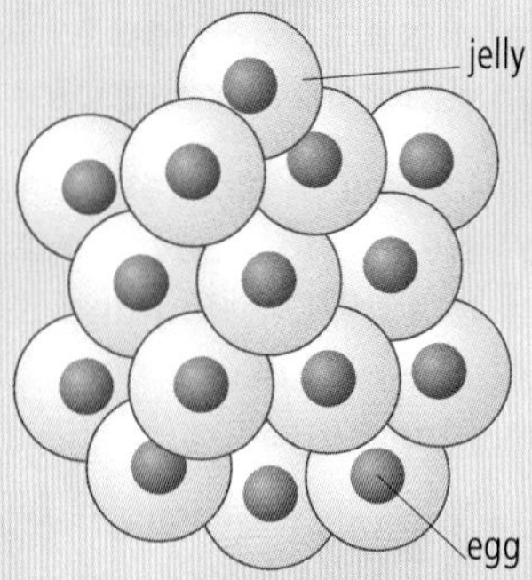

2 The diagram below shows part of a food web in a pond.

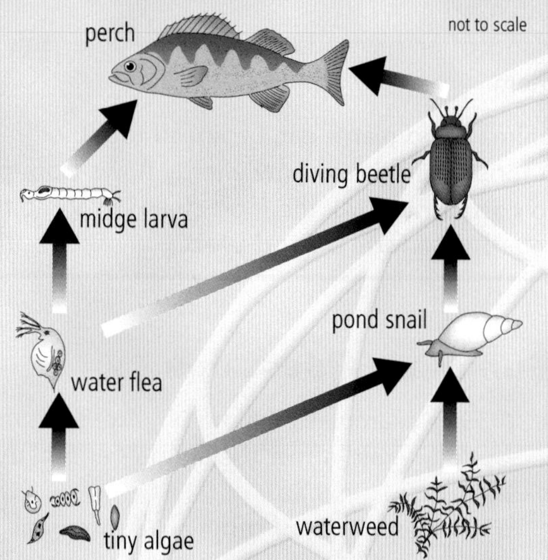

a i The numbers of tiny algae and waterweed in the pond increase. What effect will this have on the numbers of pond snails and water fleas? *1 mark*

ii Some more perch are put into the pond. What will happen to the numbers of midge larvae and diving beetles? *1 mark*

b From the food web:

i give the name of **one** predator; *1 mark*

ii give the name of its prey; *1 mark*

iii write one complete food chain which ends with perch. *1 mark*

.... → .... → .... → perch

7D Variation and classification

Introduction

There are millions of different **species** of animals and plants. Scientists **classify** them into groups of similar species. Within a species there are differences and similarities between individuals. In this unit you will find out how we classify species and how we can identify patterns of **variation** within species. Spreadsheets are a very useful tool to help store and interpret data about variation both between and within species.

You already know

- how to use keys to identify organisms
- about some of the differences between newly born animals of different species
- how different species are adapted to fit into a particular habitat

In this topic you will learn

- about the similarities and differences between different species of organisms
- about variation within a species
- why variations occur
- how and why scientists classify species of animals and plants
- different methods, including spreadsheets, of showing patterns of variation

1 Keys

a Choose a group of four or five of your classmates. Make a key that a new teacher could use to work out each person's name. The teacher should be able to do this without having to ask any questions.

b Make a list of some of the similarities and differences in the family shown in the picture above.

D1 The same but different

YOU WILL LEARN!

- individual members of a species differ from each other in many ways
- how to use a spreadsheet to store data
- how to use a spreadsheet to produce graphs
- how to use information to draw conclusions
- how to decide how valid your conclusions are

A **species** is a group of animals that can breed together to produce fertile offspring. Animals or plants of a particular species will be similar in many ways. There will, however, be differences within a species. Some species will show more differences than others, especially those that have been bred by humans.

Did you know

Some different species of animals can breed and produce offspring. For example, a horse and a donkey can mate and produce a mule. Mules, however, are sterile — they can't breed — so horses and donkeys are separate species.
In Sierra Nevada Zoo, in the USA, there is a *liger*, called Hobbs, a cross between a male lion and a female tiger.

1 Breeds of dog

Over many thousands of years humans have bred dogs to carry out a wide range of different jobs. Look at the photograph of several different breeds of dogs. All of them belong to the same species.

a Identify some of the different jobs of the dogs in the photographs. For each dog, identify the features that enable it to do its job effectively.

b In what ways are all the dogs similar?

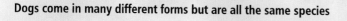

Dogs come in many different forms but are all the same species

Variation around us

All humans are members of the same species. There are many similarities between people. Yet we can easily recognise hundreds of different people because we are all different in many ways.

2 Variation in humans

Think about some of the many differences between people. Some of them can be measured easily. Others can be put into different categories, such as eye colour.

Your task is to look for patterns in variation between individuals. If you find that tall people usually have a wide arm span, then we say there is a close correlation between these two measurements.

a Collect data for all members of your class. Measure things like height, arm span and hand span. What other measurements can you easily make? Add information such as eye colour.

b Put the information you collect in a spreadsheet.

c Use your spreadsheet to produce a graph that will help you to answer the question *'Do taller people have wider arm spans?'*

d What does your graph tell you? Is this what you would expect? How valid is your conclusion? How can you improve its validity?

e Think of other questions about the patterns in your data. Use your spreadsheet to look for correlation between measurements you have made. Discuss the reliability of your evidence.

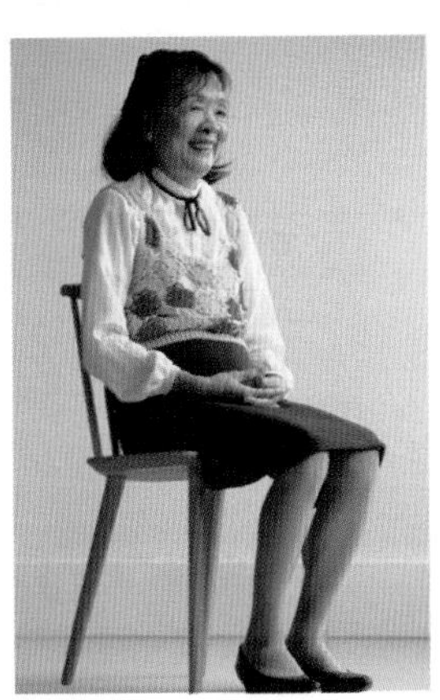

3 Patterns in variation

Variation occurs in all species of animals and plants. Look for variations in other species that you can investigate. Species that are found around your school grounds are easiest to look at. Some suggested questions to investigate are:

- *Do pink-tipped daisies have longer stems?*
- *Do longer holly leaves have more prickles?*
- *Do snails with longer shells have wider shells?*

You could look for correlation in the suggestions above. Better still, ask your own questions to investigate, based on your knowledge of the animals and plants found around your school. Make a prediction and then test it. Decide on a suitable sample size for your investigation. Use a spreadsheet to store and analyse your data. What conclusions can you draw? How valid are your conclusions?

D2 Causes of variation

YOU WILL LEARN!

- some variations are inherited
- individuals are similar to their parents but not identical
- offspring from the same parents are similar to each other but not identical
- some variations depend on the environment

We all look a bit like both our parents. We have some characteristics like our mother and others like our father. We have **inherited** these characteristics from our parents. An egg carries **genes** from the mother. A sperm carries genes from the father. A sperm fertilising an egg forms a **zygote**. This zygote contains, in its nucleus, genes from both parents. As the zygote divides to form new cells, the genes are copied. Each cell contains an identical set of genes. Half are inherited from the mother and half from the father.

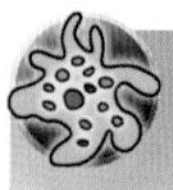

1 Which characteristics are inherited in humans?

Look at the pictures of members of the same family.

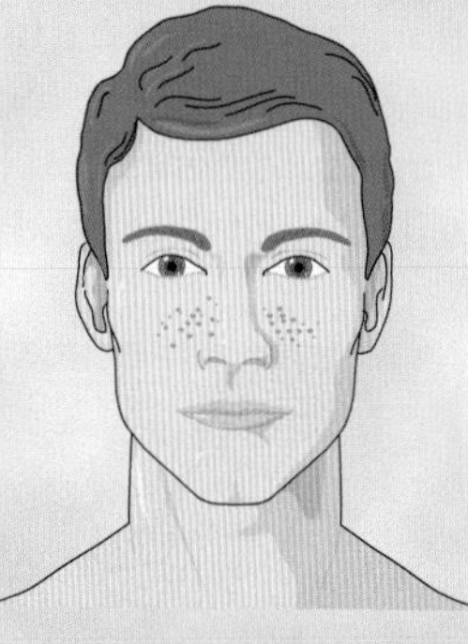

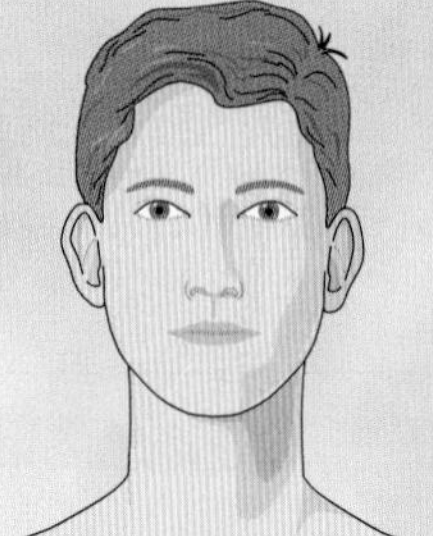
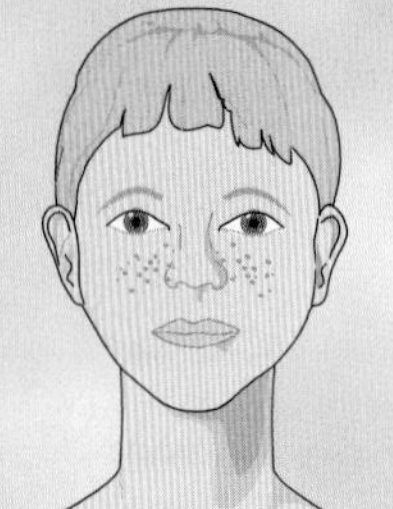
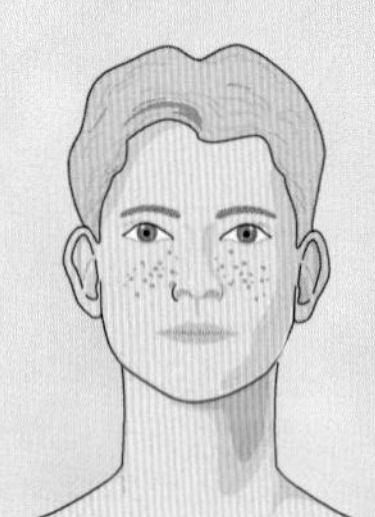
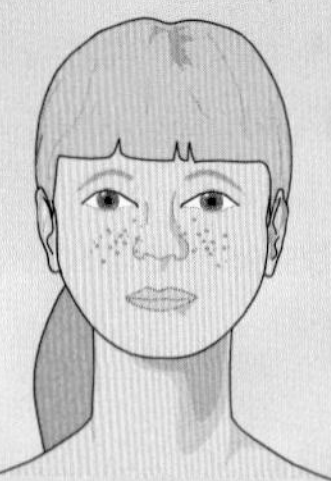

a Make a list of characteristics shown in the pictures that you think are inherited.

b Find out what is meant by **tongue rolling**. Is this an inherited characteristic?

c Some diseases and conditions are inherited. Try to find out about some of them.

d Try to make a list of other characteristics that are inherited in humans.

Did you know

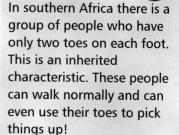

In southern Africa there is a group of people who have only two toes on each foot. This is an inherited characteristic. These people can walk normally and can even use their toes to pick things up!

Other inherited characteristics

Characteristics are inherited in all animals and plants.
Gregor Mendel was an Austrian monk. He spent a lot of his time working in the monastery garden. He was an observant man and noticed many characteristics of pea plants that he realised were inherited. He carried out experiments over many years and published his results in 1865. Sadly, no one really noticed what he had found out at the time. It was only much later that other scientists, also studying inheritance, found Mendel's work and made it well known.

2 Other inherited characteristics

a Find out more about Gregor Mendel and write about his life. Why do you think nobody noticed his work when it was first published? You could put him in a class book about famous scientists. Find out about the inherited characteristics of pea plants that he discovered.

b Find out about other characteristics that are inherited in other species of plants and animals.

Environmental variation

Not all variation is inherited. The **environment** can also affect how individual organisms develop. Bonsai trees are very small versions of normal trees. They are grown from normal seeds. If these seeds were planted in good, deep soil, with plenty of sun and water, they would develop to a normal size. Planting them in a very shallow pot and cutting back the roots regularly stunts their growth. If we collected seeds from a bonsai tree and planted them normally, then a full size tree would grow.

Both are the same age and species

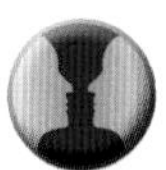

Points to discuss

Hydrangea plants are often found in gardens. Some have pink flowers, others have blue flowers. The flower colour depends on the type of soil it is growing in. In a chalky soil they are pink. In a peaty soil they are blue. Can you explain this? Look in Unit 7E for some help.

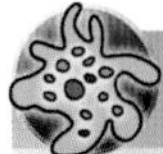

3 Environmental variation

Look at the two pictures of the same species of tree. One has grown in a sheltered place. The other has grown on a windy hilltop. Explain the differences.

Inheritance or environment?

For some characteristics, it is difficult to be sure if they are due to inherited or environmental factors. It may be a combination of both.

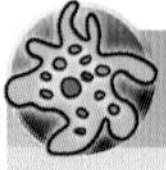

4 Is height due to inheritance or environment?

The information below gives the heights of five generations of men in the same family:

Jack	*born 1880*	*height 179 cm*
Bill	*born 1910*	*height 185 cm*
John	*born 1933*	*height 188 cm*
Phil	*born 1957*	*height 192 cm*
James	*born 1984*	*height 194 cm*

a What factors, apart from inheritance, could have affected the heights of these five men?

b Does the information help us to decide if height is due to inherited or to environmental factors?

c What other information would we need to draw a firm conclusion?

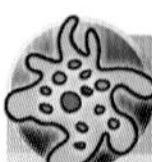

5 Leaf size

Different plants of the same species often show wide variation in the size of their leaves. Is leaf size due to inherited or environmental factors?

Design an experiment to investigate this question. Choose a plant that is found in a range of places in your school grounds. Collect data about leaf sizes. Decide what other factors might affect leaf size. Collect any other data that might be important in reaching a conclusion.

Present your findings to other members of your class. Explain what you have found out. How reliable do you think your conclusions are?

Points to discuss

Identical twins have identical genes. Non-identical twins only have some genes in common. Scientists have compared identical twins that were separated in early life with those who were brought up together.

Average difference in IQ (a measurement of intelligence)		
Identical twins brought up together	Non-identical twins brought up together	Identical twins brought up apart
3.0	8.4	5.9

(From *Freeman, Newman, and Holzinger,* Twins: A study of heredity and environment, *Univ. Chicago Press, 1937*)

- What do you think these results tell us?

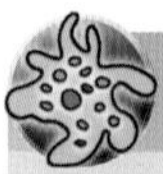

6 Inheritance, environment or both?

Look around your class. Make a list of characteristics that make us different from each other. Draw up a table to show whether these characteristics are due to inheritance, environment or both.

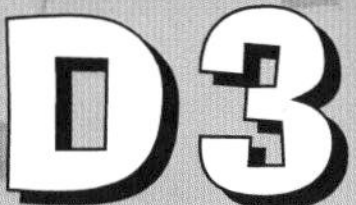

D3 Describing living things

YOU WILL LEARN!
- how to work safely with living organisms
- how to make observations to compare living organisms
- how to use different styles of writing to describe living organisms

So far in this topic we have concentrated on looking at variation within a species. It is also important for scientists to be able to compare different species. To do this we need to be able to describe organisms accurately. There are many ways of describing animals and plants. Only some of them are suitable to use in science.

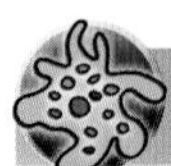

1 Styles of writing

Read these different pieces of writing which all describe animals.

Extract from *The Fish* by Elizabeth Bishop

…Here and there
his brown skin hung in strips
like ancient wallpaper,
and its pattern of darker brown
was like wallpaper:
shapes like full-blown roses
stained and lost through age.
He was speckled and barnacles,
fine rosettes of lime,
and infested
with tiny white sea-lice,
and underneath two or three
rags of green weed hung down.

(From *Elizabeth Bishop*, The Complete Poems 1927–1979, *Farrar, Straus and Giroux Inc 1979,1983*)

Extract from *Coming up for Air* by George Orwell

It was an enormous fish. I don't exaggerate when I say it was enormous. It was almost the length of my arm. It glided across the pool, deep under water, and then became a shadow and disappeared into the darker water on the other side. I felt as if a sword had gone through me. It was far the biggest fish I'd ever seen, dead or alive. I stood there without breathing, and in a moment another huge thick shape glided through the water, and then another and then two more close together. The pool was full of them. They were carp I suppose.

(From *George Orwell,* Coming up for Air, *Eric Blair 1939*)

Common Carp

Length: Average 75–80 cm.

Weight: Average 8–10 kg but females can reach 40 kg.

Body: Deep and flat from side to side. Forked tail and long dorsal fin.

Mouth: Large. Teeth are found in the throat, rather than on the jaws.

Colour: In the wild, dark grey, almost black. A wide variety of colours are seen in specimens bred in captivity.

Barbels: Two on upper lip and one each side of the mouth. These are used as touch organs.

a Each piece has been written for a different purpose. What is the purpose of each piece of writing? How can you tell?

b Use other sources of information to find different styles of writing about an animal or plant.

c Try writing an **acrostic** describing an animal or plant. Write the name of the animal down the left side of your page. Start each line with the letters you have written. For example:

__C__anine teeth are very sharp
__A__ll four paws have sharp, retractable claws
__T__ail is long and helps to keep balance

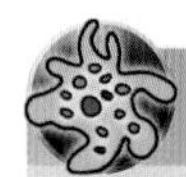

2 Describing organisms

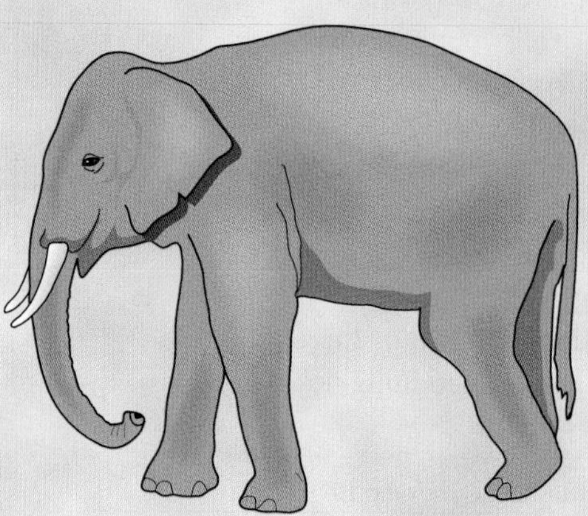

- **a** Write a **scientific** description of the animals shown in these drawings.
- **b** Use secondary sources to find extra information, such as size, diet, behaviour, etc.
- **c** Look at a range of other animals found in or around your school. Some may be kept in school while others might be collected in the school grounds. If it is not possible to find animals in school, then look for examples in books, videos, CD-ROMS or the Internet. Working in pairs, describe in detail each animal you examine. It is important that you find out the correct scientific words for different body parts. Try making a table to summarise features of all of the animals you describe.
- **d** Choose two animals that are similar but not identical. Describe features that make them similar. Describe features that show that they are different from each other.
- **e** Compare your descriptions with other members of your class. Do they match up?

Treat all animals with care.

Any that are collected from outside must be returned to where they were found.

Wash your hands after handling any animals.

Sorting into groups

YOU WILL LEARN!

- although all members of a species differ in many ways, they also have many features in common
- how to classify fingerprints into groups
- how to sort organisms into groups according to common features
- a newly discovered animal or plant might fit into an existing group or it may need a new group

Fingerprints

Fingerprints can be easily used to identify people for three reasons:

- Every person in the world has different fingerprints.
- Your fingerprints do not change during your lifetime.
- Fingerprints can be classified into different types.

1 Fingerprints

Collect about 20 or 30 fingerprints. Your teacher may have produced a set for you. If not, collect a fingerprint from each member of your class. Examine them closely. (A hand lens might be useful.) Working in a group, sort the fingerprints into groups of similar types.

a Explain what features of each type helped you to group them together.
Get a class member to give a single fingerprint on a sheet of paper. Challenge the rest of your group to identify who it came from.

b Use secondary sources to find out about fingerprints. When did the police first use them? Who came up with the idea of using fingerprints for identification? What system of classification do forensic scientists use for grouping fingerprints? Was it the same as yours?
Find out how forensic scientists take fingerprints from different surfaces. Try using their methods to take fingerprints from glass or metal surfaces.

c Produce a display of your work about fingerprints. See if you can invite a police officer into school to tell your class more about how fingerprints are used.

Points to discuss

Would you expect identical twins to have identical fingerprints? If not, then what other factors could influence how their fingerprints develop?

Did you know

The ridges on the tips of our fingers that form fingerprints help make it easier for us to grip things without them slipping.

Classifying organisms

Scientists classify animals into groups based on features they have in common. They want to ensure that a particular animal or plant can be placed into only one group and no other.

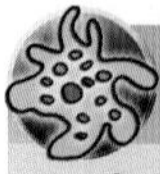

2 Grouping organisms

Josh is given a list of animals to put into groups.
Here is the result:

Live on land	*Live in water*	*Live in the air*
Frog	*Frog*	*Duck*
Duck	*Duck*	*Swift*
Snake	*Carp*	*Bat*
Horse	*Crocodile*	*Sparrow*
Ostrich	*Turtle*	
Lion	*Whale*	

a What are the problems with the system of classification used by Josh?

Look at the descriptions of organisms that you did in D3 Activity 2. Sort the organisms you looked at into groups, based on the descriptions you made.

b Explain how you decided on these groupings. Is it the same as other members of your class have made? Try to add other organisms to the groups you have made. You should be able to add a new organism to **only** one group. If it fits into two or more groups then you need to change the way in which you sorted the organisms.

Think about work you have done on **identification keys**. If you cannot remember how to use one, look at the simple example for identifying garden animals:

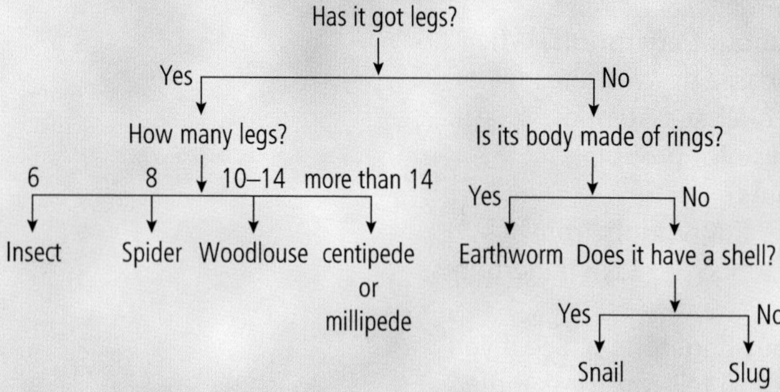

c Try to draw a similar branching key using the classification system you have used.

d Produce a display of your system of classification. Show how you can use it to classify an organism.

e Use a computer database to make a system that would help younger pupils to classify animals.

D5 How scientists classify living things

- there is a system of classifying organisms that is used by scientists all over the world
- plants and animals are separate groups of living things
- animals are divided into vertebrates and invertebrates
- vertebrates are further divided into fish, amphibians, reptiles, birds and mammals
- invertebrates are sub-divided into several groups

Scientists give every species of organism its own name. They put similar organisms in the same groups. The science of classification is called **taxonomy**. To start with they put organisms into five very large groups called **kingdoms**. These kingdoms are:

- plants
- animals
- bacteria
- fungi
- protists.

In this book we will be looking mainly at the plant and animal kingdoms.

1 Plant or animal?

It might seem obvious whether an organism is a plant or an animal. However this is not always the case. Organisms, such as **hydra** and **sea anemones**, look a lot like plants but they are animals. Scientists need a set of rules to help them to decide if an organism is a plant or an animal.

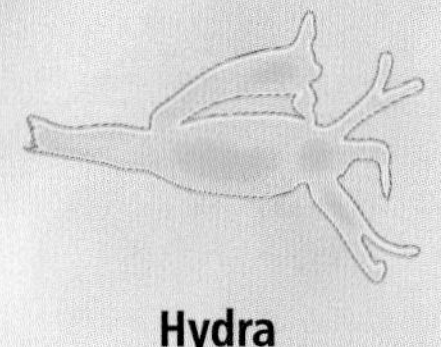
Hydra

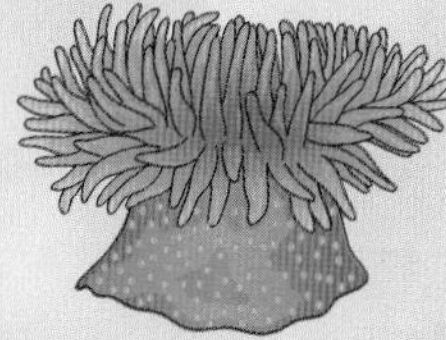
Sea anemone

Look at the work you did about cells in Unit 7A.

a Describe the features that make plants different from animals. Make a table to show the differences.

b Try to find examples of other animals that look like they belong in the plant kingdom.

2 Other kingdoms

Find out about bacteria, fungi and protists. It might be useful to work in a group of three. One person can look at each of these kingdoms.

a Write a description of each of these kingdoms.

b Draw diagrams of these organisms.

c Explain what makes these organisms different from animals and plants.
Display your work for others to see.

Once scientists have sorted organisms into kingdoms, they can divide them into smaller groups. We can divide animals into those with backbones (**vertebrates**) and those without backbones (**invertebrates**). All vertebrates have a skeleton inside their body. Vertebrates can be sub-divided into five smaller groups. Invertebrates can be sub-divided into seven smaller groups.

Vertebrates

Vertebrates are classified as shown below:

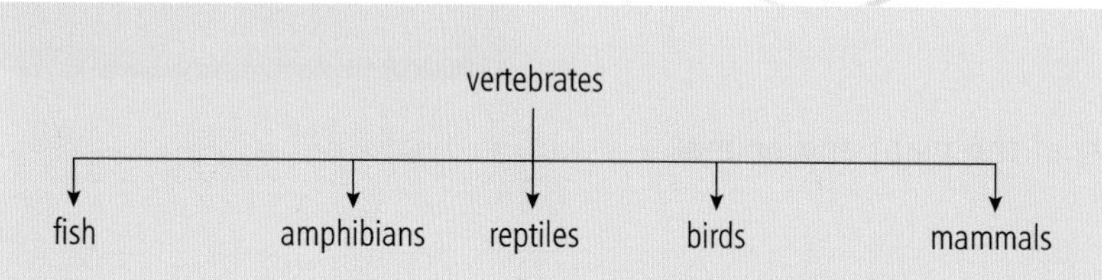

3 Classifying vertebrates

a Find out how vertebrates are classified as fish, amphibians, reptiles, birds and mammals.

b Draw a poster with branches for each group.

c Write a description for each group. This should explain the features used to place a vertebrate in a particular group.

d Decide which group the vertebrates shown on this page should be put in.

e Use other sources of information to find other vertebrates to put into groups. Use pictures to illustrate your work if possible.

f Can you find any examples of vertebrates that do not 'fit the rules' for a particular group?

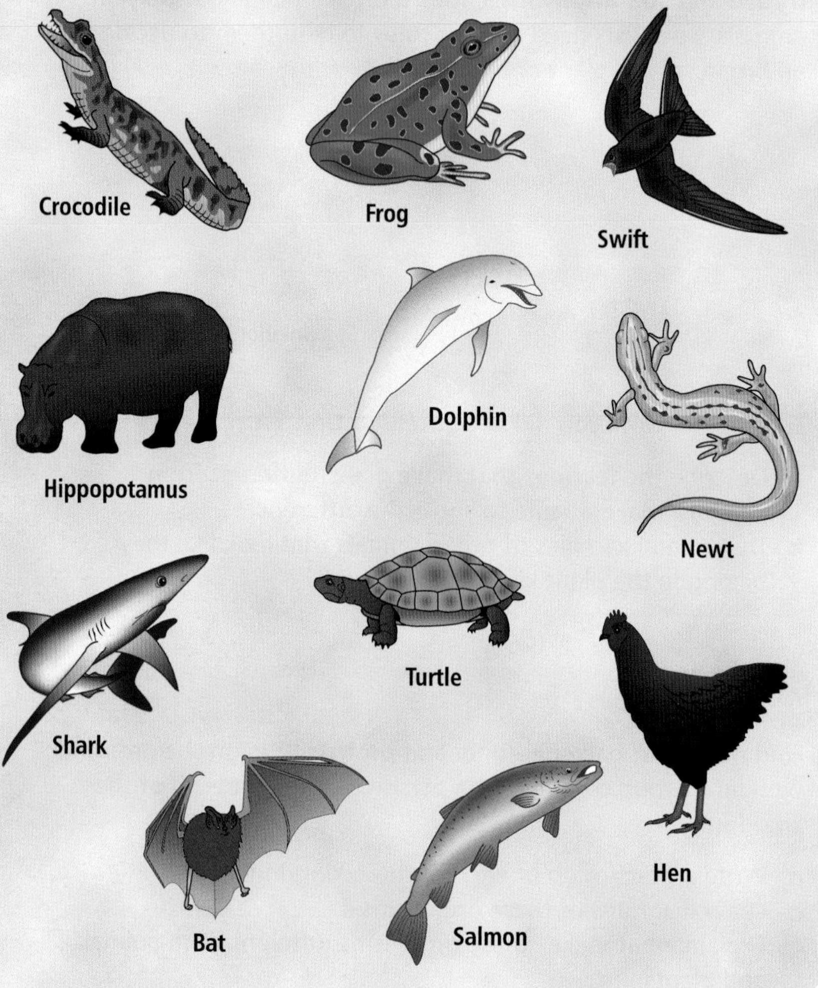

Points to discuss

- To which vertebrate group did dinosaurs belong? How did you decide?

Did you know?

The climbing perch is a fish from Asia. It can walk out of water and can even climb trees!

Invertebrates

Invertebrates can be classified as shown:

- coelenterates
- flatworms
- roundworms
- segmented worms
- molluscs
- echinoderms
- arthropods

Arthropods can be divided further into

- crustaceans
- insects
- arachnids
- myriapods

Jellyfish

Sea anemone

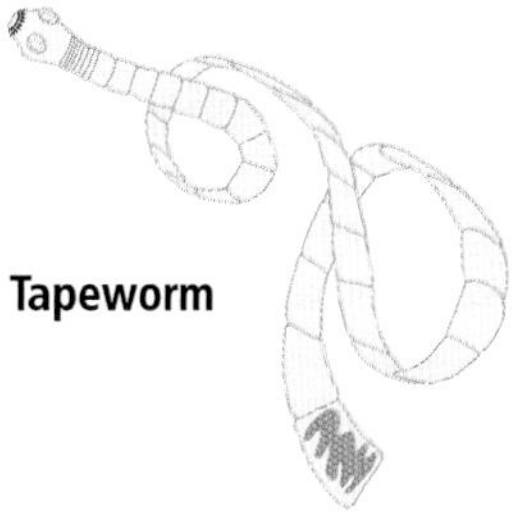

Tapeworm

Nematode worm

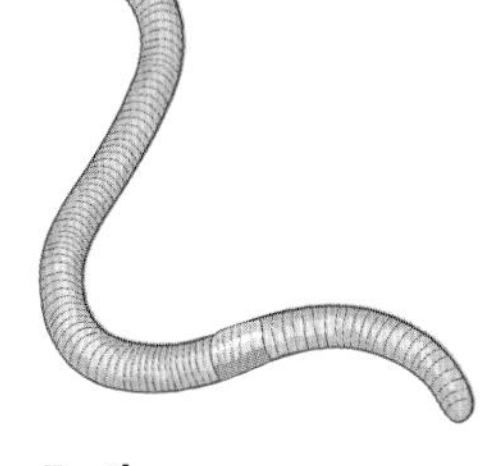

Earthworm

Snail

Octopus

Woodlouse

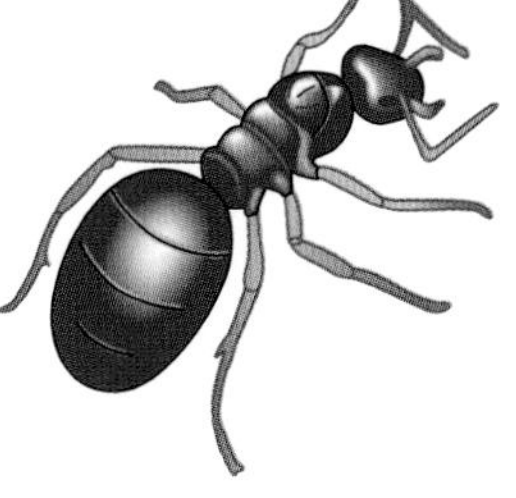

Ant

Scorpion

Starfish

Crab

Wasp

Spider

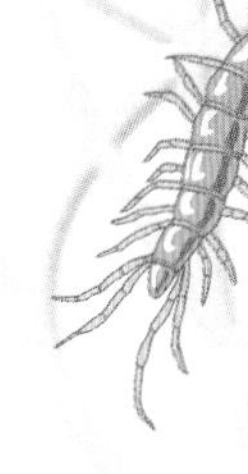

Centipede

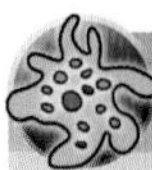

4 Classifying invertebrates

a Choose one invertebrate sub-group. Find out about the features that decide which organisms belong to that group.

b Find some examples of invertebrates in the group you are studying. Books, CD-ROMS, videos and the Internet will help you find what you need. If possible, try to find pictures to illustrate what you find.

c Present what you find to the rest of your class.

d Use information from your whole class to produce a display about invertebrate sub-groups. Describe the essential features of each group. Give examples of each group.

Did you know

About 80 % of all the animals on Earth are arthropods. That's about 10 million species! And scientists believe there could be millions more yet to be discovered.

Points to discuss

All scientists around the world use the same system of classification. They also name organisms in Latin.
Why is this helpful?

Summary

A **species** is a group of organisms that can breed together to produce fertile offspring. Members of the same species have many features in common but there will be **variation** between the individuals.

Some variations are **inherited**. They are passed on in the genes from the parents. Other variations are due to the **environment**. Some variations are due to a combination of inherited and environmental factors.

Scientists around the world use the same system of classifying organisms. They divide organisms into **taxonomic** groups. There are five **kingdoms**: plant, animal, bacteria, fungi and protists. These kingdoms can be sub-divided.

The animal kingdom can be divided into **vertebrates** and **invertebrates**. Vertebrates can be divided into **fish**, **amphibians**, **reptiles**, **birds** and **mammals**. Invertebrates can be divided into **coelenterates**, **flatworms**, **roundworms**, **segmented worms**, **molluscs**, **echinoderms** and **arthropods**.

Some animals are more difficult to classify than others.

Key words

gene
inherited
invertebrate
kingdom
species
taxonomic
variation
vertebrate

Summary Questions

1 Explain these observations.
- **a** A lion and a tiger look more alike than a dalmatian and a St Bernard, yet the lion and tiger are separate species while a dalmatian and a St Bernard are the same species.
- **b** Children with the same parents look similar but not identical.
- **c** Over the last hundred years the average height of adults in the UK has increased.
- **d** Seeds from a tiny bonsai tree will grow into a full size specimen.

2 What taxonomic groups of vertebrates do these describe?
- **a** Has feathers, lays eggs with a hard shell, has wings, breathes through lungs.
- **b** Has a body covered in scales, breathes through gills, lays eggs in water.
- **c** Has hair, lungs for breathing, young feed on milk produced by the mother.
- **d** Has a moist skin without scales, lays eggs in water, adult has lungs.
- **e** Has a dry, scaly skin, lays eggs with a soft shell, has lungs for breathing.

3 Write a description for each of the groups of invertebrates.

4 Draw a table to summarise the differences between animals and plants.

5 To which taxonomic groups do these belong:
- **a** newt
- **b** dolphin
- **c** turtle
- **d** kangaroo
- **e** bat
- **f** seahorse
- **g** eel
- **h** penguin
- **i** dogfish
- **j** shark
- **k** scorpion
- **l** squid
- **m** sea urchin
- **n** jellyfish
- **o** woodlouse
- **p** ant?

Give reasons for your answers.

6 Write accurate definitions to show that you understand the meanings of these words, when used to describe animals:
- **a** segment
- **b** abdomen
- **c** shell
- **d** limb
- **e** leg
- **f** thorax
- **g** antenna.

End of unit Questions

1 a Each of the drawings below shows an animal from a different group.

i The cat's fur traps warm air next to its body. In the drawings above, which other animal can trap warm air next to its body? *1 mark*

ii The cat is a mammal. Its body is covered with fur.
Give **one** other fact about cats which shows they are mammals. *1 mark*

b The five groups of vertebrates are:

fish amphibians reptiles
birds mammals

i Which **two** groups have bodies covered with scales? *2 marks*

ii Which **two** groups lay eggs in water? *2 marks*

2 Suzie keeps five chickens in her garden. During the night they are locked in a shed. The table shows details of Suzie's chickens.

name of chicken	sex	number of eggs laid last year
Molly	female	160
Emily	female	190
Skinny	female	150
Lucy	female	200
Elvis	male	

a Suzie wants each of her hens to lay as many eggs as possible.
She changes their food and water to give them the best recommended balanced diet.
Suggest **two** other ways she could change the hens' living conditions to encourage them to lay more eggs. *2 marks*

b Suzie plans a selective breeding programme to get chickens which lay high numbers of eggs each year.

i Which hen should she choose as a mate for Elvis at the beginning of her breeding programme? *1 mark*

ii How should Suzie choose hens from the offspring to continue her breeding programme? *1 mark*

3 a The diagram shows the family tree for a family of rabbits.

Use the words from the list below to complete the sentences *3 marks*

adapt cytoplasm genes grow
inherit letters membrane
mutate nuclei

Rabbits have the same fur colour all year round.
Young rabbits .... fur colour from their parents.
Information about fur colour is passed on from one generation to the next in the form of .... in the .... of an egg and sperm.

7E Acids and alkalis

Introduction

We come across acids everyday of our lives – often without realising it! You will find acids in oranges, fizzy drinks, vinegar and even rain. People are generally familiar with the word acid but not many know that the word comes from the Latin word 'acidus', meaning sour. Most people are unsure about alkalis, the chemical opposites of acids. However, by the end of this topic you will know a lot more!

You already know

- some substances are classified as acids
- solids can dissolve to form solutions
- mixing substances together sometimes results in new substances being made

In this topic you will learn

- about the uses and properties of acids
- how we use indicators to detect acidic and alkaline solutions
- about the pH scale
- about acids reacting with alkalis (neutralisation)

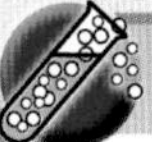

1 What can you remember?

a Name five solids that dissolve in water.
b Which acids might you find at home?
c Which acid do we find in car batteries?
d Name any acids you can see in the picture above.

E1 Using acids

YOU WILL LEARN!

- many things we use at home are acids
- not all acids are hazardous

Many people think of acids as dangerous, fuming liquids; the type of thing you see bubbling away in old horror films. But what do you think? Try Activity 1 below.

1 Ideas about acids

a Work with a partner to make a list of all your current ideas about acids. Don't look up any information, just record whatever comes to mind. You can use this list to check your progress at the end of the unit!

b Start a list of the names of any acids you know already. Your job is to add to this list as you come across new acids in your work.

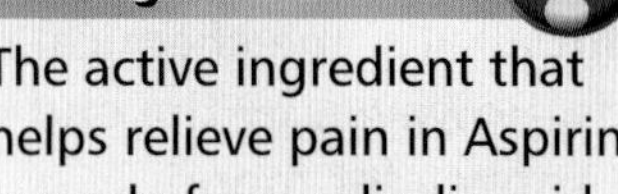

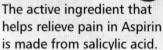

Did you know?

The active ingredient that helps relieve pain in Aspirin is made from salicylic acid.

Fizzy drinks contain acid

Acids in foods

Not all acids are dangerous! We find acids naturally in many foods. Look at the table below of acids found in some food and drink:

Food or drink	Acid it contains
oranges, lemons, limes	citric acid
apples	malic acid
vinegar	ethanoic acid
tea	tannic acid
Vitamin C tablet	ascorbic acid

Did you know?

Coca Cola contains an acid called phosphoric acid.

Points to discuss

1 The acid in oranges, lemons and limes gives these fruits their general name. What is this general name?

2 As well as citric acid, which other acid from the table above can you also find in oranges, lemons and limes?

We also ***add*** acids, not only vinegar, to our food. Food manufacturers often put additives into food during its processing. Look at the food labels shown below.

Brown flour	Vitamin drink	Breakfast cereal	Chocolate biscuit
INGREDIENTS Brown flour, malted wheatflakes, malt flour, flour treatment agent (ascorbic acid)	INGREDIENTS Water, blackcurrant juice, citric acid, sweeteners, vitamins (C, niacin (which is nicotinic acid), pantothenic acid, B6, B12, D) acidity regulator, preservatives.	INGREDIENTS Maize, sugar, malt flavouring, niacin, iron, vitamin B6, riboflavin (B2), thiamine (B1), folic acid, vitamin B12.	INGREDIENTS Sugar, vegetable oils, wheat flour, dried skimmed milk, lactose, butter oil, maltodextrin, flavourings, emulsifier (lecithin), raising agents, (sodium bicarbonate ammonium bicarbonate, tartaric acid), salt,colour (annatto).

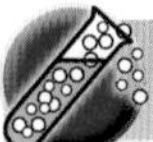 2 Food additives

a Add any new acids you see to your list of acids started in Activity 1.
b Think of two reasons why we add acids to food.
c Do some research on food additives to find out how acids are labelled in foods using **E numbers**.
d What are your views on adding substances to foods as they are processed. Present some arguments for and against, then draw your conclusion (if you can!).

Some acids preserve things

One reason that some acids are added to foods is to preserve them. This property proved very useful for archaeologists in 1983. Two workers were digging out peat from a bog in Cheshire when they discovered what looked like an old leather football. It was actually the head of a woman who had been dead for about 1750 years. The head was remarkably well preserved. It still had bits of hair and scalp attached, as well as one eyeball and some brain left! The head had not rotted away because of the acids we find in peat bogs (called humic and fulvic acids). There is also very little oxygen in a peat bog so the microbes that decompose things cannot survive there.

This is the head of 'Lindow Man'. It has been preserved in a peat bog.

 3 Preserved in acid

a Name some foods that we preserve in acid?
b Find out:
  i how peat is formed,
  ii what we use it for and why we are looking for alternatives.
c A better example of an ancient body was found later in the same bog. Find out about 'Lindow Man' and write a short newspaper report about him.

E2 Be safe with acids and alkalis

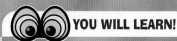

YOU WILL LEARN!

- how to recognise and interpret common hazard signs
- how to deal with acids or alkalis if they are spilt or splashed onto your skin
- that adding water to solutions of acids or alkalis dilutes them, making them less hazardous

The acids you have looked at so far have not been dangerous to handle. However, some acids (and alkalis) are very hazardous. Containers of these liquids have hazard warning signs on them. You need to know these signs to handle acids and alkalis safely.

CORROSIVE
These substances attack and destroy living tissues, including eyes and skin

IRRITANT
These substances are not corrosive but can cause reddening or blistering of the skin

HARMFUL
These substances are harmful if swallowed or breathed in or absorbed through your skin. They are not as dangerous as toxic substances, which can cause death

1 Hazard signs

Find out the hazard signs for substances that are:

a toxic
b highly flammable
c oxidising agents

It is not only in the science laboratory that you find these warnings. Some household products contain hazardous acid or alkali.

This oven cleaner spray is extremely flammable as well as causing irritation on your skin. It contains an alkali to break down grease.

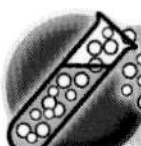

2 Unblocking sinks

a Which product contains the more concentrated alkali – the oven cleaner on the previous page or the liquid that unblocks sinks shown opposite? Explain your answer.

b How do you think the liquid unblocks sinks?

Did you know

In 1999 a man in London killed his ex-girlfriend by tricking her into drinking neat drain cleaner. It contained sulfuric acid.

Did you know

In the 1990s a serial killer in Pakistan murdered over 100 street boys, disposing of their bodies in bins of concentrated acid.

Label from a product used to unblock sinks

Transporting chemicals safely

You might have noticed the hazard signs on road tankers carrying chemicals. Look at the sign below:

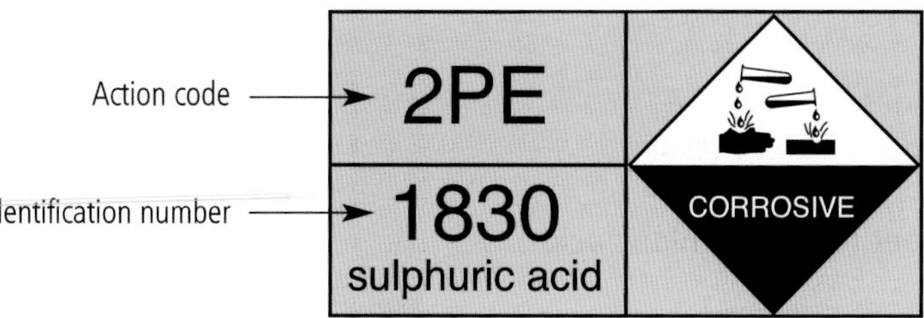

The action code tells a fire fighter at the scene of an accident how to deal with the chemical. Look at the code below:

1	Coarse spray
2	Fine spray
3	Foam
4	Dry agent

P	V	Liquid-tight chemical protective clothing	
R			DILUTE
S	V	Breathing apparatus and fire fighting kit	SPILLAGE
T			
W	V	Liquid-tight chemical protective clothing	
X			CONTAIN
Y	V	Breathing apparatus and fire fighting kit	SPILLAGE
Z			
E		PUBLIC SAFETY HAZARD	

Why do tankers like this have to display hazard signs?

3 Treating road spills

a How would you treat concentrated sulfuric acid in a road accident?

b Try to find out what is on the hazard signs on the back of a petrol tanker.

Did you know

The British use the spelling 'sulphur' but internationally 'sulfur' has become accepted. So you can use either and still be right!

Safety in the laboratory

Look at the bottles of hydrochloric acid opposite:

Did you know ?

We all have hydrochloric acid in our stomachs.
What do you think it is used for?

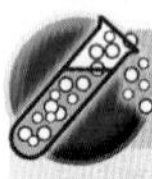

4 Acids in the laboratory

a Why do the bottles of hydrochloric acid have different hazard signs on them?
b How can you make concentrated hydrochloric acid safer to use?
c When diluting concentrated sulfuric acid, you must always add the acid to water (never add water to the acid). Look up why it is dangerous to add water to concentrated acid.

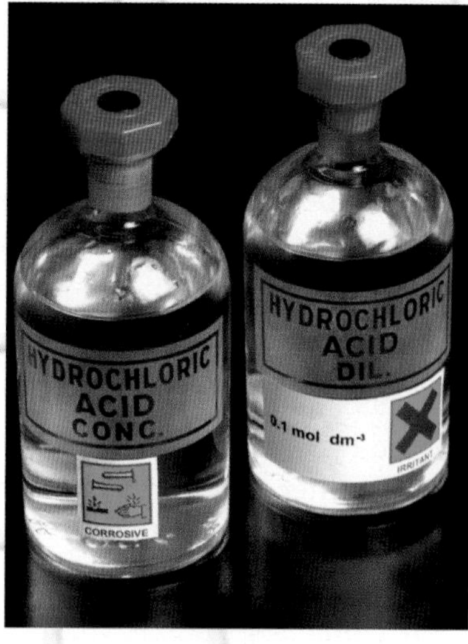

Different concentrations of hydrochloric acid.

Sometimes accidents happen in laboratories. Look at the photograph opposite: What should you do if acid or alkali accidentally splashes into your eye?
Look at the part of the student safety sheet for hydrochloric acid below:

Emergency action

• **In eye**	Flood eye with gently running tap water for 10 minutes. See doctor.
• **Vapour breathed in**	Remove to fresh air. Call doctor if breathing is difficult.
• **Swallowed**	Wash out mouth. Give glass of water to drink. Do NOT make victim vomit. See doctor.
• **Spilt on skin or clothing**	Remove contaminated clothing. Then drench skin with plenty of water. If a large area is affected or blistering occurs, see a doctor.
• **Spilt on floor,bench, etc.**	**For release of gas, consider the need to evacuate the laboratory and open windows.** For large spills, and especially for (moderately) concentrated acid, cover with mineral absorbent (eg. cat litter) and scoop into bucket. Neutralise with sodium carbonate. Rinse with plenty of water. Wipe up small amounts with damp cloth. Rinse well.

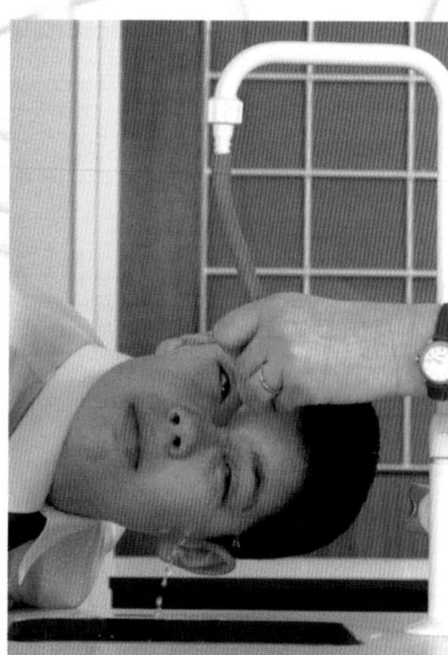

What should you always wear when handling acids or alkalis?

Why are student safety sheets particularly important when you plan your own experiments?

5 Acid spill

If concentrated hydrochloric acid is spilt, your teacher can add sodium carbonate to make it safe before cleaning it up.
Try adding some of this white powder to DILUTE hydrochloric acid in a petri dish.
What happens? How do you know when the acid spillage is safe?

Make your own indicator

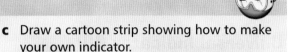

YOU WILL LEARN!

- how to use indicators to classify acids and alkalis
- how to make your own indicator
- how to design a table for your results

Indicators

Some dyes change colour depending on whether they are in acidic or alkaline solutions. We call these dyes **indicators**.
Many of the dyes can be extracted from plants. Can you think of a few plants that could give a deeply coloured dye?
You can try some of the activities below to find out about indicators. Make sure you wear eye protection and take care – they all involve using acids and alkalis.

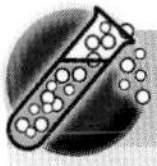

1 Making an indicator

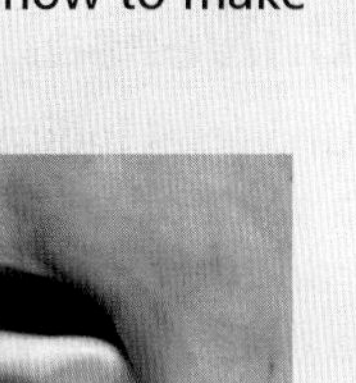

In this practical you can make your own indicator.

You can choose which plant material to use. You will have to crush and grind the plant material, using a mortar and pestle. You can add a little water and ethanol to dissolve the dye. A little sand can also help the grinding process. You can make indicator paper by staining strips of filter paper. Then leave them to dry. Or you can use the dye as indicator solution.

a What colour does your indicator go in hydrochloric acid?

b What colour does your indicator go in sodium hydroxide solution (an alkali)?

c Draw a cartoon strip showing how to make your own indicator.

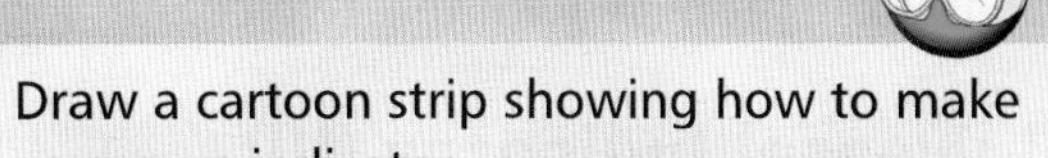

2 Testing solutions

Your teacher will give you a range of solutions to test. Your task is to use your indicator to decide which are acidic and which are alkaline.
Design your own table to show your results. It should show what happened in each test and whether each solution is acidic or alkaline.

EXCUSE ME. CAN YOU TELL ME IF THIS IS ACIDIC OR ALKALINE PLEASE?

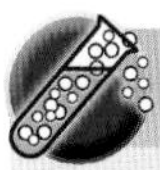

3 Different indicators

There are many different indicators. Your teacher will provide you with a range of indicators. You have to find out their colours in acid and alkali and present your results in a table.

4 Which plant material makes the best indicator?

Plan a fair test to find out the answer to this question.
Decide what you think makes a good indicator and then try out your investigation.

E4 Universal indicator and the pH scale

YOU WILL LEARN!

- the range of colours and numbers on the pH scale and what they tell us

Points to discuss

You have seen how indicators work in E3. But say you were given a solution of sulfuric acid and a solution of a weak acid, like citric acid. Would the indicators from E3 tell you which was the really hazardous solution?
Or what if you were given a concentrated solution of a strong acid and a very, very dilute solution of the same acid. Would the indicators from E3 be able to tell you which was which?
What is the problem with the 'two-colour' indicators?

HELP! HOW CAN I TELL WHICH ONE IS HAZARDOUS?

Universal Indicator (UI)

Universal Indicator is a mixture of dyes. You can buy it as a solution or as UI paper. When you add a solution, the UI can turn a range of colours. The colours have been given a number, called the **pH number** or value. The pH tells us how strongly acidic or alkaline a solution is.

The range of colours and numbers (usually from 1 to 14) is called the **pH scale**. Look at the pH scale below:

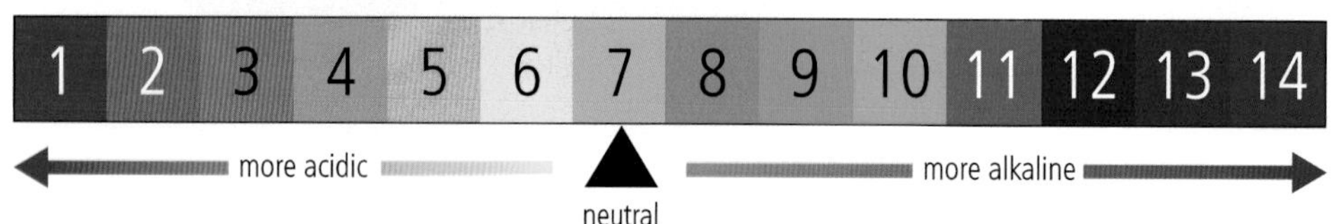

Notice that a solution that is neither acidic nor alkaline is called **neutral**. A neutral solution has a pH value of 7.

Did you know?

Concentrated solutions of strong acids have a pH value of less than 0.

1 What pH values tell us

a Use the pH scale above to complete these sentences:
The lower the pH value, the more strongly .... and h............ a solution is.
Solutions with a pH value above .... are alkaline.
A solution with a pH value of 8 is .... alkaline.
A solution whose pH is 7 is said to be ....

b Find out where the term 'pH' comes from.

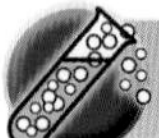

2 Finding the pH of solutions

Use Universal Indicator to test some solutions you used in E3. Include tap water and distilled water in your experiment. Record your observations and what they tell us in a table.

If you have time, take one of the strongly acidic solutions you tested. Dilute it to about 1/100th of its original concentration. Predict its new pH, then see if you were right.

E5 Neutralisation

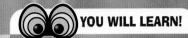

YOU WILL LEARN!

- we can get a neutral solution by adding an acid to an alkali

At the start of this unit, we said that acids and alkalis are like 'chemical opposites'. In fact, if we add just the right amount of acid to an alkali, they 'cancel each other out', and we get a neutral solution.

A chemical reaction takes place. The acid and alkali react together. In any chemical reaction new substances are made. In this case a salt and water are formed. The reaction is called **neutralisation**. We can show the reaction like this:

acid + alkali → a salt + water

This is a neutralisation reaction

Often we can't *see* any change happening when we mix an acid and an alkali. That's because the salt formed is often soluble in water. However, another sign that a chemical reaction has taken place can be observed. Try the activity below.

Did you know 

Table salt is often called 'common salt'. Its chemical name is sodium chloride. There are many other salts that can be made by adding different acids and alkalis together.

1 Temperature change during neutralisation

Take the temperature of 10 cm³ of sodium hydroxide solution in a boiling tube.
Add 10 cm³ of dilute hydrochloric acid.
Stir gently with the thermometer and take the new temperature.

a What happens to the temperature of the reacting mixture?
b Does this neutralisation reaction give out or take in energy?

Try some other mixtures of acids and alkalis and see if you can make a generalisation. ("Neutralisation reactions always ...")

We can also use Universal Indicator to show the change that happens.

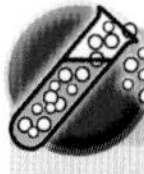

2 Getting a neutral solution (if you're skilful enough!)

Again, measure 10 cm³ of sodium hydroxide solution into a boiling tube. This time add a few drops of UI solution.

a What colour is the solution? What is its pH value?

Now measure out 10 cm³ of dilute hydrochloric acid.

b What do you predict the pH will be when you add the acid to the alkali?

Try it.

c What is the pH value now?

Use a pipette to add acid or alkali, drop by drop, and see if you can get a neutral solution.

d What colour will your neutral solution be?

Datalogging and neutralisation

We can use sensors to follow (monitor) what changes take place during a neutralisation reaction. We call this datalogging.
We can then use computers to display the results.
There are sensors that can measure the pH of a solution accurately.

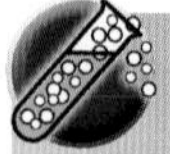

3 Monitoring neutralisation using a pH sensor

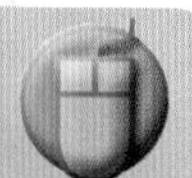

Set up the apparatus as shown below:

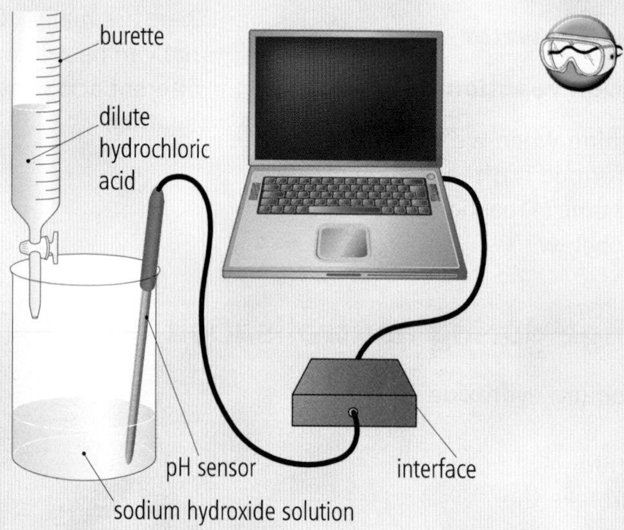

Add dilute hydrochloric acid slowly from the burette and monitor the pH using the sensor.
Display the results on a computer and print off a copy of the graph.

a How much acid was needed to neutralise your alkali?
b Describe the pattern shown on your line graph.
c Sketch the shape of the graph you would expect if you started with acid in the beaker and added the alkali to it?
d Why did you find it difficult in Activity 2 to get a neutral solution?

A pH sensor gives a more accurate pH value than Universal Indicator

Did you know

We can make solutions, called buffer solutions, that resist large changes in pH when acid or alkali are added to them. Our blood has buffer systems to reduce the effects of too much acid or alkali. If the pH of your blood falls below 6.8 or rises above 8.0 for more than a few hours, you will die.

You can also follow the neutralisation using a temperature sensor.

4 Monitoring neutralisation using a temperature sensor

Repeat Activity 3 but use a temperature sensor instead of a pH sensor.

a Predict the shape of the graph you might get.
b Check your graph against your prediction. Comment on any differences you notice.

Making a salt

We have said that a salt is made when an acid and an alkali react. In the next activity you can try to collect some of the salt.

REALLY GEORGE-I COULD HAVE NIPPED TO THE SHOPS AND BOUGHT SOME SALT BY NOW!

Points to discuss

1. What else is formed in a neutralisation reaction?
2. What will we have to do to get a solid sample of the salt that is formed?

5 Preparing a salt from a neutralisation reaction

Add 10 cm^3 of dilute hydrochloric acid to 10 cm^3 of sodium hydroxide solution in an evaporating dish. The concentration of the acid and alkali should be the same. Heat the solution on a water bath (see photo below) until about half the solution has evaporated off. (Do not let all the water evaporate from the dish). Let your dish cool down.
Label your dish and leave until next lesson.

a What do you see when all the water has evaporated?

The **salt** formed is called **sodium chloride**.

b What is this salt used for?
c Why can't you see the salt as it forms during neutralisation?
d Crystallisation dishes are wide, flat glass containers. Why do you think they have this shape?

Heating a solution of sodium chloride on a water bath

Did you know

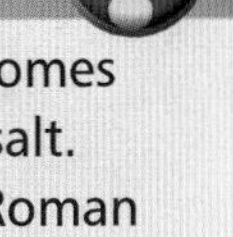

Our word 'salary' comes from the Latin for salt. In the days of the Roman Empire, soldiers were sometimes given salt as part of their wages!

E6 Useful neutralisation

YOU WILL LEARN!

- how to frame a question to investigate, plan a fair test, and compare your method and results with those from other groups
- how to evaluate indigestion remedies
- some uses of neutralisation

Points to discuss

At the start of this unit we looked at different uses of acids. But can you think of an acid that isn't useful that we might like to get rid of? How could you neutralise an unwanted acid?

Farmers neutralise **acidic soil** to make it more suitable for growing some crops. They use lime (calcium hydroxide) or limestone powder (calcium carbonate).

No doubt you've heard about **acid rain**. This can be caused by the acidic gases given off from some factories. But now more chimneys are fitted with chemical 'scrubbers' to neutralise the gases before they escape into our atmosphere. What type of substance will be used in the 'scrubbers'?

Toothpastes also contain alkalis, such as sodium hydrogencarbonate, to neutralise acids that bacteria can produce on your teeth. This, together with fluoride in the paste, helps prevent tooth decay.

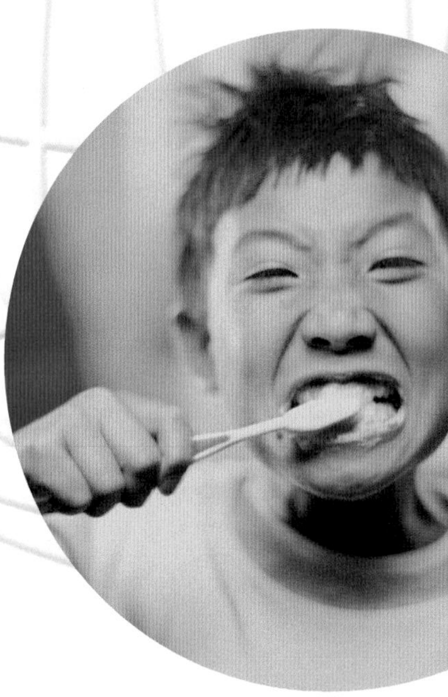

Toothpaste neutralises acids in your mouth

On page 74 we read that hydrochloric acid is found in our stomachs. It helps to break food down (and to kill bacteria). But some people suffer from **indigestion** and heartburn when too much acid is made. And that's when we take a tablet to soothe the pain. Look at some of the indigestion remedies you can buy:

1 Investigating indigestion remedies

a What do you think makes a good indigestion remedy?

Think of a question that you would like to investigate about indigestion remedies. Plan a test to find out the answer to your question. Show your plan to your teacher, then carry out your tests.

b Present your results and conclusions, together with a brief method, on a poster to share with other groups.

c Evaluate your work and that of other groups. Then make a class summary.

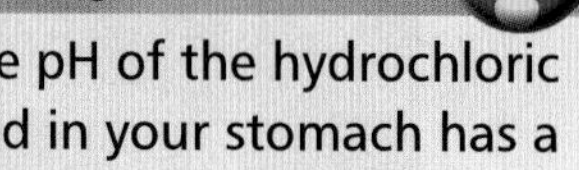

Did you know?

The pH of the hydrochloric acid in your stomach has a value around 2.0.

Summary

There are many useful acids and alkalis. Some acids and alkalis are hazardous to handle. They are very corrosive. You can make a corrosive acid or alkali safer by making it more dilute. Weak acids are often found in foods.

Indicators are dyes that are different colours in acid and alkali. Universal Indicator is a mixture of dyes. It has a range of colours. We can match the colours to numbers on a pH scale.

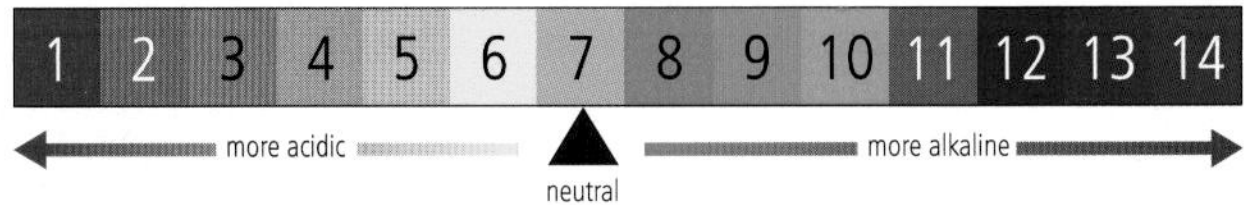

The lower the pH value, the more strongly acidic a solution is. A liquid with a pH of 7 is neutral (neither acidic nor alkaline). pH values above 7 indicate an alkali.

When acids react with alkalis they neutralise each other. They form a salt and water. There are many useful neutralisation reactions, including indigestion remedies to get rid of excess acid in your stomach.

Key words

- acid
- alkali
- corrosive
- equation
- harmful
- hazardous
- hydrochloric acid
- indicator
- pH values
- react
- sodium hydroxide
- solution

Summary Questions

1 **a** Make a list of safety rules for a new Y7 class who have never handled acids or alkalis before.
b Complete your list of acids that you have met in this unit.

2 Make a list of questions (and answers) to test a friend on this unit. You could write them in the style of 'Who wants to be a millionaire?'
Here is the first question for £100:
Which of these is not an acid?
A hydrochloric acid, B nitric acid,
C sulfuric acid, D sodium hydroxide!

3 You have been given a sample of soil and a bottle of Universal Indicator solution.
a Describe in detail how you could find the pH of the soil. (You don't want the colour of the UI masked by the soil.)
b If the soil was acidic, name two substances you could add to neutralise it.
c Why wouldn't you use sodium hydroxide solution to neutralise the soil?

4 Why do people suffer from indigestion? Find out the 'active ingredients' in one remedy.

5 **a** Ammonia is an alkaline gas. Find out some other properties of ammonia and what it is used for.
b Ammonia can be transported in road tankers as a liquid. Using the information on page 73, design a warning sign to display on the tankers. (Just write 'ammonia' where the identification number is normally shown.)

6 Wasp stings are soothed by bathing the sting in vinegar. Can you explain why this treatment works?

7 Acids have a bad reputation with many people because they are frightened by the word. You work for AA (Acids Anonymous) and have been asked to change the image of acids. Design a leaflet with the title 'Acids – You can't live without them' (or a better one of your own!).

8 Draw a concept map linking these words:
acid, salt, alkali, water, Universal Indicator, hazard, neutralisation.
The links should be labelled to explain the connections that you have made.

End of unit Questions

1 The table shows the pH of five soil samples.

soil sample	pH of soil
A	6.0
B	7.5
C	7.0
D	4.5
E	8.0

Use letters from the table to answer questions **a**, **b** and **c**.

a Which soil sample is neutral? *1 mark*

b **i** Most types of heather grow better in acidic soil. In which of the soil samples should heather grow well? *1 mark*

ii Cabbage grows better in alkaline soil. In which of the soil samples should cabbage grow well? *1 mark*

c Lime is an alkaline substance which is sometimes put onto acidic soils. What type of reaction takes place between the lime and the acid? *1 mark*

2 **a** Sunil picked yellow, red and purple primula flowers from his garden. He dipped the different flower petals into water and into two different solutions. The pH of one solution was 1 and the pH of the other was 10. The table shows the results.

colour of flower petals	in solution of pH 1	in water pH 7	in solution of pH 10
yellow	stayed yellow	stayed yellow	stayed yellow
red	stayed red	stayed red	turned green
purple	turned pink	stayed purple	turned blue

Which colour of flower petal would be most useful to make an indicator for both acids and alkalis? Explain your answer. *2 marks*

3 Water from red cabbage can be used to find out if a liquid is acidic, alkaline or neutral.

type of liquid added to the cabbage water	colour of the cabbage water
acidic	red
alkaline	blue
neutral	purple

John added three different liquids to the cabbage water.

a Use the information above to complete the table below. *3 marks*

liquid added to the cabbage water	colour of the cabbage water	is the liquid acidic, alkaline or neutral?
water	purple	i)
lemon juice	ii)	acidic
washing up liquid	blue	iii)

b What word describes chemicals which change colour in acids or alkalis? Choose from the words below:

filters indicators liquids solids

1 mark

4 The table below shows the pH of a solution of each of four gases.

gas	pH of a solution of the gas
ammonia	10
carbon dioxide	6
hydrogen chloride	1
oxygen	7

Which gas dissolves in water to form:

a an acid? *1 mark*

b an alkali? *1 mark*

c a neutral solution? *1 mark*

7F Chemical reactions

Introduction

We stay alive only because of the chemical reactions inside the cells in our bodies. In this unit we will look at chemical reactions in detail and build on your previous work about reversible and irreversible changes.

We met the reaction between acids and alkalis in Unit 7E.

Now we'll see more reactions of acids, as well as looking at burning as a chemical reaction.

You already know

- there are many gases
- new materials are formed in some changes that can't be reversed
- the pH scale measures how acidic or alkaline solutions are

In this topic you will learn

- about the new substances made in chemical reactions
- about reactions of acids that produce a gas
- about burning as a chemical reaction
- the tests for hydrogen, oxygen and carbon dioxide gases
- word equations to describe chemical reactions

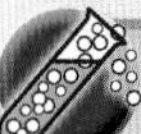

1 What can you remember?

a Make a list of five gases.
b Give an example of two changes in which new substances are made.
c Is a solution with a pH value of 8 strongly alkaline or weakly alkaline?
d Is a solution with a pH value of 1 strongly acidic or weakly acidic?

F1 What is a chemical reaction?

YOU WILL LEARN!

- chemical reactions produce new substances
- some other signs that a chemical reaction has taken place
- how to make and interpret observations

Can you remember what was made when we mixed an acid and an alkali together? Could we ***see*** any change happening? In Activity 1 you can look at some changes that you can see – but also feel the container to record other observations. (We use more than our sense of sight to make observations.)

1 Observing changes

Mix the following pairs of substances together and record all your observations (include feeling the container) in a table:

i baking powder and water (in a beaker)
ii lemon juice and bicarbonate of soda (in a beaker)
iii plaster of Paris and water (in a yoghurt pot)

a Which changes were easiest to see that a new substance was being made? What made it easy to observe?
b Which changes gave out heat and which felt cool?

Now try the second experiment again in a boiling tube. But this time add Universal Indicator solution to the lemon juice, then add the solid until the colour changes.

c What do you observe?
d How does this give us more evidence of a chemical reaction?

We can recognise chemical changes by the following observations:

- **new substances are made in reactions**
- **energy is given out or taken in during reactions**

It is often difficult (or impossible) to get the substances you start with back from the new substances made. However, there are plenty of examples of reversible chemical reactions. Try Activity 2 below to see one.

2 A reversible chemical reaction

Add a little ammonium chloride to a test tube. Put a loose plug of mineral wool in the mouth of the test tube. *Gently* heat the bottom of the test tube.

Don't let any gases escape from the test tube.

Try to explain your observations.

Did you know

A factory manufacturing ammonium-based fertilisers in Toulouse, France blew up in September 2001, killing 15 people.

New words to learn:

REACTANTS	→	**PRODUCTS**
(what we start with)		(what is formed in the reaction)

F2 Acids reacting with metals

YOU WILL LEARN!

- the test for hydrogen gas
- acids can be corrosive
- acids react with some metals, giving off hydrogen gas
- record observations, describing any pattern and identifying which results do not fit the pattern

Points to discuss

1 Can you name 10 metals?
2 Do you think that every metal will react with acids, such as sulfuric acid? Will they all corrode in acid?

You can try adding dilute sulfuric acid to some different metals in the next activity.

1 Which metals react with acid?

Add a little dilute sulfuric acid to samples of the following metals:
iron, copper, tin, zinc, magnesium, lead.
Record your observations in a table.

a How can you tell which metals react?
b Name the metals that don't react with the cold acid.
c Put the metals that do react in order, with the most reactive first.
d Lead and tin react with dilute acid under certain conditions. What do you think we could do to 'encourage' their reactions?

When metals do react with an acid, you see fizzing. One of the new substances made is a gas called **hydrogen**. In the next activity you can do a test for this gas.

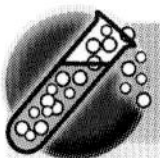

2 Testing for hydrogen

Add a little hydrochloric nitric acid to a piece of magnesium ribbon in a test tube. Insert another test tube loosely over the first tube to collect some hydrogen gas. (Hydrogen is less dense than air.) Test the gas you have collected by putting a lighted splint above the mouth of the test tube. What happens?

The test for hydrogen: the gas burns with a squeaky 'pop' when lit with a lighted splint

Most reactions of acids produce a salt as one of the products. So, for those metals that do react with acid, we can say that:

acid + a metal → a salt + hydrogen

Salts are often soluble in water, so you don't actually see them forming. But you can see the bubbles of hydrogen gas.

Points to discuss

1 How does the reaction above differ from an acid reacting with an alkali?
2 How could you collect a sample of the salt made in the reaction as a solid?

Did you know

A murderer in the 1950s was convicted only when police found his missing wife's gold tooth in a bath of concentrated acid where he worked.

F3 Acids reacting with carbonates

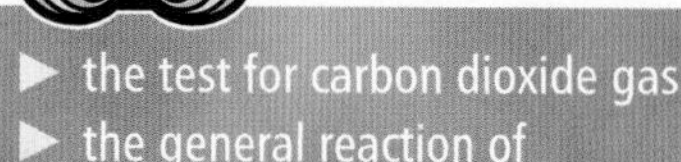
YOU WILL LEARN!

- the test for carbon dioxide gas
- the general reaction of carbonates with an acid

Do you enjoy fizzy drinks? Have you ever swallowed some too quickly and had the gas 'go down your nose'? Or left a fizzy drink open and let it go 'flat'?
The gas that gives a drink its fizz is carbon dioxide. It is also the gas produced when substances called carbonates react with acids.

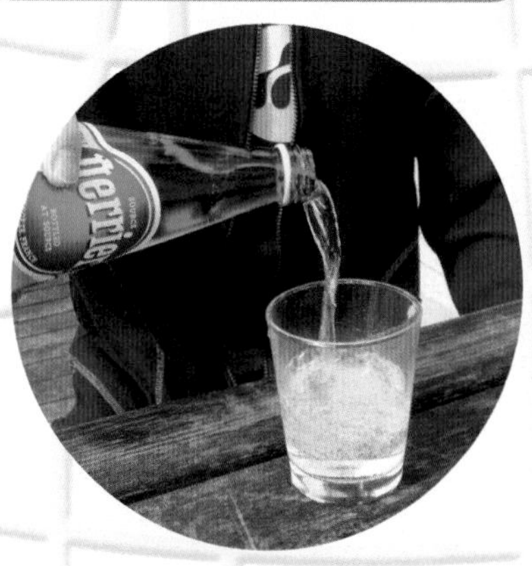

Carbon dioxide gas makes this a 'sparkling' mineral water

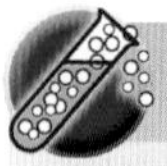

1 Testing for carbon dioxide

Set up the experiment shown opposite.
The marble chip contains calcium carbonate.

- **a** Draw a 2-D scientific diagram of your apparatus.
- **b** What do you see happen in the reaction between the marble chip and dilute hydrochloric acid?
- **c** What happens to the limewater?

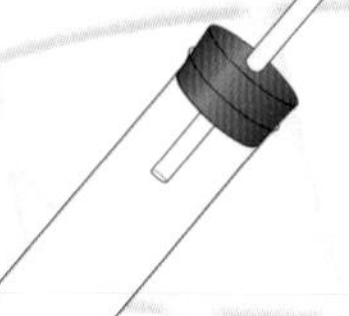
hydrochloric acid
marble chip
limewater

Test for carbon dioxide gas: limewater goes milky.

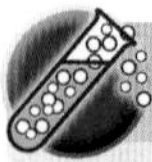

2 Carbonates plus acids

You will be provided with a range of different carbonates and different acids. Record your observations in a table.

- **a** Which gas do carbonates give off in acidic solutions?
- **b** What else do you think might be formed in these chemical reactions?
- **c** Do all the carbonates react with any of the acids provided for you?

Try adding dilute sulfuric acid to a marble chip.
Describe what happens.

- **d** Try to explain your observation above.

When acids react with a carbonate, this is the general equation:

acid + carbonate → a salt + water + carbon dioxide

This reaction is a problem when limestone (which contains calcium carbonate) in buildings and statues gets broken down by acid rain. Look at the photograph opposite:

Acid rain reacts with limestone (which contains calcium carbonate)

On the other hand, we have already seen some uses of this reaction to neutralise acids. The 'scrubbers' in factory chimneys can contain a slurry of calcium carbonate, and farmers can use the same carbonate to neutralise acidic soil.

Other substances called hydrogencarbonates react in a similar way. For example, baking powder contains a weak acid (tartaric acid) and sodium hydrogencarbonate (also known as bicarbonate of soda). When it gets wet, the two react. The bubbles of carbon dioxide produced make a cake rise.

WELL IT'S NOT ALL BAD-I THINK THIS ACID RAIN IS IMPROVING MY LOOKS

F4 The air around us

YOU WILL LEARN!
- the air is a mixture of gases
- the test for oxygen gas

As you know, oxygen is essential for life on Earth. But do you know the percentage of oxygen in the air?
Air is a mixture of gases. Only about one-fifth of the mixture is oxygen. It is the reactive gas in air.

Did you know?

The first oxygen appeared in our atmosphere only after the first primitive plant life had evolved on Earth.

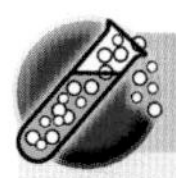

1 Finding out about air

Work in groups to find the answers to these questions. Present your information as a poster on 'Air'.

- **a** Which other gases make up the air?
- **b** What are the proportions of each gas in the air?
- **c** Why does the amount of carbon dioxide vary in different places?
- **d** What are the uses of nitrogen and argon?
- **e** Where do most scientists think our atmosphere came from?

Oxygen gas

We can make oxygen in a chemical reaction, and then collect the gas. Try the experiment below.

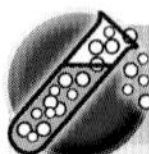

2 Making and testing oxygen gas

Set up the apparatus below to collect oxygen gas.
Allow the first bubbles to escape because these won't be pure oxygen.

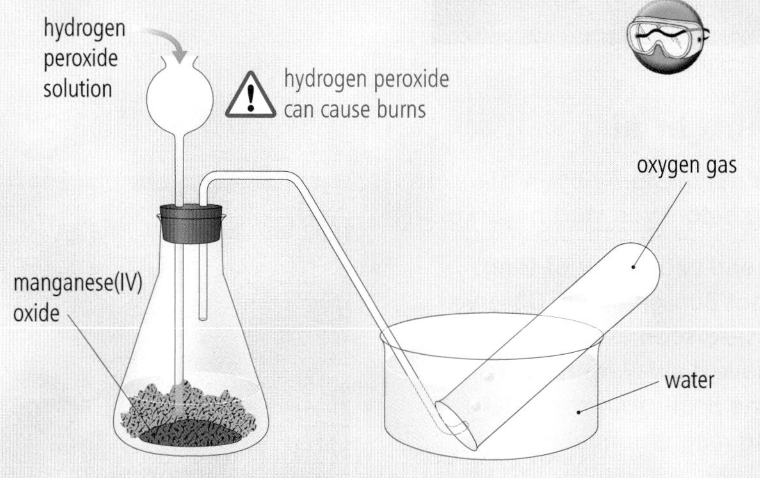

a What do you see happen in the chemical reaction?

When you have a boiling tube of oxygen you can test it. Light a wooden splint, then blow it out. While it is still glowing red, plunge it into the boiling tube of oxygen.

b What happens to the glowing splint?

Test for oxygen gas: a glowing splint re-lights.

F5 Burning materials

YOU WILL LEARN!

- burning requires oxygen
- burning is a chemical reaction that produces new substances (mainly oxides)
- how to carry out combustion reactions safely

Most students enjoy using the Bunsen burner and watching spectacular chemical reactions; so learning about burning should be fun! However, we must think carefully about doing our experiments safely.

Did you know

Fireworks get their spectacular colours from metals present in the chemicals packed inside. For example, substances containing strontium produce a crimson red flame.

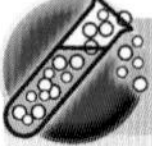

1 Burning magnesium in air

Your teacher will give you a piece of magnesium ribbon to heat. Read all the instructions below before you start heating.

Hold the magnesium ribbon at one end with a pair of tongs. Put the other end in the edge of a hot Bunsen flame. Observe the magnesium through tinted glass. As soon as the magnesium catches fire (ignites), move it away from the flame and let the reaction continue over the heat-proof mat. Make sure you are not holding the burning magnesium above the tubing to the gas tap!

- **a** Why is it a good idea to use tinted glass to observe this reaction?
- **b** Why is it a bad idea to hold the burning magnesium above the gas tubing?
- **c** Describe the new substance (the product) formed.
- **d** How does the product differ from the magnesium ribbon (a reactant) you started with?

The magnesium reacts with **oxygen** in the air. The reaction is called a **combustion** reaction. The white solid made in the reaction is called **magnesium oxide**.
We can show the reaction using a word equation.

magnesium + oxygen → magnesium oxide
REACTANTS **PRODUCT**

This tells us what we start with before the reaction (reactants) and what we end up with after the reaction (the products). When you read a word equation, the arrow (→) is read as 'gives' and + signs as 'plus'.

Magnesium powder is used in fireworks and rescue flares.

2 Heating copper in air

Hold a piece of copper foil in a pair of tongs and heat it strongly. After a couple of minutes, leave it to cool on your heat-proof mat.

a Compare the copper before and after heating.
b What is its new coating called?
c Write a word equation for the reaction.

Burning in oxygen

If magnesium burns so fiercely in air (about 20% oxygen), imagine how it will react in pure oxygen gas! Your teacher will show you some reactions in pure oxygen. The chemical name for burning is **combustion**.

Potassium reacts vigorously in oxygen. The oxide formed has a pH value of 14 when added to water

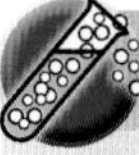

3 Combustion of elements in oxygen

In this experiment chemical elements will react with oxygen gas. An element is a substance that we can't break down into simpler substances. You will learn more about elements next year.
As you watch the demonstration, record your observations in a table as shown below.

Element	Burning in air	Burning in oxygen	pH of oxide formed
magnesium			

a Why must some elements be burned in the fume-cupboard?
b What other safety precautions are taken?
c Write a word equation for each of the reactions.
(HINT: Products might include carbon dioxide, sulfur dioxide, phosphorus pentoxide.)
d Can you spot any pattern in the pH of the oxides formed?

The 'fire triangle'

You have seen how burning requires oxygen. For a fire to continue burning, it also needs a supply of fuel, as well as heat. You can show this in a **'fire triangle'**.

If you remove one part of the fire triangle, the fire goes out. It is extinguished.

For example, firefighters will continue to hose down the scene of a fire well after it looks as though the flames have been put out. This is to make sure that any combustible material has cooled down. Without heat, the fire cannot flare up again.

The fire triangle

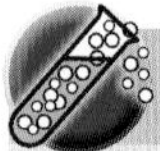

4 Putting out fires

Look at the different types of fire below:

a Explain how you could put each fire out. Make reference to the 'fire triangle'.
b Design a fire prevention leaflet for use by the public.

F6 Burning fuels

YOU WILL LEARN!

- fuels release energy when they burn
- the substances in fossil fuels contain carbon and this can form carbon dioxide when they burn
- what is formed when natural gas (methane) burns

We all rely on fuels to keep warm, to cook our food and to transport us around.

Points to discuss

1 Which fuel(s) do you use to heat your home?

2 Do you know which fuel is used to generate your electricity?

3 Which fuels do you use to get to school each day?

4 Can you think of your own definition of a fuel?

5 Can you name any fossil fuels? Why are they called fossil fuels? (You can learn more about fossil fuels in Unit 7I.)

All living things, including ourselves, are based on substances containing carbon. So it's not surprising that fossil fuels (made from ancient trees and ferns or tiny sea creatures and plants) contain lots of carbon. What do you think we get as one of the products when any fossil fuel burns?
(HINT: think back to Activity 3 on page 89.)

Did you know

The tiny sea creatures and plants, called plankton, that formed crude oil lived on Earth about 150 000 000 years ago.

The chemical name for natural gas is **methane**. Methane is made up from **carbon *and* hydrogen**. What do you think happens to the hydrogen in a fuel when it burns? Try the experiment below.

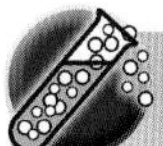

1 What happens to the hydrogen when fuels burn?

Light a Bunsen burner. The fuel is probably methane. Collect a beaker with iced water. Dry the outside of the beaker. Adjust the gas tap to get a low flame on your bunsen burner. Open the air hole slightly and gently heat the bottom of the beaker for a few seconds.

a What do you notice on the outside of the beaker? Test the outside of the beaker with blue cobalt chloride paper. This turns pink if water is present.

Wax is also made from carbon and hydrogen. Try the same experiment with a candle.

b What happens?

c Why did we need icy water inside the beaker?

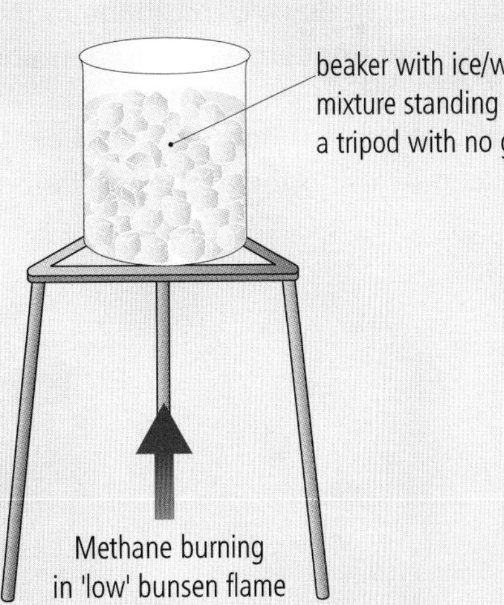

You probably know that H_2O is water. We will learn more about chemical formulae in Books 8 and 9, but you can see that water is an oxide of hydrogen. You could say that the chemical name for water is hydrogen oxide.

So the hydrogen in a fuel turns to **water vapour** during combustion.

WILL THAT BE STILL OR SPARKLING HYDROGEN OXIDE MADAM?

Look at the next experiment to find out more about the products when methane burns.

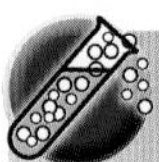

2 What happens to the carbon when fuels burn

Watch the methane burn. The gases made are drawn through the limewater by the water pump.

a Which gas do we test for with limewater?

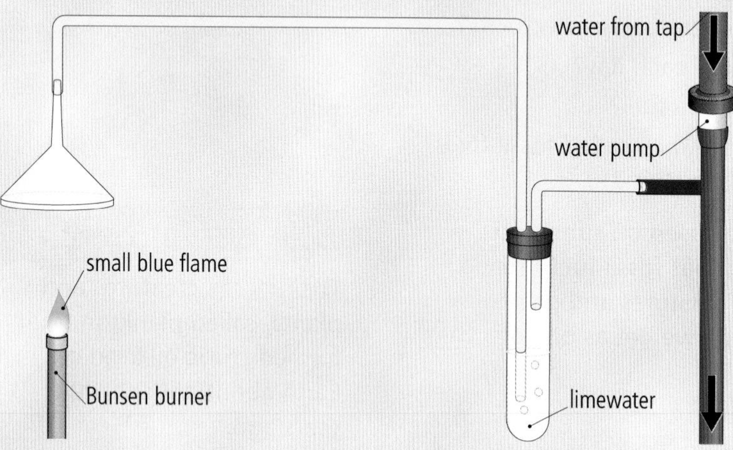

b What happens to the limewater?

c What does this experiment show? Why would running the experiment again, but just drawing air through the limewater make you more certain of your conclusion?

d What would you expect to happen if you burn ethanol in a spirit burner in place of methane in the apparatus? (HINT: ethanol contains carbon, hydrogen and oxygen.)

You can also show that both carbon dioxide and water are produced by using the apparatus below.

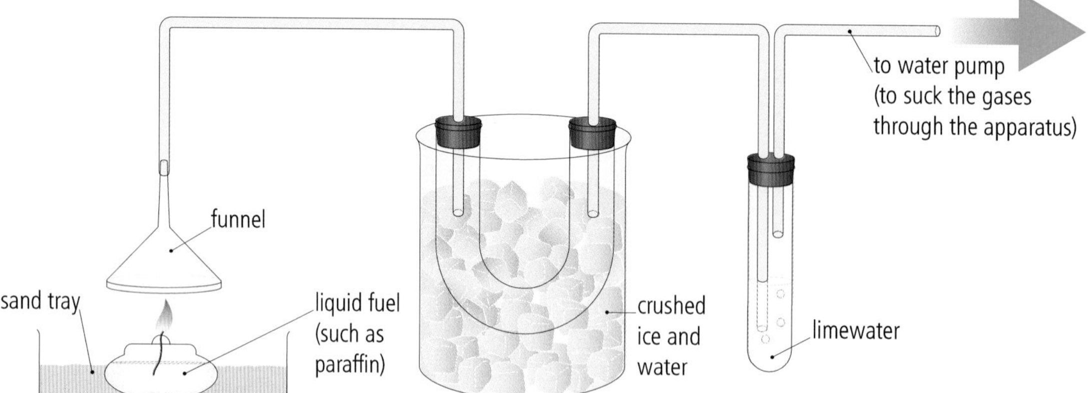

So we have found out that carbon dioxide and water are given off when fuels burn. In general, when there is plenty of oxygen available:

fuel + oxygen → carbon dioxide + water

If there is not enough oxygen present, the combustion gives off poisonous carbon monoxide gas (and possibly some carbon – soot). But we'll look at that in detail in Year 9.

Did you know

Natural gas has traces of another gas added to make it smell.

Why is this done?

F7 More about burning

YOU WILL LEARN!

- which part of the air is used up when things burn
- how to explain observations
- how to plan and carry out an investigation into burning
- how ideas about burning have developed in history

1 Using up part of the air

Carefully observe the experiment below.

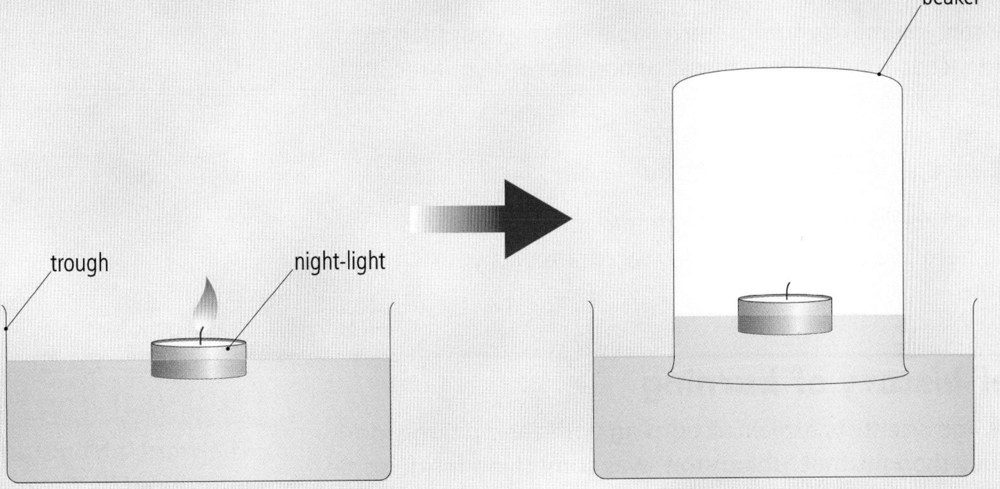
beaker
trough
night-light

a What do you see happen as soon as the beaker is put over the night-light? Try to explain this.

b Why does the night-light go out?

c Why do you think the water rises up the beaker?

d Why doesn't the water rise right to the top?

e Will this experiment give you an accurate measure of how much oxygen is in the air? Explain your answer.

f Write a word equation for the combustion of wax.

WOULD MY CANDLES BURN LONGER, AND SAVE ME MONEY, IF THERE WAS MORE OXYGEN IN THE AIR?

Once the oxygen has been used up in the reaction, the flame goes out. Carbon dioxide, which is used in some fire extinguishers, also helps to put out the flame. Where does this come from?

Points to discuss

Look at the experiment shown opposite. The small candle goes out before the big one.

1 Would you expect this to happen? Why?

2 Try to explain the results of the experiment.

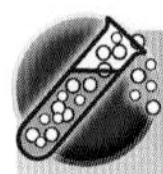

2 How does the volume of air affect the time a night-light burns?

Predict the graph you will get when you investigate this problem.

a Do you think that if you double the volume of air, the night-light will burn for twice as long? Why?

Plan your investigation. You have access to:
night-light, matches, measuring cylinders, four different sizes of pyrex beaker, stop clock (watch), sand tray, water.

b How can you make your results reliable? Show your plan to your teacher, then do your investigation. Record your results in a table, then plot them on a graph.
c Was your predicted graph correct?
d Evaluate the sources of error in your tests.

If you have time, use your graph to predict the time the night-light will burn in another beaker. How accurate was your prediction?

A brief history of burning

300 years ago scientists explained burning with their phlogiston theory. They thought that 'phlogiston' was something inside some substances. Metals were particularly rich in phlogiston. When they burned, their phlogiston was lost into the air.
This seemed a good theory and could explain many observations. In the activity above, they would say that the air in the beaker gets saturated with phlogiston. Then the flame goes out.

Did you know

The word 'phlogiston' was introduced by Georg Stahl in the early 1700s. It comes from the Greek word 'phlogios' which means fiery.

But as measuring equipment became more precise, faults were noticed in the theory. It was shown that metals actually gain mass when they are heated in air. "Hold on!" said the supporters of the phlogiston theory, "That must be because a metal's phlogiston has negative mass." In other words, they defended their theory. One of the scientists who went on to discover oxygen gas, Joseph Priestley, still believed in phlogiston when he died. He called oxygen 'dephlogisticated air'.

However, another scientist, Antoine Lavoisier, suggested a theory of burning based on the reactive gas (which he named oxygen) in the air. This added on to metals when they burned and that's why they got heavier. This idea gradually became accepted as more experimental evidence was gathered that supported the theory of 'oxidation'.

Antoine Lavoisier (1743–1794) is known as the Father of Modern Chemistry. Find out about his unfortunate death in Activity 3

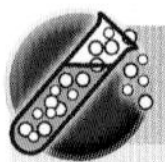

3 Research about burning

Find out about the roles of Georg Stahl, Joseph Priestley and Antoine Lavoisier in our changing ideas about burning. You could add your findings to a class book about famous scientists.

Summary

In a chemical reaction, we get new substances formed. We can represent these using word equations, in which

reactants → products

Examples include

1. **acid + a metal → a salt + hydrogen**

   Many metals react with acid, giving off hydrogen gas. The hydrogen burns with a squeaky 'pop' when tested with a lighted splint.

2. **acid + a carbonate → a salt + water + carbon dioxide**

   The carbon dioxide turns limewater milky.

3. **metal + oxygen → metal oxide**

   When substances burn in air, they react with the oxygen present to form oxides. They are called combustion reactions.

4. **fuel + oxygen → carbon dioxide + water**

   Fuels containing carbon and hydrogen burn in air to give the products shown above. There are also other products formed if the supply of oxygen is limited.

   We can test for oxygen gas by showing that a glowing splint relights.

Key words

calcium carbonate
carbon
carbon dioxide
combustion
hydrogen
magnesium
methane
oxygen
product
reactant
word equation
zinc

Did you know

At present it takes 5 tonnes of rocket fuel to send 1 tonne of equipment into space.

Summary Questions

1 Name the reactants and products in these chemical reactions:
- **a** sodium + oxygen → sodium oxide
- **b** sulfur + oxygen → sulfur dioxide
- **c** ethanol + oxygen → carbon dioxide + water

2 Copy and complete these word equations:
- **a** iron + sulfuric ..... → iron sulfate + ...
- **b** calcium ..... + nitric acid → calcium chloride + carbon dioxide + ...
- **c** zinc + oxygen → .....
- **d** carbon + oxygen → .....
- **e** methane + oxygen → ..... + ...

3 These questions refer back to Question 2.
- **a** How could you positively identify the gas given off in **2a**?
- **b** Draw the apparatus you could use to positively identify the gas in **2b** and give the result of the test.
- **c** Draw the apparatus you could use to test for both the products in **2e**.

4
- **a** Name two metals that do not react with dilute acid.
- **b** Think of two ways to speed up the reaction of a metal with an acid.
- **c** You want to collect a gas jar of hydrogen gas from the reaction between zinc and sulphuric acid. Draw the apparatus you could use. (HINT: hydrogen gas does not dissolve in water.)

5
- **a** Write a word equation to show the reaction of magnesium burning in air.
- **b** What is another word you can use to describe a burning reaction?
- **c** Describe the difference you see when magnesium ribbon burns in air compared to burning in pure oxygen.
- **d** Try to explain the difference you see in part **c**.
- **e** How are the reactions in part **c** similar?
- **f** What safety precautions should you take when burning magnesium in oxygen?

End of unit Questions

1 A teacher designs a flow chart to show how to find the names of three gases.
What are the missing words below? *4 marks*

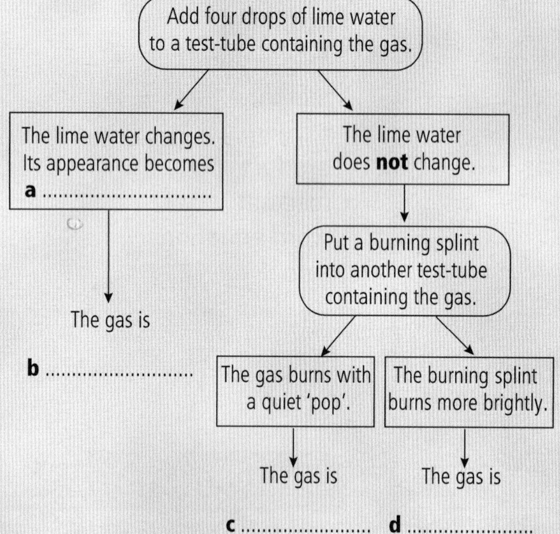

2 The diagram shows a key which can be used to identify different chemicals.

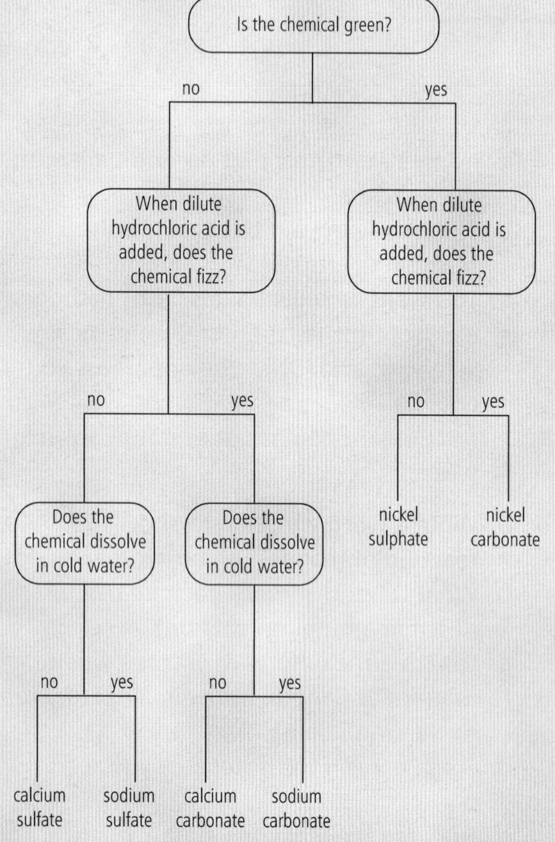

a Use the key to identify chemicals A, B and C.

i Chemical A is a white powder. It fizzes when dilute hydrochloric acid is added. It dissolves in cold water. *1 mark*

Chemical A is .....

ii Chemical B is a green powder. It does **not** fizz when dilute hydrochloric acid is added. *1 mark*

Chemical B is .....

iii Chemical C is a white powder. It does **not** fizz when dilute hydrochloric acid is added. It is insoluble in cold water. *1 mark*

Chemical C is .....

b Nickel carbonate is green. It is the nickel that makes nickel carbonate green, **not** the carbonate. Explain, using information from the key, how you know that this is true. *2 marks*

3 The diagram below shows a candle burning in air under a bell-jar.

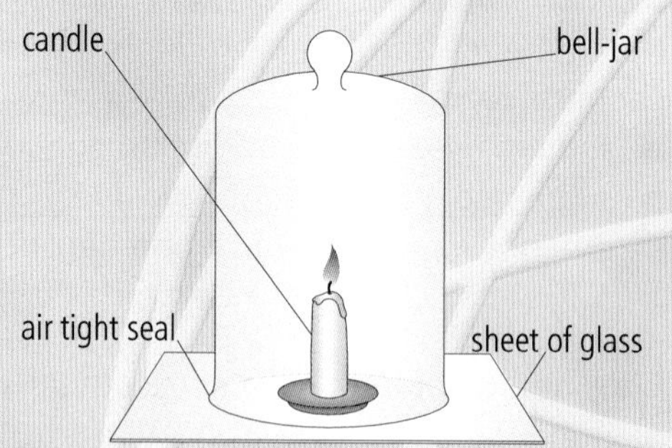

a i When the candle burns, there is a reaction. Give the names of **two** of the products of this reaction. *2 marks*

ii As the candle burns, some of the candle wax is used up. Give **two** other observations which would show that a chemical reaction is taking place. *2 marks*

7G Particles

Introduction

In this unit you will be extending your previous work on solids, liquids and gases. You will have plenty of opportunities to make observations and to build up a 'model' that helps explain the way materials behave.

You already know

- the properties of solids, liquids and gases
- that the same material can exist as a solid, liquid or gas
- about melting, freezing, evaporation and condensation

In this topic you will learn

- about the particle model, to explain differences between solids, liquids and gases
- the way experimental evidence is explained by, and can affect, scientific theories and models

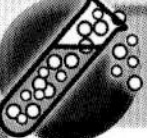

1 What can you remember?

As a quick reminder of your previous work:

a Think of five solids, five liquids and five gases. These should not be objects (e.g. table/chair) or trade names (e.g. Coca Cola).

Talk to a friend about:

b the differences in the way that solids and liquids behave,

c the differences in the way that liquids and gases behave.

G1 Explaining observations

YOU WILL LEARN!

- how to use your knowledge to interpret and explain observations
- how to discuss and evaluate the ideas of other people

Ever since humans gained the power to think, people have been trying to explain their observations.

Points to discuss

Imagine you are a cave person, living before science as we know it had ever been thought of. Think of some explanations to explain why:

1 There are sometimes droughts.
2 There are sometimes floods.
3 The Sun appears in and disappears from the sky in the same directions every day.
4 The Moon and stars appear at night.

Try some of the following experiments. You can use your own ideas to explain the things you see.

1 Comparing masses

Measure the mass of the blocks, which are the same size but made of different materials.

a Record your results in a table.
b Try to explain your results.

2 Bar and gauge experiment

Put the metal bar into the gauge. Now heat the metal bar and try to fit it in the gauge again. (You can also do this with a metal 'ball and ring' apparatus.)

a What happens?

b Try to explain why this happens.

Leave the apparatus to cool on a heat-proof mat after your experiments.

3 Sweet smells

Open a bottle of perfume and place it in the middle of your group. Who can smell it first?

a Name two other liquids that smell strongly.
b Explain how the smell gets to your nose.

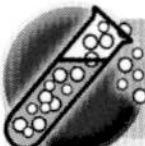

4 Dissolving crystals

Sprinkle a spatula of copper sulfate crystals into half a beaker of cold water.
Do the same thing again but use hot water.

a What do you notice in the two beakers?
b Why do you think this happens?

5 Heating a metal bar

Stick a paper clip to the end of a metal bar using petroleum jelly. Rest the bar on a tripod and heat the other end.

a What happens?
b How does this happen?

Allow the metal bar to cool after the experiment

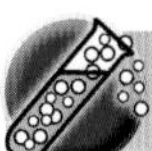

6 Stretching elastic

Hang some slotted masses on an elastic band.

a What would happen if you carried on adding more and more masses?
b What happens if you take all the masses off?
c Explain why elastic behaves like this.

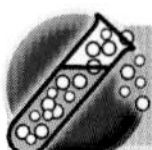

7 Adding masses to a thin wire

Hang a thin piece of metal wire from a clamp. Start adding masses to the end of the wire. Make sure you wear eye protection and protect feet from falling masses.

a What happens as you add each mass?
b What happens eventually?
c Can you explain your observations?

Did you know

The property whereby metals can be stretched out into wires is called ductility. Metals are said to be ductile.

8 Squeezing solids, liquids and gases

Collect three sealed syringes – one containing air, one with water and one with a cylinder of wood. Try pushing in the plunger on each syringe.

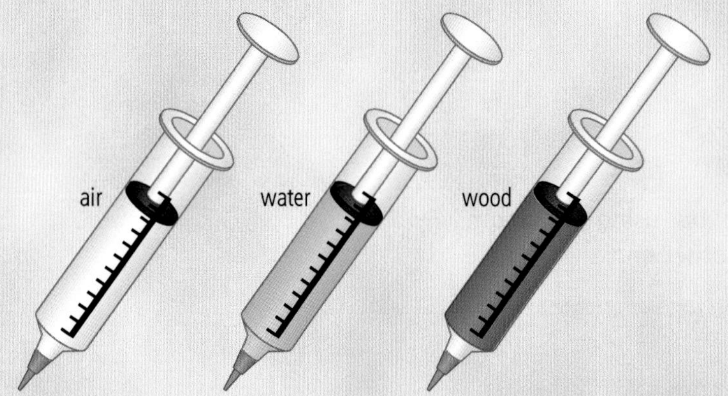

a What differences do you notice?
b Try to explain these differences.

Points to discuss

Now discuss your observations and explanations with people from other groups.

1 Did other people observe different things to you?
2 Does anyone disagree with your explanations?
3 Do you think anyone else's explanations are better than yours? Why?
4 Have you changed any of your ideas as a result of listening to other people?

Now watch this demonstration.

9 Ammonia and hydrogen chloride

Look at the demonstration set up by your teacher:

a Describe what you see happening inside the tube.
b Try to explain your observations.

G2 Tricky solids, liquids and gases

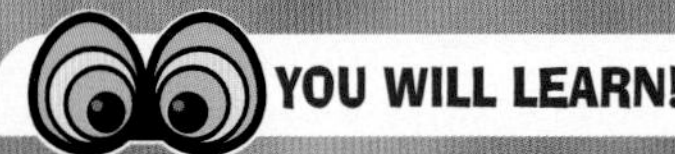

- some materials are not easy to classify as solids, liquids or gases
- how to evaluate your theory in the light of evidence obtained

You already know about the properties of solids, liquids and gases. But we can find some substances difficult to classify. See how you do in Activity 1.

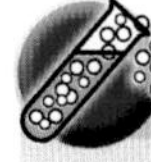

1 Which are the solids, liquids or gases?

Look at each of the materials in the materials exhibition and classify them as a solid, a liquid or a gas. Explain your reasoning behind each choice. You can use a microscope to help if you want.

Substance	Solid, liquid or gas?	Reasoning
sugar		
toothpaste		
wallpaper paste		
talcum powder		
sauce		
cling-film		
hair gel		
hair spray		
sponge		
Blu-Tack		

Now share your ideas with another group. Do you disagree over any classifications? Try to agree on a final version of your table before discussing your results as a class. Have you changed any of your ideas since you tried the *Points to discuss* on the previous page?

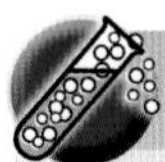

2 Making a key

Using the properties of solids, liquids and gases, make a key to help classify substances.

Try your key out on some of the materials from Activity 1.

G3 Early ideas about particles

YOU WILL LEARN!

- how the ancient Greeks started to think up theories to explain the world around them
- how scientists create 'models' to explain evidence

The first people to think that substances are made up of tiny particles were the ancient Greeks. This idea was developed by **Democritus**, a wealthy Greek philosopher, who was born in 460 BC. He got the idea originally from his teacher called Leucippus.

Democritus believed that particles (which he called atoms) were so small that they couldn't be seen. He thought that these particles could be different shapes and sizes. He also said that they can move around and be arranged in different ways. Democritus used these ideas to explain the world around him.

Democritus was born in 460 BC

Explaining observations using ancient Greek ideas

Imagine water flowing in a river.
Democritus and his followers thought that the particles of water must be smooth and round. This explains why they can slip past each other easily.

But now imagine a piece of iron.
Democritus thought its particles must be rough and jagged. Their edges must be sharp because it must be difficult for the particles to slip past each other. They get locked together into a solid shape.

So Democritus had used his imagination to construct a 'model' of how nature works.

Scientists use models to help them explain the evidence they gather. This evidence can be gathered from observations and measurements made in nature or in experiments set up in laboratories. Sometimes the evidence is from mathematical studies.

EVERYTHING IS MADE FROM TINY PARTICLES
THAT SOUNDS GREEK TO ME

1 Applying the 'ancient Greek model' of particles

Try using the ideas of Democritus to:

a **i** explain three of the activities you observed from G1
ii draw the particles in water
iii draw the particles in a piece of iron.

b Find out about another ancient Greek who helped develop scientific ideas at that time. Write about their ideas and anything that you can find out about their lives.

Did you know

Democritus died when he was 90 years old.
In which year did he die?

Did you know

Another, more famous Greek philosopher called Aristotle, argued against the ideas of Democritus and his particles. This hindered the development of Science for centuries because most people went along with Aristotle's ideas.

G4 Particle theory

YOU WILL LEARN!
- sometimes new evidence requires us to change scientific models or theories
- solids, liquids and gases are made up of tiny particles
- how to explain the differences between solids, liquids and gases using the particle model
- how to apply particle theory to explain gas pressure and new observations

Nowadays we have more evidence about the tiny particles that make up solids, liquids and gases. Some of the ancient Greek ideas are useful, but many have had to be changed to explain new evidence.

ARE YOU SURE MY NOSE IS THAT BIG?

Models are sometimes changed in the light of new observations and opinions!

We still think that everything is made up of particles that are too small to see and that different materials contain different particles. However, we will now use a model in which all the particles (that Democritus called atoms) are the same shape (like tiny balls). The main difference between different particles is their mass rather than their shape.

We now also explain things like chemical reactions by thinking of atoms joined to each other and then 'swapping partners'. You will learn more about this in Y8. But now let's use the particle model to explain the differences between solids, liquids and gases.

Particles in solids

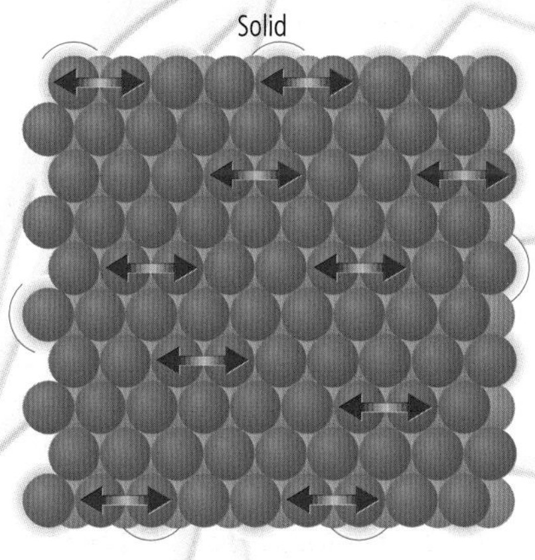

The particles in a solid are touching each other. They are vibrating but are fixed in their positions.

As we heat a solid, its particles start vibrating more vigorously. That's why a solid expands when it gets hot. If we supply enough energy, the particles shake about so much that they break free from their neighbours and the solid **melts**.

Particles in liquids

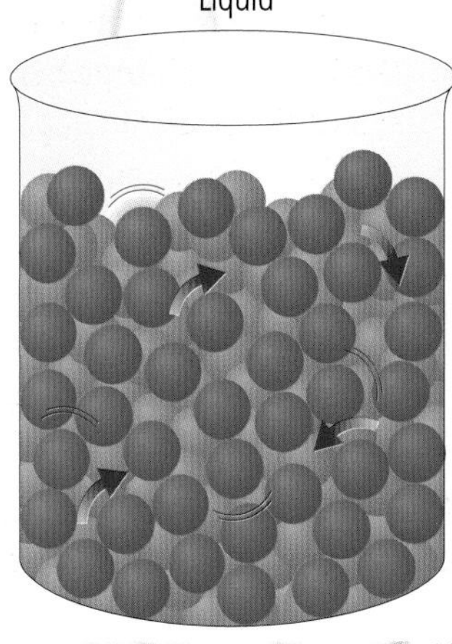

The particles in a liquid are still touching. But there is no regular pattern and they are not fixed in place. They can slip and slide over each other.

As we heat a liquid, the particles move around more quickly. Greater numbers of particles have enough energy to escape from the surface of the liquid. The liquid **evaporates** more and more quickly until it eventually **boils**.

Particles in a gas

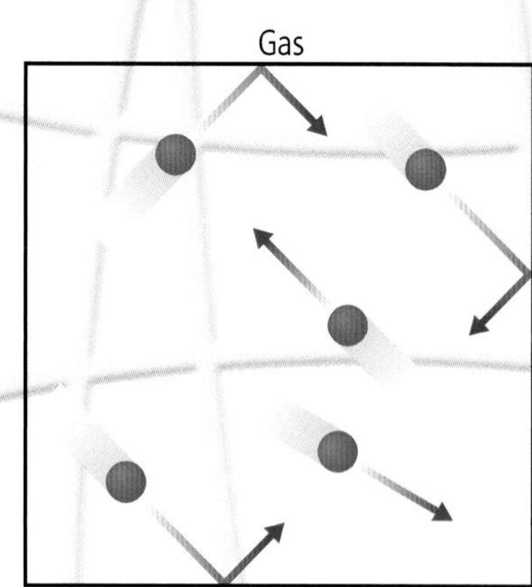

The particles in a gas are constantly zooming around all over the place. There are big gaps between the particles.

As the particles bash into the walls of their container they exert a force that causes **gas pressure**.

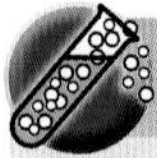

1 Explaining properties

Copy and complete these sentences using the particle theory.

- **a** Solids have a fixed shape because .....
- **b** Liquids have no fixed shape because .....
- **c** Liquids can flow because .....
- **d** Gases take up a large volume because .....
- **e** Air pressure is caused by .....

Applying the particle theory

Now try, or watch, some of the experiments below.

2 Explaining more observations

1. Using forceps leave a few crystals of potassium manganate(VII) in the middle of an agar plate.
2. Carefully draw up some water, then some blue ink, into a syringe so that they form two separate layers.
3. Watch a demonstration of bromine liquid placed in a gas jar which is then covered by a second gas jar. We call the movement of one substance through another (without us having to stir them up) **diffusion**.
4. Your teacher will boil some water in the bottom of a can. Then just as heating is stopped, a bung is placed in the top of the can.
   - **i** Explain each of your observations of the above experiments using particle theory.
   - **ii** Discuss the observations you made in G1. This time apply the particle theory to explain them. Have you changed many of your ideas since the start of the unit.

Did you know

The most famous experiment ever performed to demonstrate gas pressure was conducted in 1654. A scientist called Otto von Guericke greased the rims of two copper hemispheres and stuck them together. After pumping the air out of the copper sphere, he tied two teams of eight horses to each side of it and tried to pull the hemispheres apart. He knew that it could not be done. Can you explain why?

Summary

We can explain the properties of solids, liquids and gases using **particle theory**. This describes a model that matches the observations we make of how materials behave.

In a solid the particles are lined up next to each other. They are fixed in position but do vibrate.

In a liquid the particles are still very close together but can slip and slide over each other.

In gases the particles whiz around and there is lots of space within the gas. As they collide with the walls of their container they produce a force that causes **gas pressure**.

Diffusion is when substances mix without us stirring them up. This happens automatically through liquids and gases because their particles are free to move around.

Key words

diffusion
evidence
gas pressure
model
particle
theory
vibration

Did you know

When liquid water turns into ice its volume actually increases. Weird but true! The particles in ice are arranged in a very 'open' structure.

Summary Questions

1 **a** Imagine you and your classmates are the particles in a solid. How would you be arranged in the classroom? Describe any movement you would make.
b How would your movement in the solid change if you imagine that the temperature rises.
c What happens to you and your classmates when the solid melts?
d How would you all pretend to be a gas?

2 Explain the following observations using the particle theory.
a Metal railway tracks expand on hot days.
b 1 cm^3 of gold has a mass of 18.9 g, whereas 1 cm^3 of aluminium has a mass of 2.7 g.
c You can smell a fish and chip shop from across the road.
d There are 'No Smoking' signs in petrol stations.
e Although you can pour sugar out of a container, it is still classified as a solid.
f The tar on a road gets sticky on a very hot day.

3 **a** Describe what happens to the particles of air when you blow up a balloon.
b Why can you compress a gas but not a solid?

4 Look at the experiment below:

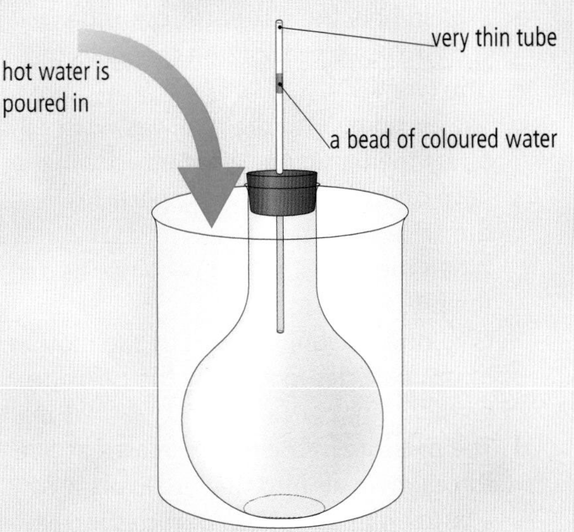

a Describe what you think would happen in the thin tube.
b Explain your answer to **a** using the particle theory.

End of unit Questions

1 The diagram below shows particles in a gas, a solid and a liquid.
Each arrow, A, B, C and D, represents a change of state.

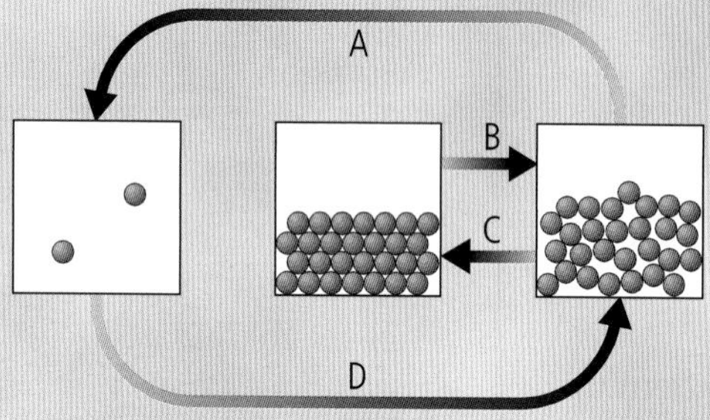

Choose from the following words to complete the sentences below.

boiling condensing distilling evaporating filtering freezing melting

a Change of state A is called .....
b Change of state B is called .....
c Change of state C is called .....
d Change of state D is called ..... *4 marks*

2 Sue pumps up a bicycle tyre. As she does so, she notices that the pump becomes hot.

a Explain how the gas particles inside the tyre exert pressure on the walls of the tyre. *1 mark*

b The air going into the tyre was warmed up by the pumping. What effect will this have on the motion of gas particles in the air in the tyre? *1 mark*

c When the air in the tyre becomes hotter, the pressure rises.
Give **one** reason, in terms of the motion of gas particles in air, why the pressure rises. *1 mark*

d The pressure in the tyre increases as Sue forces more air into the tyre.Explain why a larger number of gas particles increases the pressure in the tyre. *1 mark*

3 a What happens to the length of a metal bar when you heat it? *1 mark*

b Explain why this happens. *2 marks*

c If you heat the metal bar to a high enough temperature, it will melt. Explain what happens in terms of the particles in the metal. *2 marks*

d Explain why some metals are more dense than others. *2 marks*

4 A pen cap floats in a plastic lemonade bottle three-quarters full of water.
If you squeeze the bottle the pen cap sinks to the bottom.
If you then let go of the bottle, the pen cap floats to the surface.

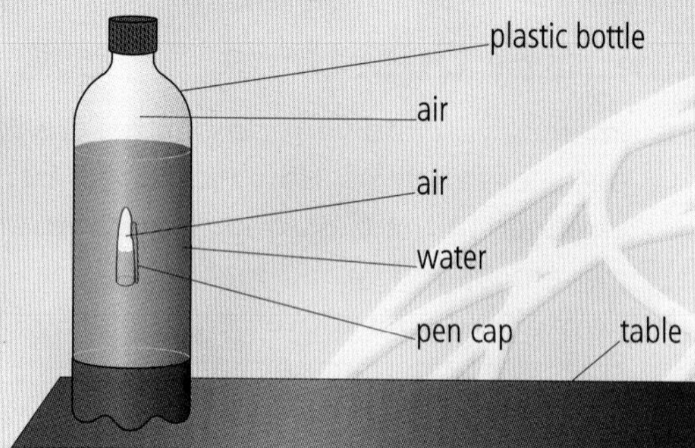

a When the bottle is squeezed what, if anything, happens to:

i the distance between the air particles inside the bottle? *1 mark*

ii the distance between the water particles inside the bottle? *1 mark*

iii the pressure of the air trapped inside the pen cap? *1 mark*

iv the volume of the air trapped inside the pen cap? *1 mark*

b Explain why the pen cap sinks when you squeeze the bottle. *2 marks*

7H Solutions

Introduction

In this unit you will find out more about dissolving and separating mixtures. You will have a chance to use the particle theory from Unit 7G to explain the different techniques you will use.

You already know

- that some solids dissolve in water and others don't dissolve
- how to separate some mixtures of solids and liquids
- that not all liquids contain water
- that all materials are made up of tiny particles

In this topic you will learn

- more techniques for separating mixtures
- how to distinguish between a pure substance and a mixture
- how to apply particle theory to explain techniques of separation
- about saturated solutions and solubility curves

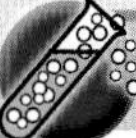

1 What can you remember?

a Write down the names of any liquids besides water that we use to dissolve things.

b How would you separate bits of soil from a sample of water?

H1 Mixtures and dissolving

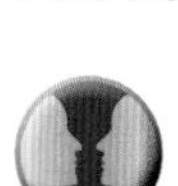

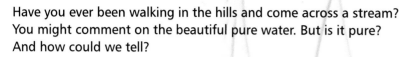

YOU WILL LEARN!

- some solids dissolve in liquids and others do not
- mixtures can be separated
- many common materials are mixtures
- the meaning of the words soluble, solute, solvent and solution

Have you ever been walking in the hills and come across a stream? You might comment on the beautiful pure water. But is it pure? And how could we tell?

Points to discuss

1 What is the difference between a pure substance and a mixture?
2 If you collected a sample of water from a stream, how could you check if it was pure water?
3 Have you separated solids from liquids before? Name five solids that do ***not*** dissolve in water?
4 Have you eaten or drunk any 'pure' substances today?

Look at the labels from some household goods below.

TOMATO SAUCE
Tomatoes, spirit vinegar, glucose syrup, sugar, salt, spice and herb extracts, spice garlic powder

Furniture polish
Beeswax, linseed oil, turpentine

Baking powder
Wheatflour, Raising agent; diphosphate, sodium hydrogen carbonate

BLEACH
less than 5% sodium hypochlorite, non-ionic surfactant, anionic surfactant

Icing sugar
Icing sugar, anti-caking agent E554

VINEGAR
5% ethanoic acid

Points to discuss

Look at the labels above:

1 Are any of the products pure substances?
2 Which products are solutions?
3 Why are mixtures so important in the food industry?
4 Can you think of any pure substances used in cooking?

1 Which liquids are mixtures?

In this experiment you will be given several liquids. Your task is to think of a way to decide whether each liquid is a pure substance or a mixture.

a Describe your method and let your teacher check it. Have you planned the same method for each liquid?
b What happens when you try it out?
c What did you find out?
d Try to explain your experiment using particle theory.

Dissolving

You know that some solids dissolve in liquids. We call the solid that dissolves the **solute**. We say that the solid is **soluble** in that liquid.

The liquid that dissolves the solid is called the **solvent**. The mixture formed by the solid and liquid is called a **solution**.

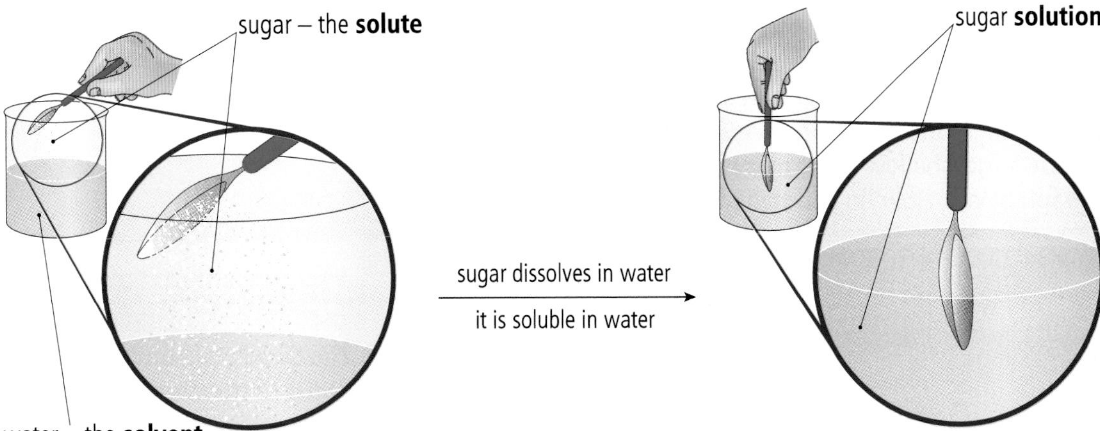

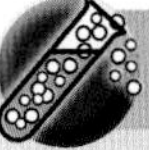

2 Which solids are soluble?

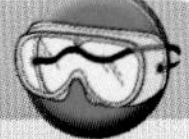

Plan an experiment to see which of the following solids are soluble in water:

potassium chloride, calcium carbonate, sodium nitrate, iodine, copper carbonate, magnesium sulfate, copper sulfate.

Record your results in a table.

Avoid touching any solids or solutions you test.

3 Solvents other than water

Different liquids dissolve different solids to different extents! In this experiment you can try a similar method to Activity 2, but this time use a different solvent. You can try ethanol or propanone. What happens in your tests?

Ensure there is no naked flame present.

4 Removing stains

You have accidentally drawn on a tablecloth at home with a black felt tip pen. See which of the three solvents we have used in H1 would be best at removing your mistake.

Did you know

Substances called chloroalkanes are very good solvents. They are used by dry cleaners. A liquid called dichloromethane is used as a paint stripper because it can even dissolve dried paint.

H2 Extracting salt from rock salt

- how to get salt from rock salt
- how to evaluate the method used by how much salt is extracted from the rock salt
- salt comes from a variety of sources and has many uses

We have already seen how we can make a sample of common salt (sodium chloride) on page 79. We used a neutralisation reaction. But our salt would be very expensive if it was made like that in industry. Fortunately, we can find sources of sodium chloride in nature.

Have you ever been swimming in the sea and swallowed a mouthful of water? If you have, you'll know that seawater is salty. In hot countries they can get the salt out of seawater (**extract** it) in salt pans. These are large, shallow tanks that hold the seawater. Look at the photograph below. How do you think this works?

Salt can be extracted from seawater

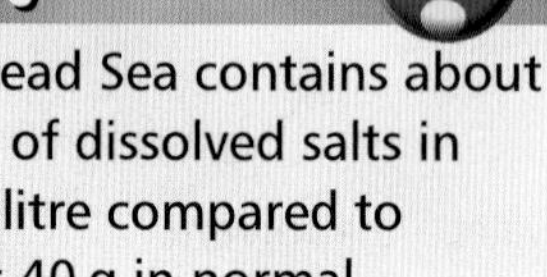

The Dead Sea contains about 350 g of dissolved salts in every litre compared to about 40 g in normal seawater.

How does that affect the properties of the seawater from the Dead Sea?

We also extract salt from underground deposits of **rock salt**. The rock salt can be mined from seams by digging it out.

The sodium chloride in rock salt is mixed with sand and bits of rock. This is fine if you are using the salt to grit icy roads in winter. But if you want to produce table salt, people aren't going to like bits of sand in their food! In the next experiment you can purify rock salt.

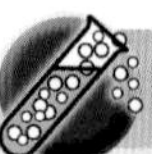

1 Purifying rock salt

Imagine that you work for a chemical company. You have taken samples from seams of rock salt in three different places. You now have to decide which is the best place to mine the salt.

Plan an experiment that will tell you which rock salt contains the highest proportion of salt. Remember that sodium chloride is soluble in water. You will have access to an electric balance.

$$\textbf{Yield of salt (\%)} = \frac{\textbf{mass of pure salt}}{\textbf{mass of rock salt}} \times \textbf{100}$$

a Write a report for your board of directors advising them which rock salt is best. Explain how you arrived at your decision. Use diagrams to help them understand your enquiry.

b What else would you need to know before you decide which site is best to mine?

Salt lowers the freezing point of water

Solution mining

The fact that salt dissolves in water can be used to extract it from underground seams of rock salt without the need to build a traditional mine.

Look at the diagram below:

Did you know

The seam of rock salt that lies under Cheshire is up to 2000 metres thick in places.

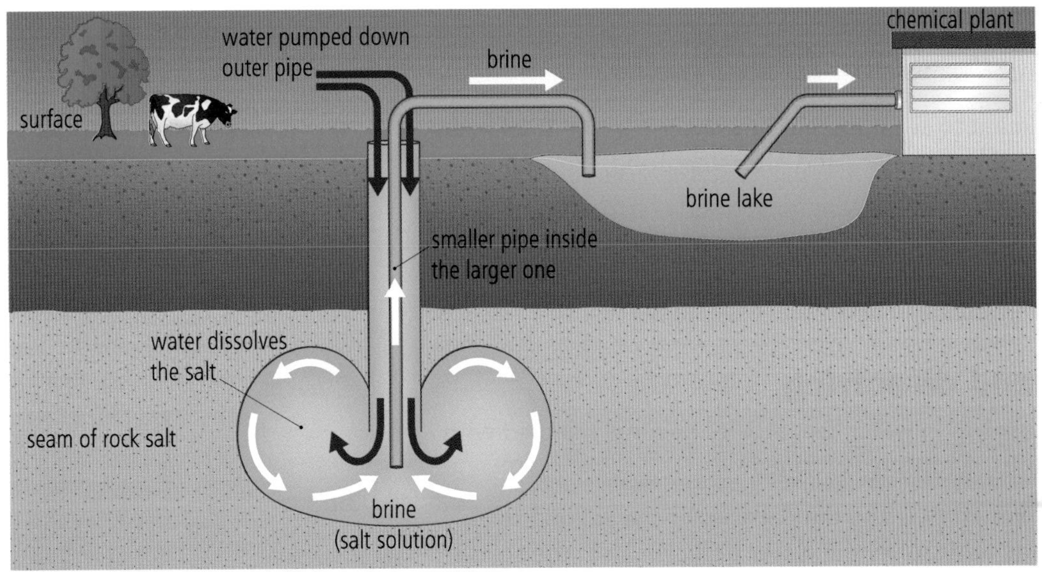

Points to discuss

1 Use the diagram above to explain how solution mining works.
2 Which method used to extract rock salt from the ground do you think is better for the environment? Explain why.

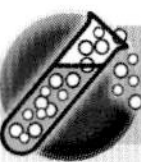

2 Finding out more about rock salt

Do some research to find out:

- **a** how rock salt was originally formed – use the word **evaporite** (a type of rock) in your answer,
- **b** where we have deposits of rock salt in this country,
- **c** why subsidence can be a problem associated with mining rock salt. How do chemical companies guard against this now?

Salt is a very important ***raw material*** (substance you start with to make new products) in the chemical industry.

Did you know

Over a million tonnes of salt are extracted from salt lakes in Spain each year.

3 Products from salt

Do some more research to find out:

- **a** Why is the chemical industry based on salt called the chlor-alkali industry?
- **b** Find the names of the different substances we get from salt.
- **c** How are these substances obtained from salt?
- **d** What products do these substances go on to make?

You can present your information in a variety of ways. You might choose a poster, a documentary report or an information leaflet.

H3 Explaining dissolving

YOU WILL LEARN!

- how to compare the mass of solute and solvent before and after dissolving takes place
- how to apply the particle theory to explain dissolving

In the last unit we found out about the particle theory. It gives us a way of explaining the things we observe. Try out Activity 1, then use the particle theory to explain your experiment.

1 What happens to the mass?

Plan an experiment to see if there is any change in the total mass of a solute and solvent before and after dissolving. (You can use salt and water.)

Make a prediction, explaining your reasoning, before you start your experiment.

Particles and dissolving

When a solid dissolves in water, its particles become mingled with the water particles. A mixture is formed.

Water particles are attracted to the particles of the soluble solid. As the solid starts to dissolve, the water particles 'pull' the solid's particles away from their neighbouring particles. The particles of solid are 'dragged off' into the solution and become surrounded by water particles.

The water particles are moving constantly. So they keep the particles of solid spread throughout the solution.

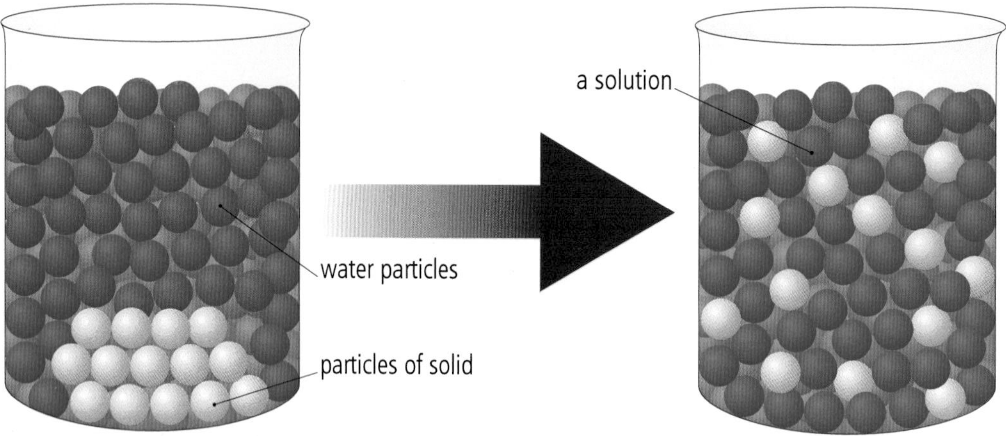

2 Applying the model of dissolving

Use the model of dissolving described above to explain:

a why there is no change in the mass of a solvent and solute before and after they are mixed,
b why a solute cannot be separated from a solution by filtering,
c why you think some solids are insoluble in water.

H4 Distillation

YOU WILL LEARN!
- we can separate a solvent from the substances dissolved in it by distillation
- how distillation works

We have seen how to separate a solute from a solution in H2. What happened to the solvent when you extracted salt from its solution? But what happens if you want to collect the solvent from the mixture?

Points to discuss

1. Think of the problems a country with very little fresh water will face.
2. If the country has a large coastline, it has plenty of seawater available. Why can't it use this water directly for most purposes?
3. How do you think the country could purify the seawater?

1 Separating water from a solution

Add a few drops of food colouring to 20 cm^3 of water in a boiling tube. Set up the apparatus shown opposite. Then heat the mixture very gently. Don't let the coloured mixture shoot through the delivery tube.

a What collects in the receiving tube?

b Explain how your experiment worked, using the words evaporated and condensed.

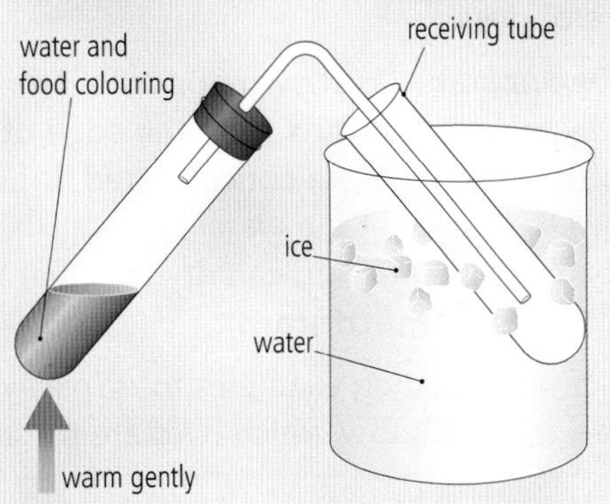

In the experiment above it is quite tricky to collect all the water from the mixture, as some evaporates from the receiving tube. Can you think of a way to improve the yield of water?

Early Arabian chemists were the first to perfect the process of distillation. **Distillation** is the process whereby a liquid is separated and collected from a solution. The solution is heated so that the liquid evaporates. The gas is then cooled and condenses. The pure liquid is collected.

Here is the apparatus you can use to do a simple distillation.

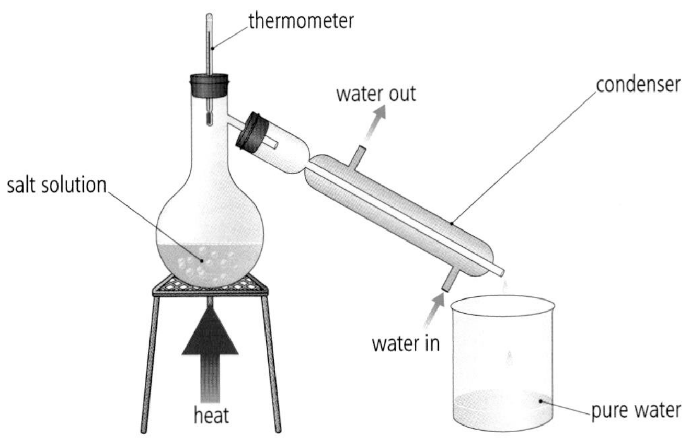

Simple distillation

2 Research on distillation

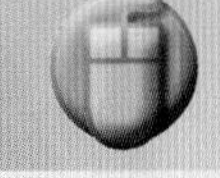

a Find out more about the Arabian chemists who first developed apparatus for distilling mixtures.

b Find out which countries obtain supplies of water from the sea.

c Describe how a desalination plant works.

H5 Chromatography

YOU WILL LEARN!

- we can use chromatography to separate mixtures of solutes that dissolve in a particular solvent
- how chromatography is used to compare and identify substances
- how scientists use evidence gained from chromatography

Have you ever spilled water onto your exercise book by mistake? If you have, you will have noticed how inks 'run' on your soggy pages. Some inks seem to 'blur' at the edges as other colours appear. This process is the basis of a technique called chromatography. **Chromatography** is used to separate mixtures of different solutes.

A solvent carries the solutes along a piece of absorbent paper. You can try this out in the experiment below.

1 Separating dyes

See if the water-soluble inks contain one dye or a mixture of dyes.

Set up the apparatus as shown opposite. The wick is made by making two cuts from the edge of the filter paper to its centre. Make a concentrated dot of ink just above the wick. Let the water soak up the wick and spread out the ink. You can dry the filter paper (now called a **chromatogram**).

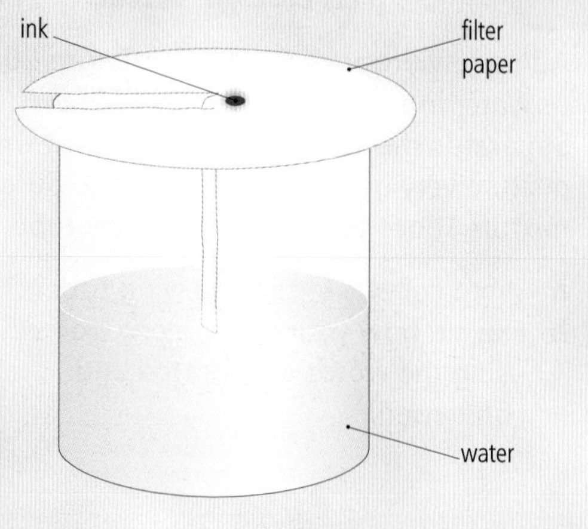

a Use some interesting examples to display your results.
b Make a table to show which dyes are present in each ink.
c What would happen if you used permanent ink in your experiment? Try it if you have time.

How chromatography works

The particles of the solute (different coloured dyes in Activity 1) are 'carried' along the paper by the particles of solvent (water in Activity 1). Do you remember how we used the particle model to explain what happens when a solid dissolves? (See page 112.)

Well, chromatography is similar. The particles of the solvent are attracted to the particles of the solute. The stronger the attraction between the particles of solvent and solute, the further the solute is carried along before being left behind on the paper.

If an ink was made up of the three dyes in this cartoon, what would its chromatogram look like?

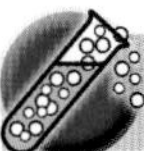

2 Other ways to make a chromatogram

Try these two methods to produce a paper chromatogram using the inks from Activity 1.

Which of the three methods tried so far do you think produces the best chromatograms? Why?

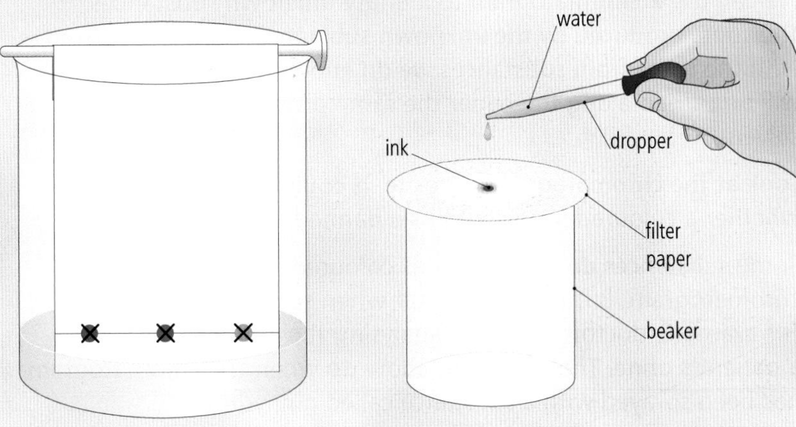

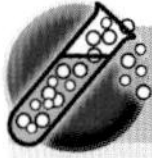

3 Investigating food colourings

You will be provided with a range of food colourings to test.

To make a good chromatogram you need to start with small, concentrated dots of food colouring.
Follow these steps:

1 Draw a pencil line 2 cm from the bottom of your chromatography paper.
2 Mark with a pencil cross the places along the line where you will spot the food colourings. Label the colours under each cross in pencil again.
3 Dip a capillary tube into the food colouring.
4 Quickly dab the end of the tube onto its cross on the line. You want a small circle – don't let it spread out!
5 Let the dot dry, then dab again on the same spot.
6 Repeat this three or four times.
7 When you have done this for each food colouring, set up the chromatogram as shown above. Make sure the water level starts below your spots of food colouring.

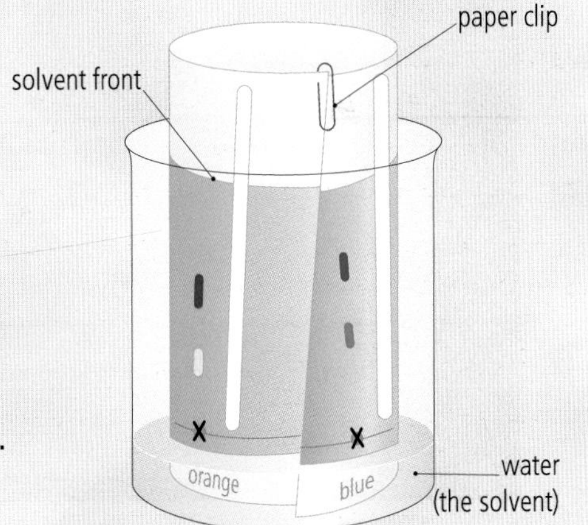

What conclusions can you draw from your chromatogram?

So far, we have looked at paper chromatograms but you can use other materials to run the solvent through and other solvents (besides water). Try the experiment below.

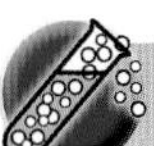

4 Thin layer chromatography

In this experiment see if you can find out more about Universal Indicator solution.

Use a capillary tube to make a small, concentrated spot near the base of a microscope slide covered in a white coating. Stand the microscope slide in a beaker with a little solvent. You can try some different solvents, as well as water.

How many substances can you detect?

Ensure there are no naked flames present.

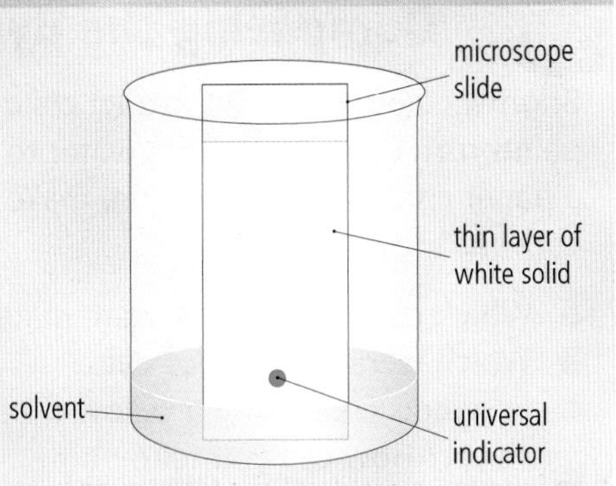

Using chromatography

We can use a chromatogram to identify unknown substances. The spots produced by the unknown substance can be compared with the spots from substances we do know. The same substance will be carried along the paper the same distance by the same solvent.

Look at the chromatogram opposite. It could be used to check whether a coloured food contains a banned dye.

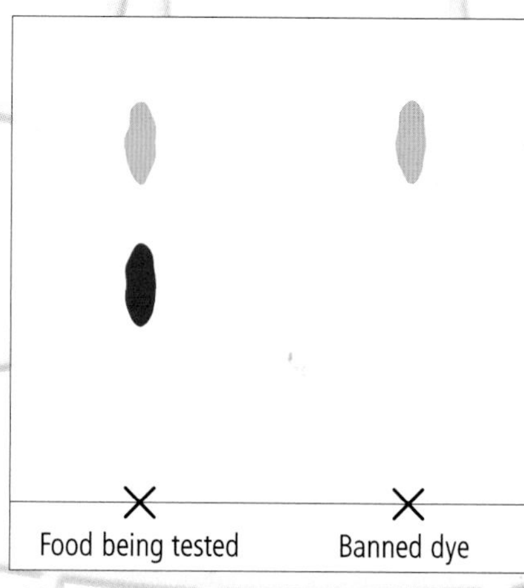

This chromatogram shows a food scientist that the colouring does contain a banned dye. What colour do you think the food has been coloured with?

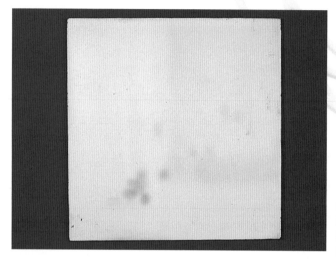

Some substances do not appear as coloured dots on a chromatogram. But they do appear when sprayed with a stain. For example, doctors might be analysing the amino acids in a patient's urine. The spots only show up when the chromatogram has been sprayed with a substance called ninhydrin. Look at the chromatogram below:

Amino acids only show up as purple spots when sprayed with a substance called ninhydrin

Forensic scientists use chromatography to identify unknown substances found at the scene of a crime. Chromatography can also reveal forgery when someone has written or printed in what looks like the same colour as the genuine ink; it can reveal any differences in the ink used.

Scientists now often use gas chromatography to separate mixtures. Instead of using water and paper, the heated sample is carried by gases through a column containing a resin. Complex instruments identify the substances coming from the end of the column.

Did you know

Chromatography is used to detect illegal drugs in race horses.

5 Comparing the dyes in sweets

Brightly coloured sweets attract children to buy them. Use a thin paintbrush dipped in a little water to spot each colour to make a paper chromatogram. Again, make the spots as small and concentrated as possible.

a Which colours of sweet were made with a single dye?
b Which were mixtures of dyes?
c In sweets containing a yellow dye, is it the same dye in each sweet? How can you tell?

H6 Saturated solutions

YOU WILL LEARN!

- how to make a saturated solution
- that the solubilities of different solids vary in a particular solvent
- solubility in water is usually expressed in grams per 100 grams of water (at a particular temperature which is stated)
- some solids dissolve more in some liquids than others

We will now find out if there is a limit to how much solute can dissolve in a solvent.

1 Making saturated solutions

You can test one of these solids:
sodium chloride (common salt)
sodium hydrogencarbonate (bicarbonate of soda)
potassium nitrate

Add a small spatula of your solid to 15 cm^3 of water in a boiling tube. Put a bung in the tube and shake it.

a Does the solid dissolve? How can you tell?

Your task is to find out if there is a limit to the number of spatulas of solid that will dissolve.

b How will you tell when no more will dissolve?
c How many spatulas dissolved in your experiment?

A solution in which no more solute can dissolve is called a **saturated solution**.

2 Changing solvents

Repeat Activity 1 but this time use ethanol instead of water.

a Is your solid soluble in ethanol?
b How many spatulas dissolved before the solution became saturated?
c Is your solid more soluble in water or in ethanol?
d Find some groups that tested the other two solids. What did they find?

Ensure there are no naked flames present.

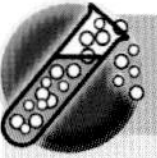

3 Changing volumes

a What do you think will happen to your results if you increase the volume of solvent used in Activities 1 and 2?
b Predict how many spatulas of the solid you used in Activity 1 will dissolve in 20 cm^3 of water.

Now test your prediction.

c Evaluate your experiment. How could you have improved your accuracy?

Ensure there are no naked flames present.

We need some units when we talk about the solubility of a solid. By convention the units have been chosen as **g/100 g** of water. This tells us how many grams of solute dissolve in 100 grams of solvent.

For example, ***the solubility of sodium chloride in water is 36 g/100 g of water at 25 °C***. (100 g of water has a volume of 100 cm^3).

H7 Solubility curves

YOU WILL LEARN!

- many solutes are more soluble at higher temperatures
- how to collect solubility data to draw a solubility curve
- how to make comparisons and predictions from solubility curves

Did you notice that the solubility of sodium chloride on the previous page quoted the temperature (i.e. 36 g/100 g of water ***at 25 °C***)? We have to do this because the solubility of a solute varies with temperature.

1 Solubility of potassium nitrate

Measure out 8 g of potassium nitrate. Heat some water to 60 °C in a small beaker. Use a graduated pipette to transfer 10 cm^3 of the hot water to a test tube. Now add the 8 g of potassium nitrate to the test tube, stopper and shake. This should form a solution that is almost saturated. Let the test tube cool down and note the temperature when the first crystals appear.

a At what temperature does the solution become saturated?

Now cool the test tube under a cold tap and observe what happens.

b What do you see happen in the test tube?
c Why does this happen? What pattern have you spotted?
d How could you get the solid to dissolve again?

We can find the solubility of a solid at different temperatures by observing when crystals first appear from a cooling solution. At this point of crystallisation, the solution is saturated. You can try this for potassium nitrate. You should already have one result from Activity 1.

When you have several results, you can plot a graph showing how the solubility changes with temperature. This is called a **solubility curve**.

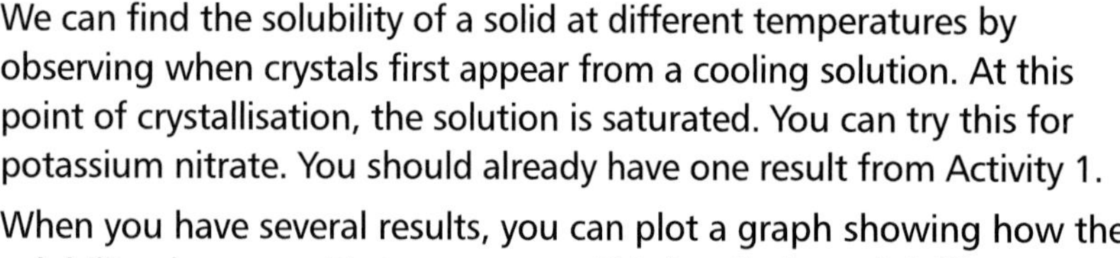

2 Plotting the solubility curve of potassium nitrate

Work with other groups to get five readings to plot on a graph. The range of temperatures should be between 20 °C and 60 °C. The method you use to obtain your data is similar to Activity 1. Here are some approximate figures to help decide how much potassium nitrate each group should use:

- at 20 °C, its solubility is between 25 and 35 g/100 g of water;
- at 60 °C, its solubility is between 100 and 120 g/100 g of water.

Think about how to make your results as reliable as possible. Record the results in a table.

a Copy and complete using your answer to **a** in Activity 1:
At .....°C, 8 g of potassium nitrate dissolve in 10 g of water.
Therefore its solubility at .....°C is ..... g/100 g of water.
b Convert all your results to solubility in g/100 g of water, and draw your graph.

Using solubility curves

Now use your solubility curve to make some predictions.

3 Predictions from your solubility curve

Using your solubility curve from Activity 2:

a Predict the solubility of potassium nitrate at a temperature between two points on your graph.
This is called **interpolation**.

b Predict the solubility of potassium nitrate at 10 °C. To do this you will need to extend your line. This is called **extrapolation**.

If you have time, test your predictions by experiment.

Look at the solubility curves of copper sulfate and sodium chloride below:

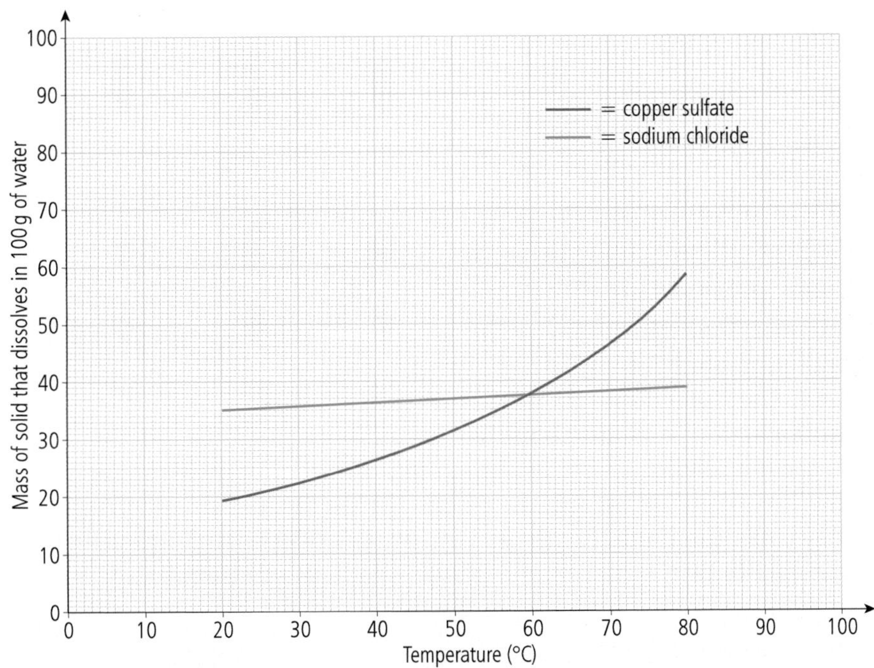

4 Using solubility curves

Use the graph above to answer these questions.

a How much copper sulfate will be needed to dissolve in 100 g of water to form a saturated solution at 25 °C?

b Is the solubility of copper sulfate or sodium chloride affected more by temperature?

c At 40 °C, which substance is more soluble in water?

d At 80 °C which substance is more soluble in water?

e At what temperature do both substances have the same solubility?

f What will be the solubility of copper sulfate at 90 °C?

g You add 60 g of copper sulfate to 100 g of water at 70 °C.

i How many grams of copper sulfate remain undissolved after stirring?

ii How could you check your answer by experiment?

h How much copper sulfate will dissolve in 25 cm^3 of water at 80 °C?

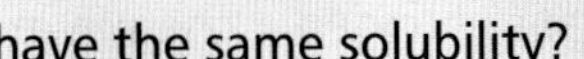

Summary

When solids dissolve in a liquid their particles become intermingled. The solid is called the **solute**, the liquid is the **solvent** and the resulting mixture is a **solution**.

We can collect the solvent (liquid) from the solution by **distillation**. If a solvent contains two or more solutes, we can separate the solutes by **chromatography**.

A solution that will not dissolve any more solid is a **saturated** solution.

The **solubility** of a substance varies with temperature. This can be shown on a solubility curve.

Key words

chromatogram
chromatography
distillation
filtration
insoluble
saturated solution
soluble
solute
solution
solvent

Summary Questions

1 Explain the following observations using the particle theory:
- **a** A solid dissolves in water.
- **b** The two dyes in an ink are separated using paper chromatography.
- **c** Pure water is collected from a solution of salty water by distilling the mixture.

2 Customs officers at an airport are suspicious of a flask carried by a passenger. They think the colourless liquid it contains might have an illegal drug dissolved in it. The flask is taken to their forensic laboratory.
- **a** How could they test to see if a solid is dissolved in the liquid?
- **b** Draw the apparatus they could use if they wanted to collect the solvent to test separately.
- **c** How might they test the original liquid to see if it contains more than one substance dissolved in it?

3 Police arrest a man on suspicion of forgery. They believe he has changed a cheque made payable to his company from £5000.00 to £50 000. They take a fountain pen found in the suspect's office for testing. They also have the ink from the firm that wrote out the original cheque. Forensic scientists produce a chromatogram of the two inks. Look at the chromatogram in the next column. Write a report for the court explaining exactly what the chromatogram shows. The jury will need your expert advice!

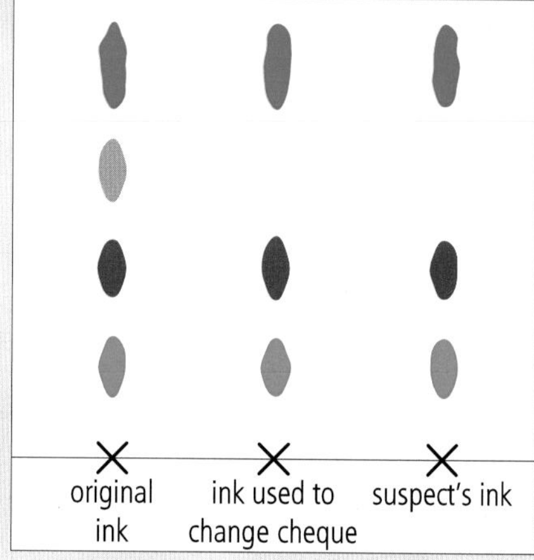

4 **a** Use the data below to plot a solubility curve for potassium chlorate:

Temperature (°C)	Solubility (g/100 g water)
0	3.5
20	7.5
40	14.0
60	24.0
80	37.5

- **b** What is the solubility of potassium chlorate at 50 °C?
- **c** How much potassium chlorate will dissolve in 5 g of water at 35 °C?
- **d** If you add 30 g of potassium chlorate to 100 g of water at 80 °C, then let it cool, at what temperature will the first crystals appear?

End of unit Questions

1 Emma dissolved some salt in some water to make salt water.

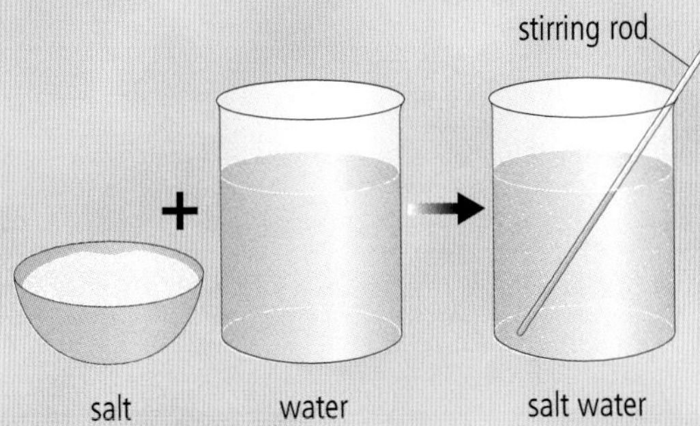

a Which words from the list below describe: **i** the salt, **ii** the water and **iii** the salt water?

solution	solute
sediment	filtrate
solvent	substance

3 marks

b What two things could Emma do to make the salt dissolve more quickly? *2 marks*

c Emma dissolved 5 g of salt in 50 cm^3 of water. Now she wants to make some salt water which is only half as concentrated. What should she do? Choose from these options:
Dissolve 10 g of salt in 100 cm^3 of water.
Dissolve 5 g of salt in 100 cm^3 of water.
Dissolve 10 g of salt in 50 cm^3 of water.
Dissolve 5 g of salt in 25 cm^3 of water.
1 mark

2 Sunil crushed petals from 3 different flowers separately in some liquid and poured off the coloured solutions. Then he put drops of each coloured solution into the middle of different pieces of filter paper.

The solutions spread out on the filter paper. The diagrams show his results.

solution from yellow petals — yellow ring
solution from red petals — yellow ring, purple spot
solution from purple petals — purple spot

a What is the name of this method of investigating coloured substances? *1 mark*

b Sunil made notes on his experiment. Some words are missing. Complete the sentences. *3 marks*

When I crushed a flower in a liquid it produced a coloured solution.
This is because a coloured substance had ..... in the liquid. This shows that the liquid is a ..... for these coloured substances.
My experiment shows that one of the flowers probably contained two coloured substances. This was the ..... flower.

3 Cathy has two orange drinks, X and Y. She uses chromatography to identify the coloured substances in the drinks. Her experiment is shown below.

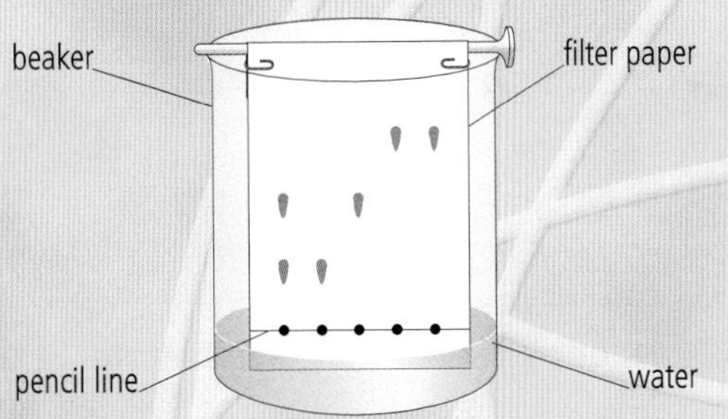

Cathy made the chromatogram below using drink X, three food colourings, E102, E160, E110, and drink Y.

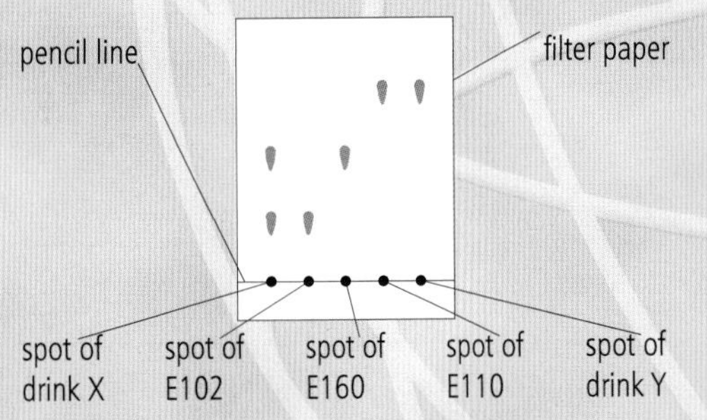

a i Use Cathy's chromatogram to identify the two coloured substances in drink X. Write down their E numbers. *2 marks*

ii Copy Cathy's chromatogram and draw another spot to show what it would look like if drink Y contained E102 as well. *1 mark*

iii Chromatography separates the coloured substances in a drink. How can you tell from a chromatogram how many coloured substances there are in a drink? *1 mark*

b i The spots show up well on filter paper. Give one reason why filter paper is used in this experiment. *1 mark*

ii The line across the bottom of a chromatogram should be drawn with a pencil, not with ink. Why should the line not be drawn with ink? *1 mark*

4 The graph shows how the solubility of two salts in water changes with temperature. The solubility is the number of grams of the salt which will dissolve in 100 g of water.

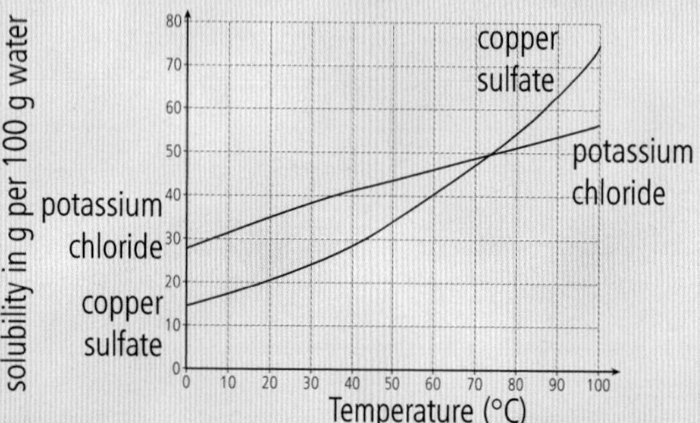

a Describe how the solubility of copper sulfate changes with temperature. *1 mark*

b Use the information in the graph to answer the questions below.

i What is the solubility of potassium chloride at 40 °C? *1 mark*

..... g per 100 g of water

ii At what temperature are the solubilities of the two salts the same? *1 mark*

iii What is the largest mass of copper sulfate which can be dissolved in 50 g of water at 60 °C? *1 mark*

c Why is the solubility of salts in water normally given only for temperatures between 0 °C and 100 °C? *2 marks*

5 a The apparatus in the diagram below is used to obtain pure water from impure water.

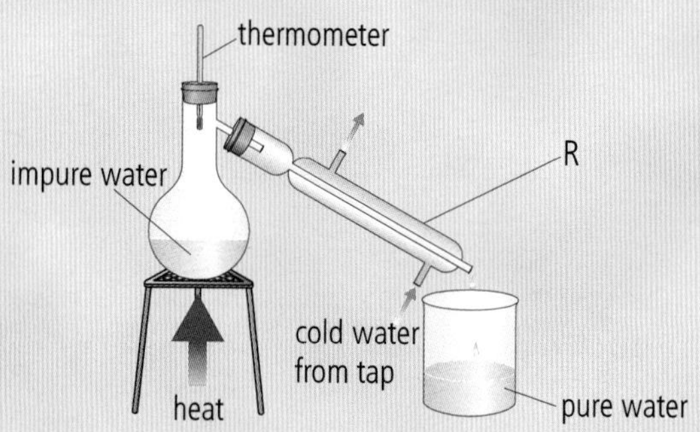

i What temperature would the thermometer show? *1 mark*

ii What is the function of the piece of apparatus labelled R? *1 mark*

iii Give the name of the process which purifies water in this way. *1 mark*

b Look back to the apparatus in part **a**. Name the change of state which occurs:

i in the round-bottomed flask.

ii in the piece of apparatus labelled R.

2 marks

6 The table below gives information about four gases. It shows the volume of each gas that will dissolve in 1000 cm^3 of water at two different temperatures.

gas	volume dissolved in 1000 cm^3 water at 20 °C	volume dissolved in 1000 cm^3 water at 60 °C
ammonia	680 000 cm^3	200 000 cm^3
carbon dioxide	850 cm^3	360 cm^3
hydrogen chloride	442 000 cm^3	339 000 cm^3
oxygen	30 cm^3	19 cm^3

Use the information in the table to answer the following questions.

a i Which **one** of the four gases is the most soluble at 60 °C? *1 mark*

ii Which **one** of the four gases is the least soluble at 20 °C? *1 mark*

b How does a rise in temperature affect the amount of gas which will dissolve? *1 mark*

7I Energy resources

Introduction

We all use large amounts of energy in our everyday lives. Traditionally most of our energy has come from burning fuels like fossil fuels or wood. Nowadays our energy sources include materials that don't have to be burned, such as nuclear fuels, and a wide range of 'alternative' energy sources, such as renewable energy resources. You will learn about how we obtain energy from these different sources, some of the things the energy is used for, where living things get their energy from and what they use it for. You will also find out about the advantages and disadvantages of different energy sources and how to choose the right energy source for a particular task.

You already know

- several types of fuel and places where fuel is used
- the energy in fuel is released when the fuel is burned
- the change that takes place when fuel is burned is irreversible
- humans and other animals get their energy from the food they eat

In this topic you will learn

- how to use energy transfer diagrams to represent the changes taking place when fuels are used
- to compare the advantages, limitations and environmental impact of different fuels
- the range of renewable energy resources available and what they can be used for
- the energy requirements of different people and the transfer links between the Sun, energy resources and people

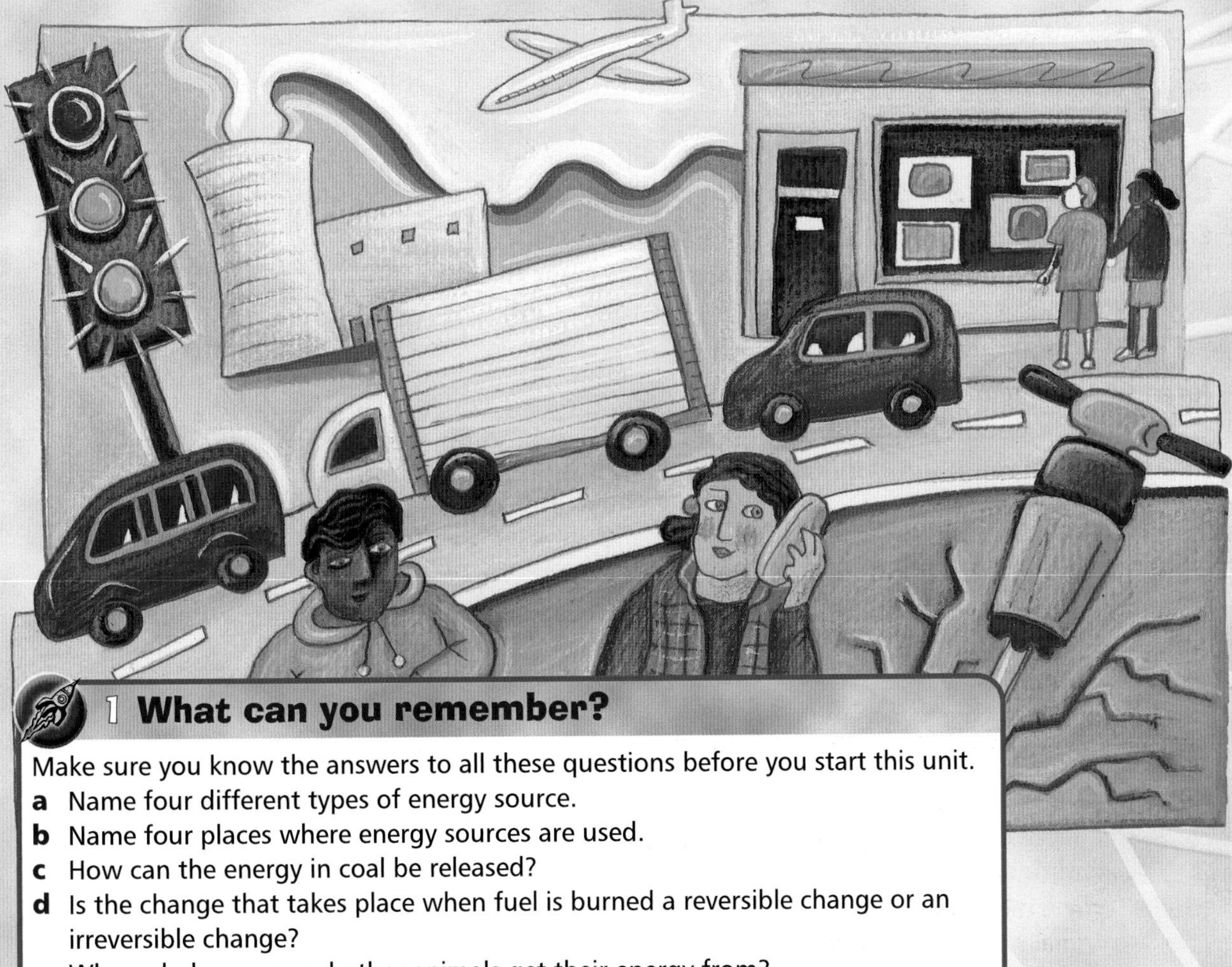

1 What can you remember?

Make sure you know the answers to all these questions before you start this unit.

a Name four different types of energy source.

b Name four places where energy sources are used.

c How can the energy in coal be released?

d Is the change that takes place when fuel is burned a reversible change or an irreversible change?

e Where do humans and other animals get their energy from?

I1 Getting energy from fuel

YOU WILL LEARN!

- how to draw and describe energy transfer diagrams
- how to compare the energy from different fuels
- the factors that influence the type of energy source used for different purposes
- how fuel use can affect energy transfer links between the Sun and Earth

Points to discuss

1 Name at least 10 different fuels and say what they are used for.
2 Is there anything that all your types of fuel have in common?
3 Write a definition of a fuel. It should include the word 'energy'. (You could also try to define energy!)

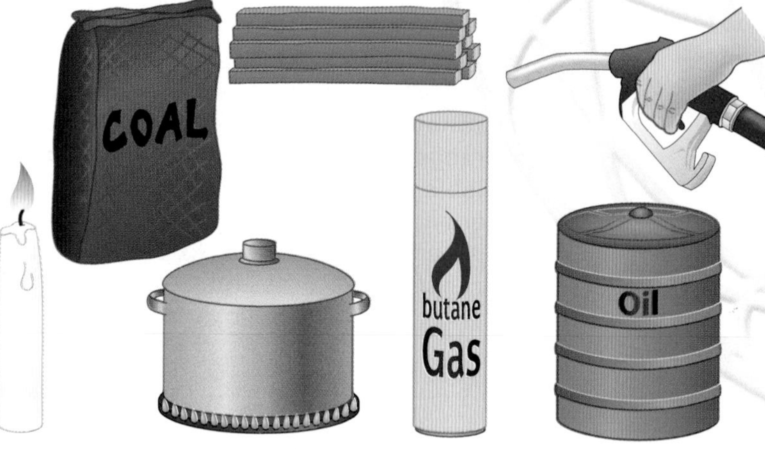

Some of the fuels we use

Energy transfer diagrams

Energy is always needed to make changes happen. This energy has to come from somewhere. **Energy transfer** diagrams show how energy moves and how it changes from one form to another.

For a candle burning to light a room:

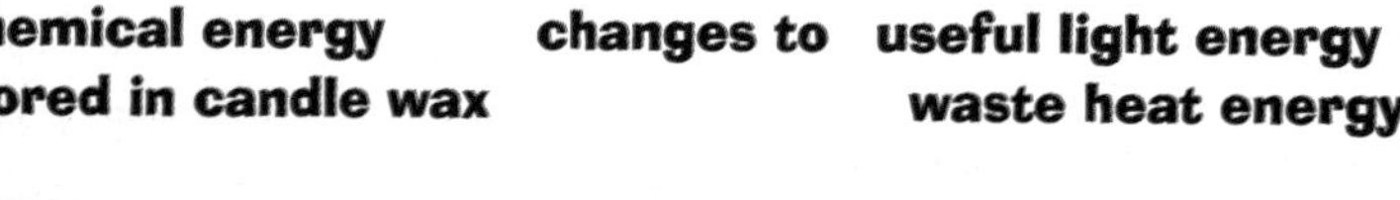

Chemical energy stored in candle wax **changes to** **useful light energy + waste heat energy**

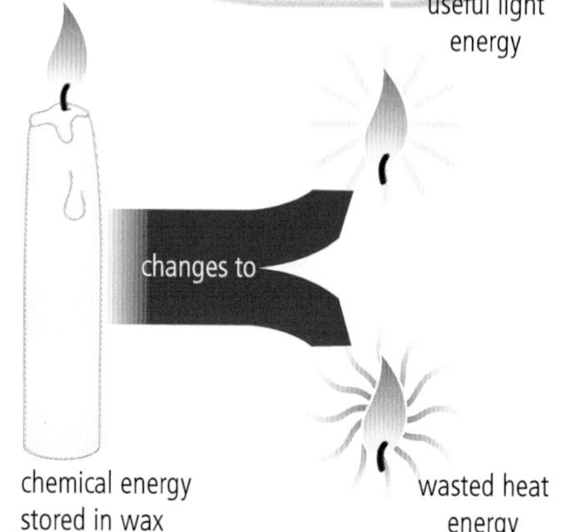

1 Drawing energy transfer diagrams

Draw some energy transfer diagrams of your own for the situations listed below. Think very carefully about what provides the energy, the changes that produce useful energy, and the form of the energy that is wasted.

a Burning petrol to make a car move.
b Pushing a swing.
c Cycling up a hill.
d An electric fire heating a room.

Which cyclist will use up the most energy?

Not all fuels are the same. Some types of fuel give out more energy than others.

2 Comparing energy from different fuels

Design an investigation you could do in your science laboratory to compare the energy given out by different types of fuel.

Remember! A good scientist:

- plans exactly what their experiment is going to look for;
- assesses any hazards and plans a safe way to work;
- makes results as accurate and as repeatable as possible;
- doesn't try to hide any unusual or unexpected results! (They might be the scientific breakthrough everyone has been looking for!)
- ensures any comparisons are fair;
- chooses a clear way to present the results;
- decides what conclusions, if any, can be drawn from their results.

When your plan has been checked by your teacher, carry out your investigation.

As there are many hazards in this investigation, your teacher may choose one group's investigation to carry out as a class demonstration.

These are unsafe scientists – check all the hazards in your investigation

a Can you present your results as a table or a chart to make the comparison between different fuels clear?

b What conclusions did you draw from your investigation?

c Explain how you used your results to reach these conclusions.

d Were there any factors that might have affected your results?

Efficiency

An **efficient** fuel is one that produces a lot of energy from a given amount of fuel. What are the advantages of using an efficient fuel? When we choose fuel for a particular purpose we usually have to consider more than just efficiency. For instance, you would not put coal in a car, or petrol on a domestic fire.

What factors make solar power and batteries suitable energy resources to use in a calculator?

Points to discuss

1. What factors, other than efficiency, would affect your choice of fuel?
2. Think of some examples where different types of energy source are used. Why do you think these energy sources were chosen?

Points to discuss

1 The fuel used to power spacecraft is hydrogen but oxygen is needed as well. These are stored separately as liquids and mixed before the hydrogen is burned to power the spacecraft. Think about why both elements are needed, and why they are stored separately.

2 Walkers and climbers usually use small canisters of liquid butane or propane gas as fuel for their cooking stoves. In very cold weather the canisters have to be warmed up by holding them before the stove will light. Why do you think this is?

Spaceshuttle taking off

More energy transfers

Most burning fuels release 'greenhouse gases', which cause global warming. Some gases, such as carbon dioxide, let the Sun's radiation through but stop some of the heat from Earth radiating back out again. So gradually the Earth warms up.

The energy diagrams show how it happens.

The energy given out to space is less when we have greenhouse gases in the air.

So Earth gradually warms up.

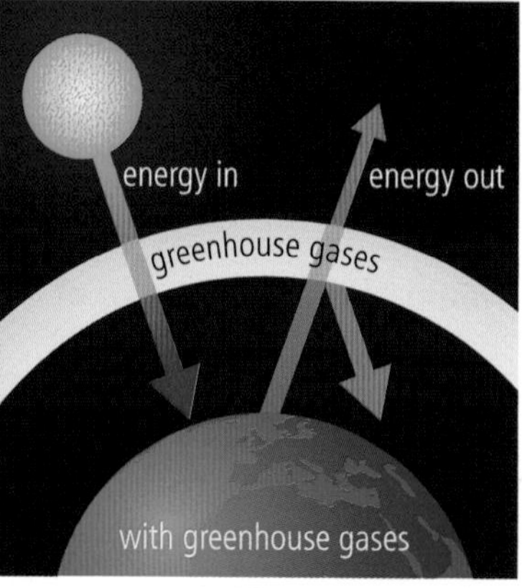

Greenhouse gases make the Earth warm up

Did you know

Liquid aircraft fuel is not **flammable**. Only the vapour burns. **NEVER** attempt to test this with even tiny amounts of fuel. If the vapour above the fuel catches light, a very serious fire will result.

12 What are fossil fuels?

YOU WILL LEARN!
- how fossil fuels formed and how long they may last
- why the conservation of fossil fuels is important
- some ways to conserve fuels

Fossil fuels are those that were made by the decay of organic material (plants and animals) that lived many millions of years ago. Coal, oil, natural gas and the fuels made from oil are all fossil fuels.

The diagram shows how fossil fuels form.

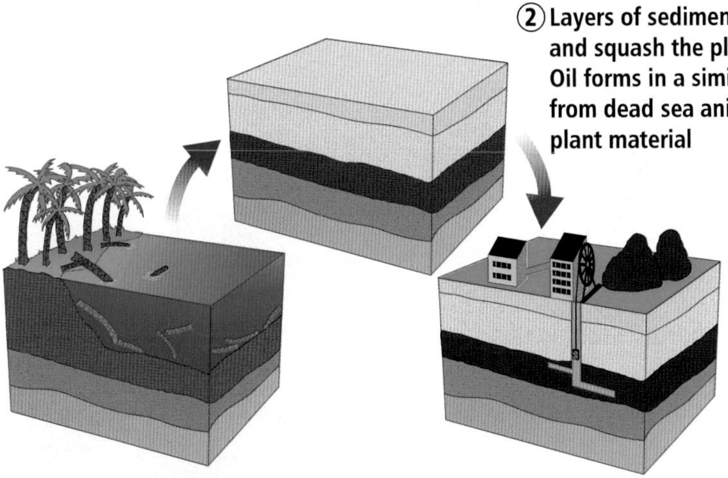

② Layers of sediment build up and squash the plant material. Oil forms in a similar way from dead sea animal and plant material
① Coal forms from plant material that does not decay immediately, usually because it is under water
③ 300 million years later miners dig shafts and tunnels to reach the coal. Liquid oil is reached by drilling holes down to it

Points to discuss

1 It is quite common to find fossils in pieces of coal. Why do you think this is?
2 Where did the energy stored in fossil fuels come from originally?

The timeline shows how long different fossil fuels may last.

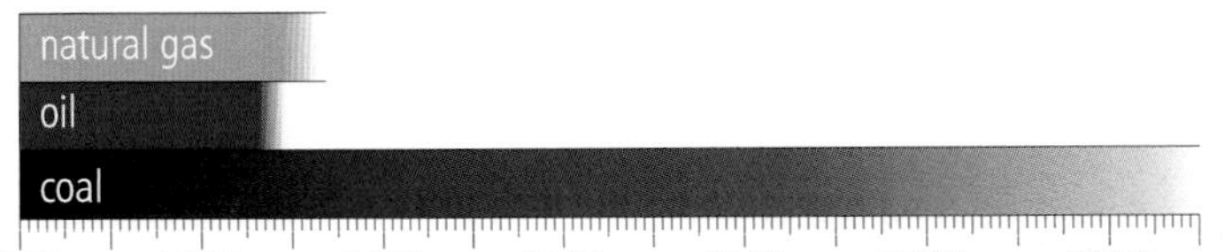

These are only estimates of how long different fuels will last

Fossils are often found in coal

These estimates are not accurate, and they keep changing. This is because they depend on:

- how much fossil fuel has yet to be discovered,
- whether or not the rate at which we use fossil fuel changes,
- whether or not the fuel can be extracted cheaply enough for people to buy. This changes as technology improves.

The present rate of **fuel consumption** for the world is increasing. Suggest some reasons why.

1 Alternatives to fossil fuels

Using books, a multimedia encyclopedia, or the Internet:

- **a** Find out some of the uses of different fossil fuels.
- **b** Group the uses you have found into those where some other type of fuel could be used and those where there is no suitable substitute.
- **c** Write a short commentary (one or two paragraphs) on how our lives will be affected as fossil fuels run out.

Obviously, fossil fuels will last longer if we use them at a slower rate. There are ways we can all act (both on a personal scale and on a larger scale) to save energy, making the supplies of fossil fuels last longer.

Points to discuss

1. List ways in which individuals can save energy? How is this energy saved?
2. What can we do, as individuals, to encourage industries and governments to use less energy?

Recycling

Many of the materials we use can be recycled. Usually, less fuel is used to recycle materials than to make new ones, so recycling is a way of saving fuel.

We can all save energy

2 Recycling

- **a** Find out some of the materials that can be recycled.
- **b** How are they recycled?
- **c** Does recycling materials have any benefits other than saving fuel?

How many materials do you know that can be recycled?

Wash your hands after handling waste materials. Wear rubber gloves if at risk from sharp objects.

3 Design a poster

Design a poster or a cartoon strip to encourage people to save energy.

Did you know

Every glass milk bottle is reused up to 100 times. Even after it has been broken the glass can be recycled and used again.

What are renewable energy resources?

YOU WILL LEARN!

- how energy from the Sun can be used
- how to explain some of the uses, advantages, limitations and environmental impact of different renewable energy resources
- how to describe some of the features of nuclear power

Energy from the Sun

We know that fossil fuels will not last for ever. For decades some scientists have been doing research into other means of supporting our modern 'energy rich' lifestyle.

The energy in fossil fuels came originally from the Sun, and has been stored for millions of years. Some research concentrates on finding and improving ways to use energy from the Sun directly.

Did you know

The Earth receives more energy from the Sun in 15 minutes than all the people in the world use in a year.

Points to discuss

- How many examples can you think of where the Sun's energy is used as 'fuel'?

1 Using the Sun's energy

Find the best way of using the Sun's energy to heat a small volume of water.

There are many things you could vary. Here are a few:

- the material the container is made from
- the colour of the container
- whether or not the container is insulated.

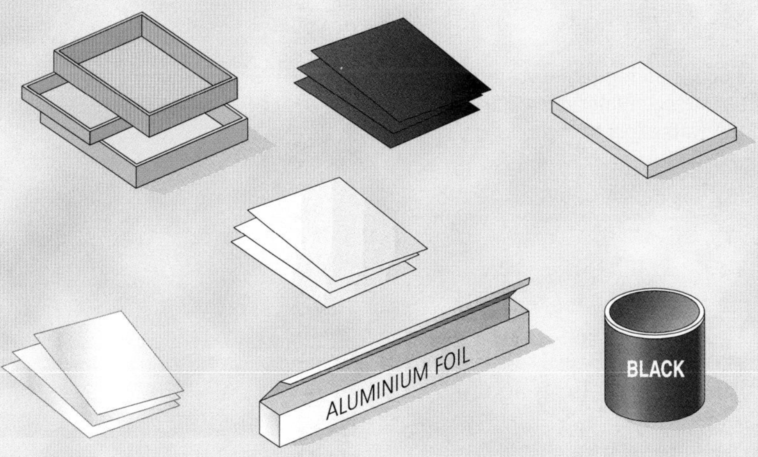

If you have time, you could also experiment with the position of the container (where the Sun shines from) and whether you use anything (such as glass, plastic, metal foil) to cover the container.

a Write one or two short paragraphs to describe your results, and to explain what conclusions you drew from them.
b Were there any limitations or uncertainties?

Renewable energy resources

Renewable energy resources are those that can be replaced as they are used up. These energy resources can be divided into two types.

1. Those where the energy comes almost directly from the Sun:
- 'traditional fuels' such as wood, animal dung, crop wastes
- solar panels, where the Sun's energy is used to warm water for heating
- electricity generated using solar cells

2. Those where the energy comes indirectly from the Sun:
- wind or water power
  It is the Sun warming some parts of the Earth more than others that causes the currents of air and ocean currents. These can be used to drive machinery or generate electricity. Warmth from the Sun drives the water cycle that causes rivers to flow.
- wave power
  The gravitational pull of the Moon and the Sun causes the tides that drive some water powered electricity generators.

The table below gives very brief details about some renewable energy resources.

Energy resource	Details
Traditional fuels	Relatively cheap and easy to produce. Give off carbon dioxide that contributes to global warming.
Solar cells	Use the Sun's energy to generate electricity. Work best in countries with a lot of sunshine.
Hydroelectric power	Uses a downhill flow of water to turn turbines to generate electricity. Used in mountainous areas with fast flowing rivers, or where dams can be built across very large rivers.
Tidal barriers	Use the rise and fall of tidal water to turn turbines to generate electricity. Can damage or destroy wildlife habitats by changing the water flow to them.
Wind generators	Use the wind to drive round sails to drive turbines to generate electricity. Are often described as an 'eyesore'.

2 Renewable energy resources

Choose one renewable energy resource. Find out more about it. Make a poster or leaflet either advertising it or advising against its use.

Non-renewable alternative energy resources

Those where the energy source is not the Sun.
- Geothermal energy comes from heat from the centre of the Earth. Heat from inside the Earth is used to heat water and generate electricity. Most common in areas with hot springs, though it is possible to drill down to layers of warmer rock in other areas too.
- Nuclear energy comes from the breaking up of radioactive atoms.

Solar panels on roof top

Wind farms

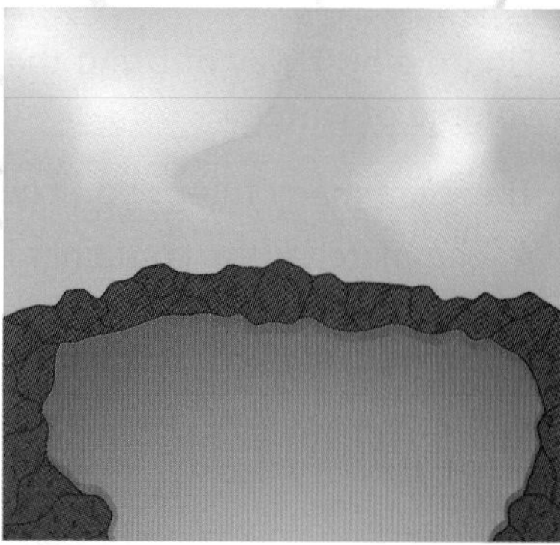

Hot springs

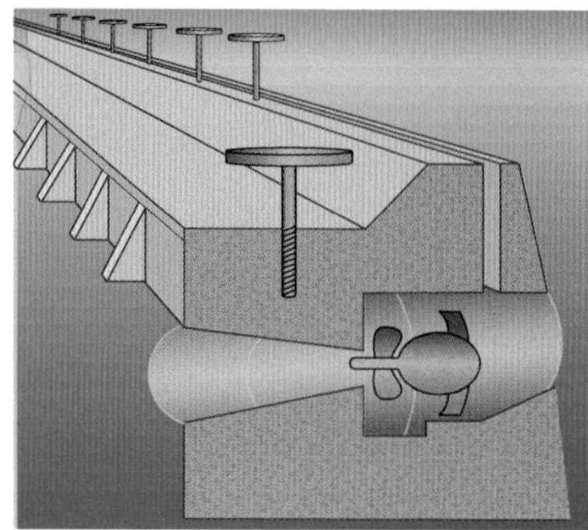

Tidal barrier

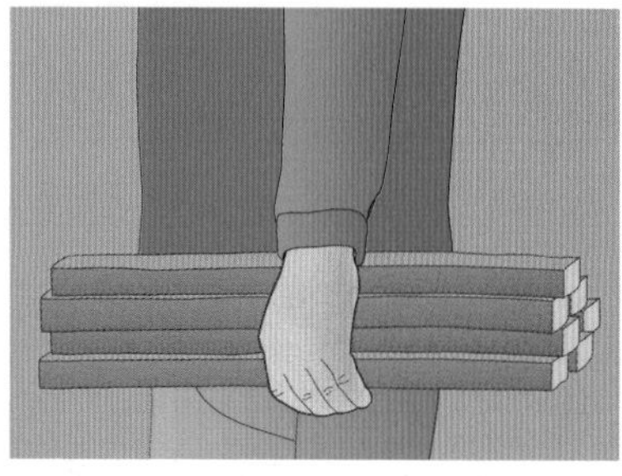

Firewood

Nuclear power

Nuclear power uses the heat energy released by splitting radioactive atoms (nuclear fission). Uranium ore, mined in many places around the world, is processed into fuel rods. The rate of nuclear fission is controlled so the energy is released slowly and used to heat water to generate electricity.

Nuclear power is not a renewable energy source: eventually the uranium supply will run out. The known supplies of uranium are enough to last hundreds of years.

Like any other energy resource, nuclear energy has good and bad features. Supporters say:

- it is a cheap form of energy
- it causes no air pollution
- it supplies about 4 % of energy used worldwide. This is only a small fraction of the amount it could supply.

Critics say:

- radioactive waste from nuclear power stations remains dangerous for centuries or even millennia. Safe storage facilities have to be built to house the waste
- accidents at nuclear power stations can release radioactivity into the environment. This can cause cancers in people, especially children, and can destroy farmland and cause serious environmental damage.

Did you know ?

The world's worst nuclear reactor disaster happened at Chernobyl on April 26th 1986. An improperly supervised experiment went wrong, causing an explosion which blew off the reactor's protective covering. 31 people died in the accident. 100 000 people had to move away from their homes, many permanently. Prevailing winds blew radioactive dust across Europe and Britain. The total number of radiation-caused deaths is still not known.

Nuclear power station

3 Decision time

Find out more about some aspect of nuclear power.

a Imagine someone wants to build a nuclear power station near your home. Will you be for it or against it?

b Hold a debate. Present your arguments 'for' and 'against' to a 'Planning Committee'. What will they decide?

Points to discuss

Imagine life 100 years in the future. Oil and natural gas are rare, and far too expensive to burn. Supplies of coal are limited.

What sources of energy will you use? Be imaginative! Be inventive!

These buildings use less energy than most buildings

4 How much have you learnt?

Make your own diagram to show how much you have learnt about different energy resources. Choose the design shown or design your own.

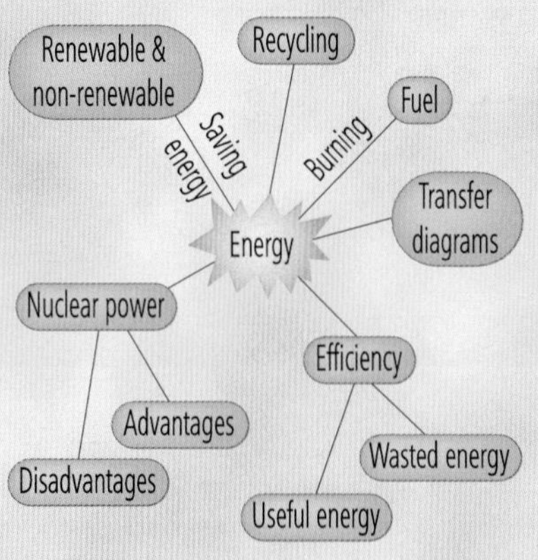

Did you know

Crude oil is not the only source of fuel to use in cars. A car has been developed that runs on vegetable oil. This is a renewable source of energy, made from plants like oil seed rape. The cars do not need new oil, they can run on used oil from chip shops and restaurants, provided the bits are filtered out from the oil first.

Did you know

Water is made from hydrogen and oxygen. Hydrogen can be used as a fuel. Much scientific research is concentrating on finding ways to use water as a source of energy. If the research is successful, the Earth has enough supplies of water to provide for all our energy requirements for millennia.

How do living things use energy?

YOU WILL LEARN!

- how to compare the energy obtained from different foods
- how the energy requirements of humans vary
- how energy transfers take place in food chains

Energy for activity

Have you ever come back from a swimming session or a football game and said "I'm hungry"? You are most likely to feel hungry when you have been active.

Humans and all other animals get the energy they need from their diet, the food they eat. Food is the 'fuel' for animals.

You already know that some foods seem to satisfy hunger better than others. After running a marathon you wouldn't choose a stick of celery to fill you up!

People who use more energy need to eat more

1 Comparing the energy in different foods

Plan an investigation to find out how much energy is stored in different types of food. **Remember:** Anything that will burn can be used as fuel to provide energy.

Ideally your investigation should:

- compare different types of food
- compare your results with those of a different group.

Look at your results for different foods.

a Do the 'high energy' foods have anything in common?
b Why do you think herbivores (animals that eat just plants) spend so much of their time eating?

Joules

The energy in food is measured in **joules**.

1 joule = energy needed to lift 1 N a height of 1 m
(An average sized apple weighs about 1 N.)

On food packaging the energy is generally given in kilojoules (kJ).

1 kJ = 1000 J

Approximate energy requirements are

12-year-old boys – 11 700 kJ per day
12-year-old girls – 9700 kJ per day
male office worker – 11 000 kJ per day
female office worker – 9800 kJ per day

The energy you use to climb up a hill can be found using the equation below:

energy (in joules) = your weight (in N) × height of hill (in m)

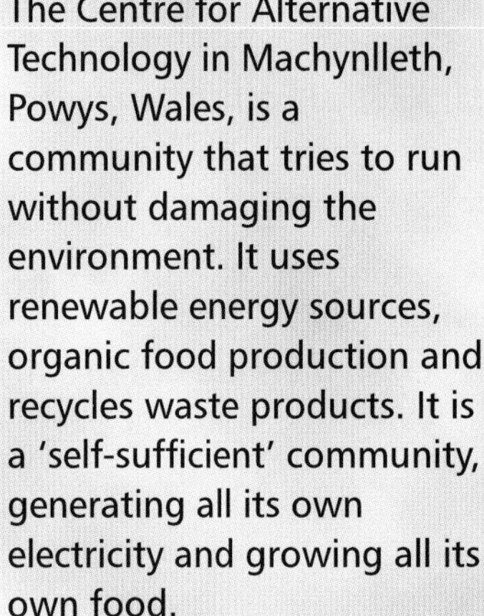

Did you know

The Centre for Alternative Technology in Machynlleth, Powys, Wales, is a community that tries to run without damaging the environment. It uses renewable energy sources, organic food production and recycles waste products. It is a 'self-sufficient' community, generating all its own electricity and growing all its own food.

Points to discuss

1 How high is the hill you 'ought' to be able to climb using the food you eat each day?

How far could you climb using the energy in a bag of sweets?

2 Why do you think you need so much food energy if you are not climbing this height hill each day?
Hint: try to think of **all** the things your body uses energy for.

Different people need to eat different amounts of food to supply the energy they need.

Points to discuss

1 Discuss what things affect how much energy someone uses.
2 What happens if a person's energy intake from food is not balanced by the energy they use?

2 Planning suitable meals

Use the 'nutritional information' section on food packaging to discuss and plan a set of suitable meals for:

a a 12-year-old boy on an activity holiday,
b a female office worker trying to lose weight.

Remember:
- eating just chocolate bars is not healthy
- crash diets are not healthy either. Weight loss should be gradual.

Choosing the right food can be tricky

Sir Ranulph Fiennes nearly died because he used more energy than he ate

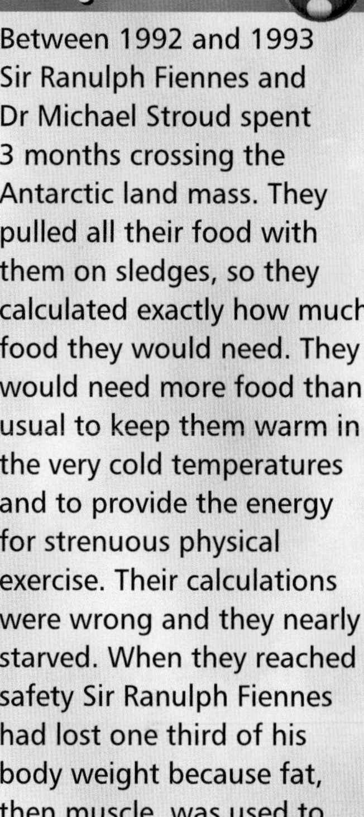

Did you know?

Between 1992 and 1993 Sir Ranulph Fiennes and Dr Michael Stroud spent 3 months crossing the Antarctic land mass. They pulled all their food with them on sledges, so they calculated exactly how much food they would need. They would need more food than usual to keep them warm in the very cold temperatures and to provide the energy for strenuous physical exercise. Their calculations were wrong and they nearly starved. When they reached safety Sir Ranulph Fiennes had lost one third of his body weight because fat, then muscle, was used to provide the energy he needed.

Food chains

Food chains show how living things get their energy. Plants at the bottom of the food chain use the Sun's energy to 'produce' their own food. Herbivores eat plants, and carnivores eat herbivores. Some organisms do not fit into this simple pattern of 'producer → primary consumer → secondary consumer'. For example, fungi

- grow on dead plant or animal material
- do not photosynthesise.

Some plants and animals have symbiotic relationships (they depend on each other). Zoanthids

- are like sea anemones
- are green because they have microscopic plants called zooxanthellae living within their cells
- have most of their energy provided by photosynthesis of the zooxanthellae.

Points to discuss

1 Where does the energy needed by fungi come from?
2 What do you think the zooxanthellae gain from their symbiotic relationship with zoanthids?

A zoanthid

Points to discuss

If a group of teenagers all complete the same mountain bike course, use your knowledge of energy to decide who is going to do most work:

1. a heavy person or a light person,
2. a person on a heavy bike or a light bike,
3. a person who completes the course quickly or a slower person.

Muscles and energy

Every time you move, muscles have to do work to move your body from where you start to where you finish. How much work this is, depends on your weight and how far your muscles have to move you. Of course if you are on a bike, you have to add the weight of the bike to your weight to get the total weight that your muscles are moving. If you go uphill, your muscles are doing extra work lifting you against the force of gravity. Going downhill is easier though! Going faster does not mean you do more work, only that you do it in a shorter time.

Most of your energy is used for the life processes that keep you alive. Only a relatively small proportion of it is used in the exercise you do. That is why adults sometimes spend weeks going to the gym to 'burn off' the extra food they consumed at Christmas. Alcoholic drinks contain large amounts of energy.

While your muscles are working they produce waste-heat energy. This is why you get hot when you exercise. Normally your body loses the waste-heat energy by sweating or by sending warm blood to just under the surface of your skin (you looked flushed and hot). Sometimes this waste energy is very useful. When you are very cold some of your muscles contract rhythmically. You shiver. The heat your muscles produce like this helps warm you up.

Did you know?

Teenagers usually have a higher power to weight ratio than adults. This means that a healthy teenager can work faster than a healthy adult of the same weight. That is why teenagers can generally climb or cycle up hills faster than their parents.

Summary

When **fuels** are burned, the **energy** stored in the fuel is **transferred** to heat, movement and other forms of energy. Much of the energy is transferred to 'waste' forms of energy.

It is important to conserve fuels because **fossil fuels** will run out and, at present, the amount of energy available from **renewable energy resources** is limited.

Renewable energy resources often have less environmental impact than fossil fuels but they can be more expensive and are often less easy to use.

People get their energy from the food they eat. **Food chains** show how the Sun's energy is transferred through plants then, in food, to the various creatures in the food chain.

Key words

diet
efficient
energy
energy transfer
flammable
food chain
fossil fuel
fuel
fuel consumption
joule
nuclear power
renewable energy

Summary Questions

1 Make your own glossary (list of meanings) for the key words. Keep your definitions short.

2 Draw an energy transfer diagram to show the energy changes that take place in the following situations. Remember to include 'wasted energy' as well as 'useful energy'.
- **a** When a car is driven.
- **b** In a fan heater.
- **c** When an electric drill is used.

3 Suggest four ways in which people could reduce the amount of energy resources they use. State briefly how they work.

4 It has been suggested that dinosaurs were made extinct when dust from a huge meteor impact blocked out the Sun, plunging Earth into 'night time' for about 2 years.
- **a** How would this affect the amount of energy reaching Earth?
- **b** Why would this affect the dinosaurs?
- **c** Many types of plants and animals survived. Suggest how they might have done this.

5
- **a** Describe some of the advantages of recycling used items, rather than making new items from raw materials.
- **b** What types of materials can be recycled?
- **c** For one material in part **b**, explain how it is recycled.
- **d** What factors would you consider before deciding whether or not it was worth recycling a particular type of material?

6 Both coal and wood can be burned on a domestic fire to provide heating for a house.
- **a** Suggest how you might attempt to find out which fuel was more efficient.
- **b** What other factors would you consider when deciding which fuel to use?

7 List as many different energy resources as you can think of. Group them in three different lists:

List A – Energy resources where the energy comes directly from the Sun.

List B – Energy resources that come indirectly from the Sun, where the energy has been stored in some form.

List C – Energy resources where the energy source is **not** the Sun.

8 Choose one type of renewable energy resource and one use of your chosen energy resource. Draw an energy transfer diagram to show the energy changes taking place as your energy resource is used.

9 When you eat foods, you are taking in energy. How does your body use this energy? How does the type of activity you do affect the type of foods you need to eat?

End of unit Questions

1 Fossil fuels are used to generate electricity, but over half of the world's population uses biomass as a fuel.

a What is 'biomass', which is used as a fuel? *1 mark*

b Biomass and fossil fuels are both energy resources. What is the original source of this energy? *1 mark*

c Give the names of three fossil fuels which are often burned to generate electricity. *1 mark*

d Fossil fuels are often described as non-renewable energy resources.
Explain why they are called 'non-renewable'. *1 mark*

e There are advantages and disadvantages of burning different fuels.

i Give **one** advantage of using biomass rather than fossil fuel as an energy resource. *1 mark*

ii Give **one** advantage of using fossil fuel rather than biomass as an energy resource. *1 mark*

iii Give **one disadvantage** of using both fossil fuel and biomass. *1 mark*

2 Some pupils are designing a web page about energy resources. Their design is shown below. It is not quite finished.

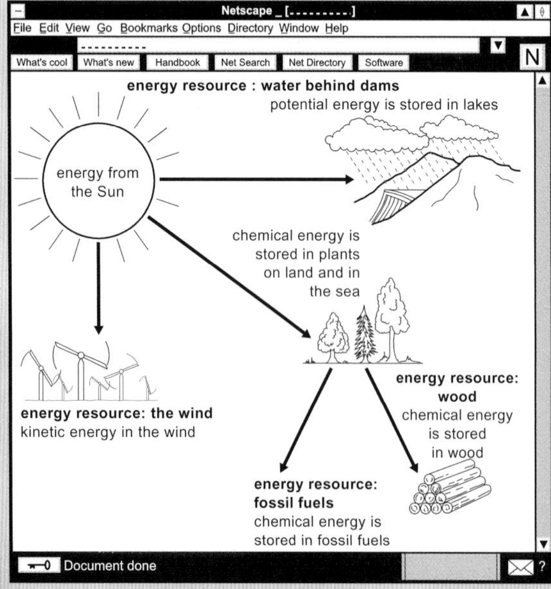

a To complete the web page, the pupils want to add a drawing of some fossil fuels. Give the names of **two** fossil fuels. *2 marks*

b Four energy resources are labelled on the web page:
water behind dams **the wind**
fossil fuels **wood**
How many of these can be used to generate electricity? *1 mark*

3 The tides can be used to generate electricity. A dam is built across a river estuary, as shown below:

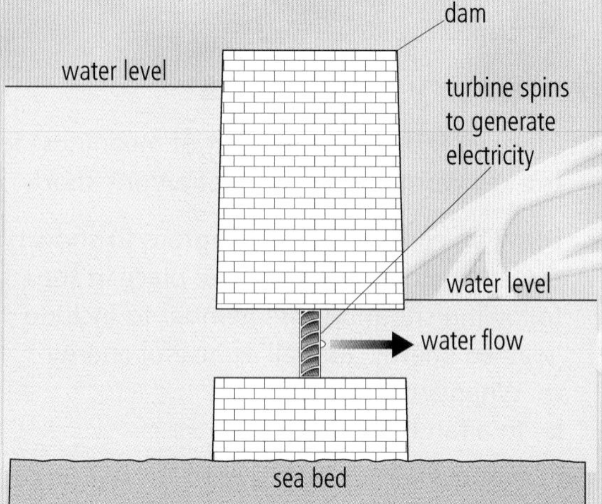

a The water is higher on one side of the dam than on the other. As the water begins to flow through the dam it turns a turbine. The turbine generates electricity.
Describe the useful energy changes which take place in this process. *2 marks*

b Explain why tides are classified as a renewable energy source. *1 mark*

c Give **one** way, **other** than from the tides, of generating electricity by using the sea. *1 mark*

d Apart from cost, give **one** advantage and **one** disadvantage of an oil-fired power station compared with a tidal power station. *2 marks*

7J Electrical circuits

Introduction

Electrical circuits are part of our everyday lives. Almost all of our modern technology, from our computers and televisions to the lights in our sports centres and the engines in our cars, contain some electrical circuits. In this unit you will learn ways of measuring and controlling the electricity in circuits, how electrical circuits transfer energy and why electricity flows at all! This unit also covers some electrical dangers and some electrical safety features.

You already know

- that electrical devices only work if they are in a complete circuit
- how to connect up an electrical circuit
- how to use circuit diagrams to represent your circuits

In this topic you will learn

- how to measure current and compare its size in different circuits
- about current flow in series and parallel circuits
- about developing models to explain current flow in circuits
- about the energy transfer in circuits and how to relate this to voltage
- why electricity can be hazardous, and how some electrical safety devices work

1 What can you remember?

Look at the circuit opposite. Identify all the features that will prevent the bulbs lighting up. State briefly what you could do to correct each fault.

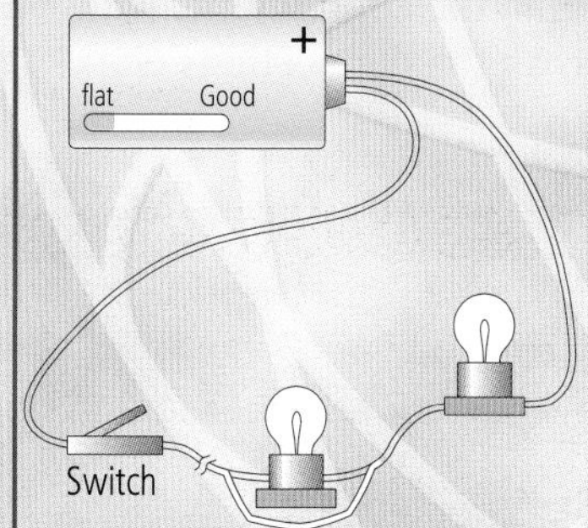

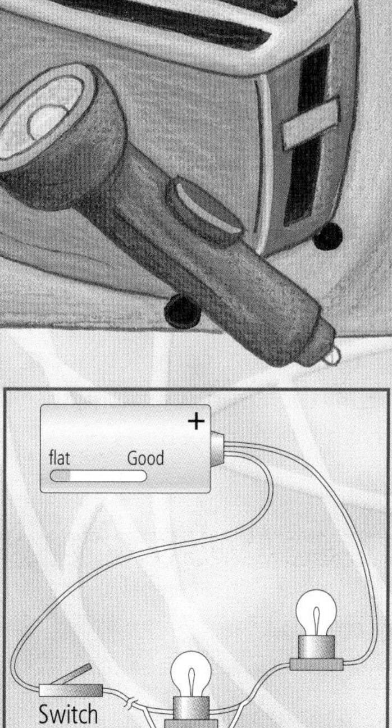

Can you see what is wrong with this circuit?

J1 Making electrical circuits work

YOU WILL LEARN!

- how to find and correct faults in an electrical circuit that does not work

Circuit diagrams

Circuit diagrams show how **circuits** are built. Each electrical **component** has its own symbol.

Points to discuss

How many symbols do you know? What do they look like?

Circuit diagrams do not tell you everything.
The diagram opposite could be the circuit diagram for a torch, a lamp on a miner's helmet, the flashing lights found in the soles of some trainers, a mains powered desk lamp or the ceiling light in a room. They are all represented by the same circuit diagram.

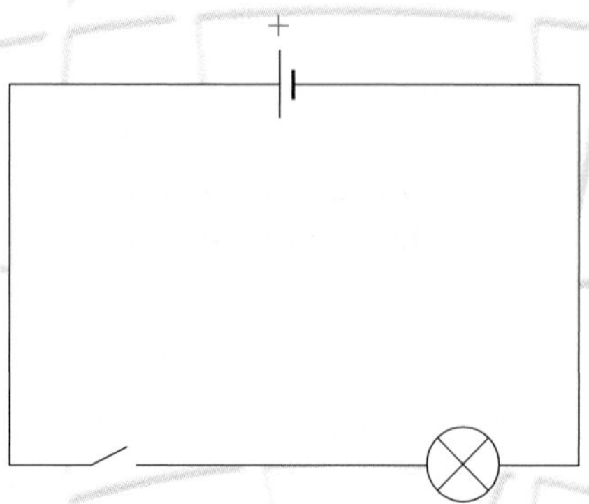

Circuit diagrams do not tell you everything

1 Understanding circuit diagrams

Take apart a hand held torch. (Be careful. Remember where all the bits go!)

a Can you identify all the components shown in the circuit diagram?
b Can you find the electrical connections between all the components?
c Can you put it back together so that the torch works again?

Could you put this torch back together?

What do I do if it won't work?

Be an electrical detective. Ask yourself these questions.

- Is it put together correctly? Check it against the circuit diagram, following the 'complete loop'.
- Do all the components work? Check each one in turn.
- Do all the connections work? Check them one at a time.

2 Finding electrical faults

Build a circuit that works. Draw the circuit diagram. Make a fault in the circuit.
Challenge your partner to find out what is wrong with the circuit.

J2 What happens in a circuit?

YOU WILL LEARN!

- how to use an ammeter to measure and compare current in circuits
- what resistance is, and how it affects current
- the difference between current and voltage

Electric current

The flow of electricity through something is called an electric **current**. It can be measured using a device called an **ammeter**.

1 What does current flow through?

From work done at Key Stage 2, you may well know what materials electricity will flow through. These materials are **conductors**.

a Predict whether or not an electric current will flow through a pencil.

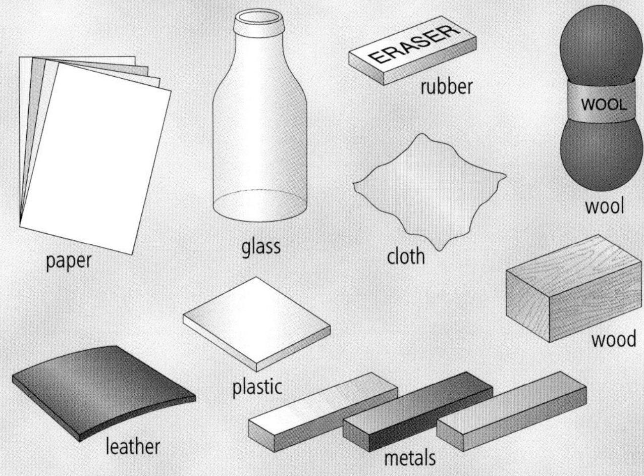

Which of these materials conduct electricity?

Build a circuit to test your prediction. Test the wood and the 'lead'. Test other materials as well, if you have not already done so at Key Stage 2.

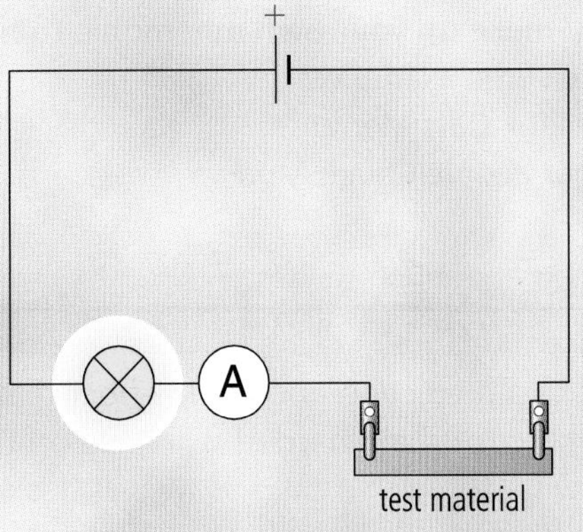

Circuit to test for conductors

Use an ammeter to measure the size of the electric current (the amount of electricity flowing round the circuit).

b Was your prediction correct?

2 How does resistance affect current?

An electrical **resistor** is a component that resists the flow of electric current (makes it hard for the current to flow):
Build this circuit.

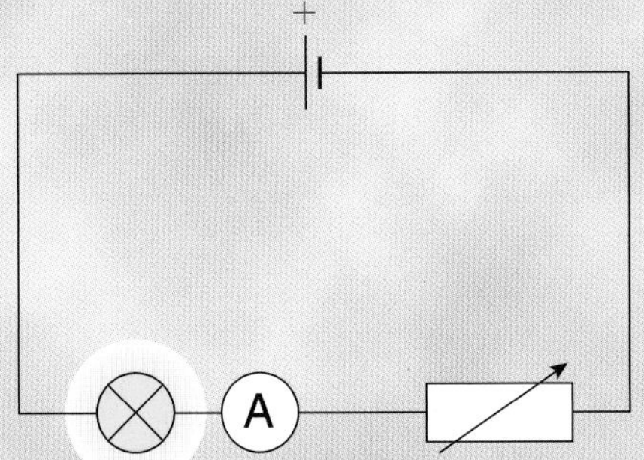

Circuit to find out how resistance affects current

Try putting the ammeter in different places.

a What can you say about the size of the current in different places round the circuit? Find out what effect the variable resistor has.

b How does the brightness of the bulb change?

Take the variable resistor out of the circuit. Find out the effect on the size of the current (the reading on the ammeter) of connecting more than one bulb in series.

c Draw your circuit diagram.

d What happens to the size of the current when there are more bulbs?

e Use the idea of electrical resistance to explain this.

Points to discuss

1 What is voltage? Jot down all the things you know about voltage.
2 Where have you seen voltages written down?
3 What do you associate voltages with?
4 Why are batteries made with different voltages?
5 What effect does a different voltage have on a bulb?

Electric iron

Morphy Richards
Made in U.K.
Customer freephone 0800 424868
CE BEAB Approved
220-240V ~ 50/60Hz : 350W

Radio

ALBA CXS 70
Stereo radio cassette recorder with CD
FM 88 - 108 MHz
MU 540 -1600 KHz
AC 230-240V ~ 50Hz
DC 9V (LR14 x 6 or equivalent)

These labels tell you what voltage the equipment needs in order to work

Voltage

Voltage can be defined as:

- Voltage pushes the current round a circuit
- Voltage Pushes – Current Moves

Can you make up your own mnemonic to help you remember this? Here are some examples:

- Very Pink Cats Meow
- Vulgar People Chuck Mud

3 Voltage and brightness

a Make a prediction about the effect that increasing the voltage (pushing harder) will have on the amount of current flowing through a bulb. How will this affect the brightness of the bulb?

Build a circuit to test your prediction. (Hint: you will need a power supply with a knob to adjust the voltage, called a variable voltage supply, a bulb, an ammeter and a voltmeter.)

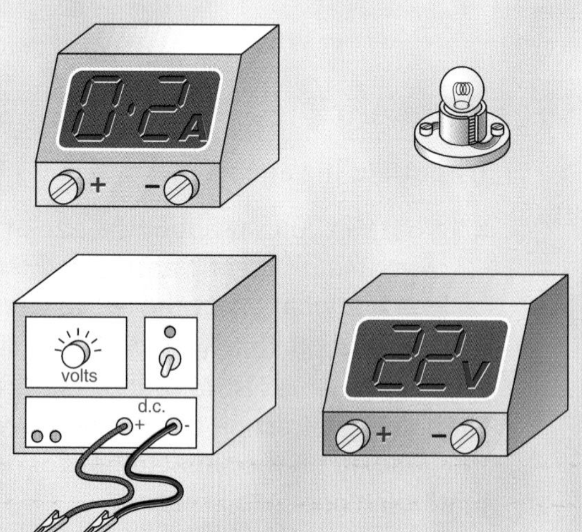

b Was your prediction correct?

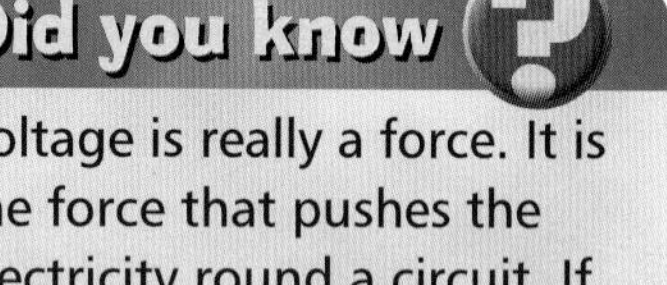

Voltage is really a force. It is the force that pushes the electricity round a circuit. If the voltage is large enough, it can even push electricity through a non-conductor like air. That is how lightning happens. The high voltage of the cloud pushes a spark of electricity through the air to the ground.

Does it matter which way round electric cells are connected?

Look at an electric cell. Can you find a + symbol? The 'push' of the cell comes from this end.

Most people refer to electric cells as 'batteries' in everyday life. To be more precise, a battery is a series of cells linked together. For example, most car batteries contain six cells.

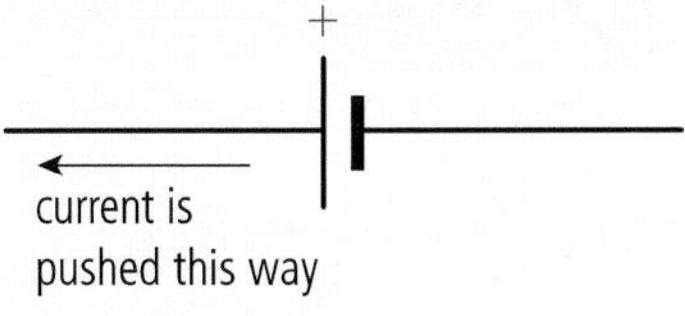

Current is 'pushed out' from the positive side of the electric cell

4 Electric cells

Connect a cell to a small motor, or to a hand-held fan.

a Which way is the cell pushing the current? Which way does the motor/fan turn?

Turn the cell round, so it pushes the electric current the other way.

b What happens to the motor or the fan?

Build this circuit.

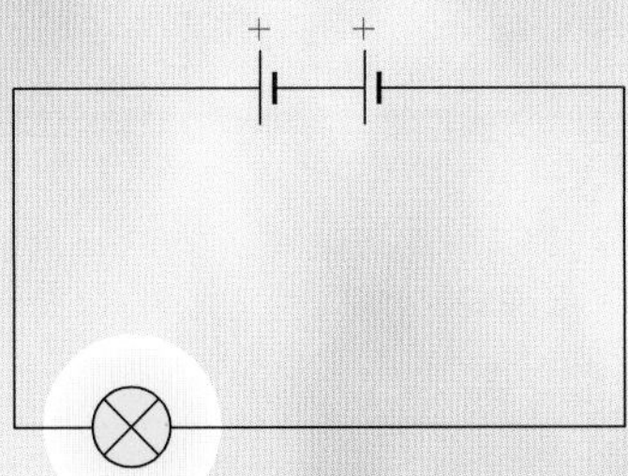

Find out what happens when you turn one cell round, and when you turn both cells round.

c Use the idea of voltage pushing current to explain what you see.

It is important to fit electric cells the correct way round

In the 19th century, when scientists didn't know what caused an electric current, they decided that current is 'pushed out' from the positive side of the cell. We still use this convention even though we know that electric current is electrons flowing the other way.

Did you know

Some electrical components let current flow through them in one direction but stop current flowing the other way. That is why many electrical appliances have to have the cells fitted a certain way round.

J3 Parallel circuits

YOU WILL LEARN!

- the difference between series and parallel circuits
- what happens to current in a parallel circuit

Parallel circuits

We call it a **parallel** circuit if there is more than one route the electric current can take.
Circuits with only one path are called **series** circuits.

Points to discuss

Decide which of these are series circuits and which are parallel circuits.

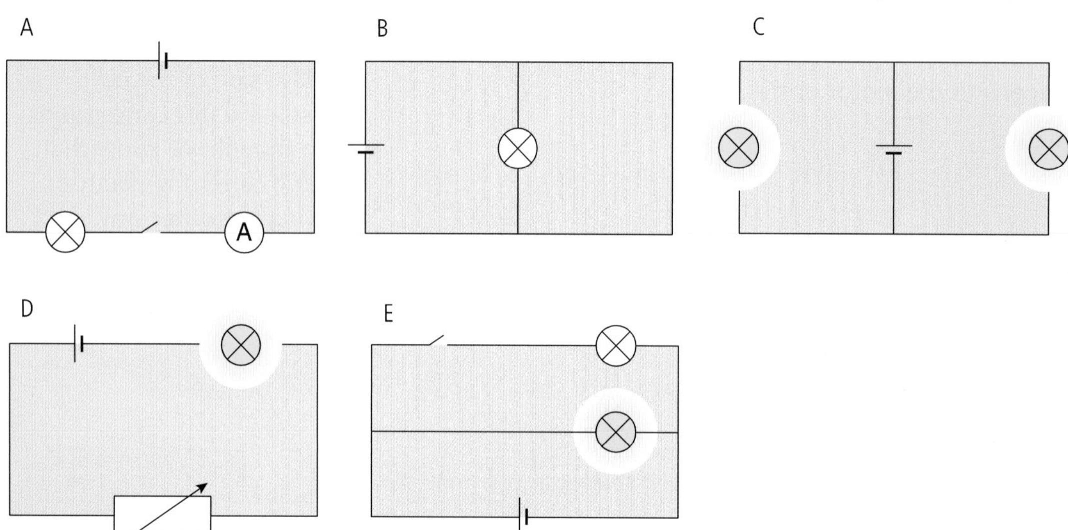

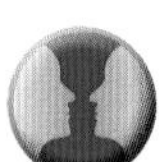

Points to discuss

1 What do you think happens to the current in a parallel circuit? Imagine the electric current as people being pushed along a corridor, or marbles being pushed along a marble run.
2 What will happen to the current when it is easier for current to go along one of the wires than the others? (Think about people when the corridor divides, or marbles when the marble run divides.)
3 Make a prediction about the current at the labelled points in the circuit opposite.

1 Current in parallel circuits

Make the circuit shown opposite, with two bulbs connected in parallel. Measure the current at the places that are labelled.

a What do you notice?
b Is it what you expected?

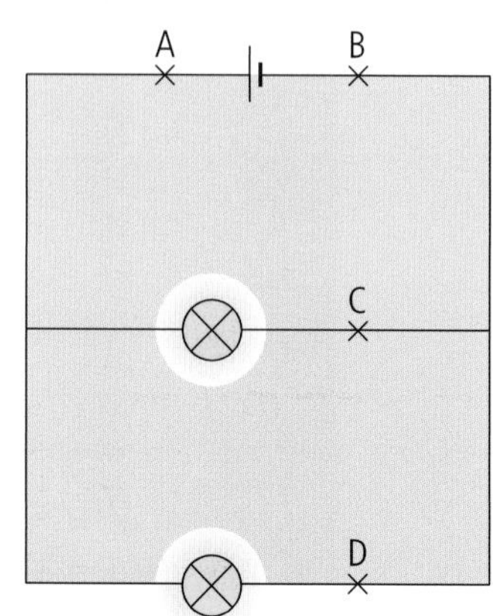

What can you say about the current at the labelled points?

J4 What happens in electrical circuits?

YOU WILL LEARN!

- the energy transfers that take place in electrical circuits
- one or more 'thought models' to explain electricity

You have already learnt that:

- current flows in complete circuits
- current is the flow of electricity
- increasing resistance makes less current flow in the circuit
- voltage pushes – cells push the electricity round the circuit
- high voltages push harder than low voltages.

1 Cells and batteries

If you leave a torch switched on, the bulb will eventually stop shining.

a Use the words 'push', 'electricity', 'current' and 'cell' or 'battery' to describe what has happened.

b What could you do to show that it is the cell or battery that has stopped working, not the bulb?

Think about the energy changes in the torch:

c Describe them.

d Draw an **energy transfer diagram**.

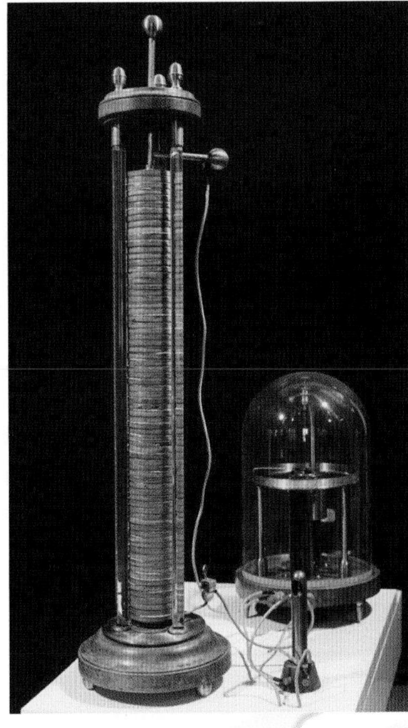

One of the earliest batteries

Energy in electric cells

Cells have chemicals inside them that can push electricity through conductors. Chemical energy stored in the cell is transferred into electrical energy in the wires, then into light and heat energy in the bulb.

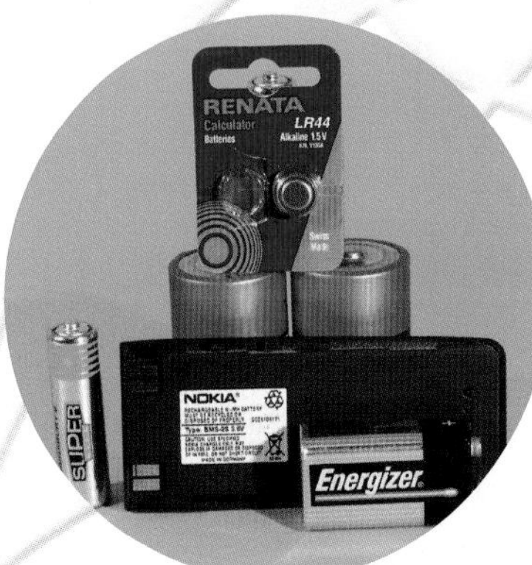

Electric cells and batteries come in many shapes and sizes

2 A closer look at cells

a Look on battery labels. How many chemicals can you find the names of?

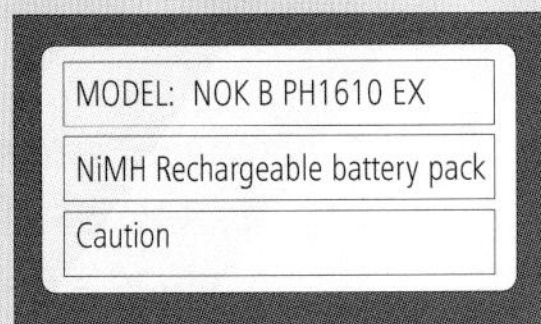

MODEL: NOK B PH1610 EX
NiMH Rechargeable battery pack
Caution

How many different chemicals can you find in cells and batteries?

Hazard: the chemicals in cells are dangerous (corrosive or poisonous). Do not open cells yourself.

b Use ideas of energy to explain why cells and batteries go 'flat' in circuits. (Hint: think of the energy changes when you push a ball across the floor.)

Did you know?

Electric cells eventually go flat even if they are not connected to anything. This is because their stored chemical energy is very slowly used up pushing tiny amounts of electricity through the air. Cells have a 'shelf life' of several years.

Thought models of electricity

A thought model is a way of imagining something, to make it easier to understand. People can have different thought models. If your model helps you get the right answers, it doesn't matter if nobody else 'looks at it like that'.

Try this thought model.

- Current (bits of moving electricity) is like people in corridors, or marbles on a track.
- Voltage is like someone pushing the people, or marbles.
- Bigger voltage = harder push.
- A resistor is like the corridor, or track, getting narrower so the people, or marbles, can't get through very easily.

Current is not 'used up' around the circuit (people don't disappear out the windows of the corridor) but current does carry energy from the cell to the components in the circuit.

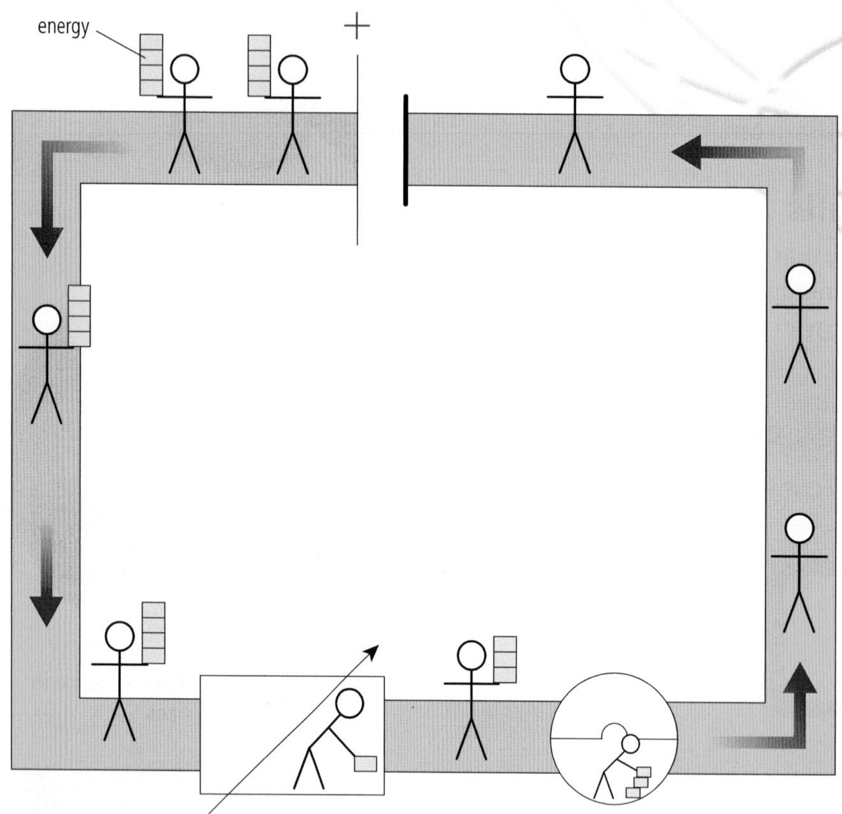

This thought model uses people to carry packets of energy round the circuit. In a real circuit, current carries the energy round the circuit

Points to discuss

Use this thought model to explain these facts.

1. Increasing the voltage makes a bulb brighter.
2. Two bulbs connected in series are dimmer than one bulb on its own.
3. If two identical cells are connected positive to positive, no current flows in the circuit.
4. In a parallel circuit, the total current is found by adding the current in each branch of the circuit.
5. Can you think of other thought models to explain electricity in circuits?

J5 Useful circuits but what are the hazards?

YOU WILL LEARN!

- some examples of real-life series and parallel circuits
- what electrical fuses are, and why they are used
- why mains electricity is dangerous
- how to describe some examples of electricity in nature

1 Is series or parallel best?

Series and parallel circuits are used for different purposes. Look at the real-life examples of circuits below. Decide whether the components are in series or in parallel and work out why.

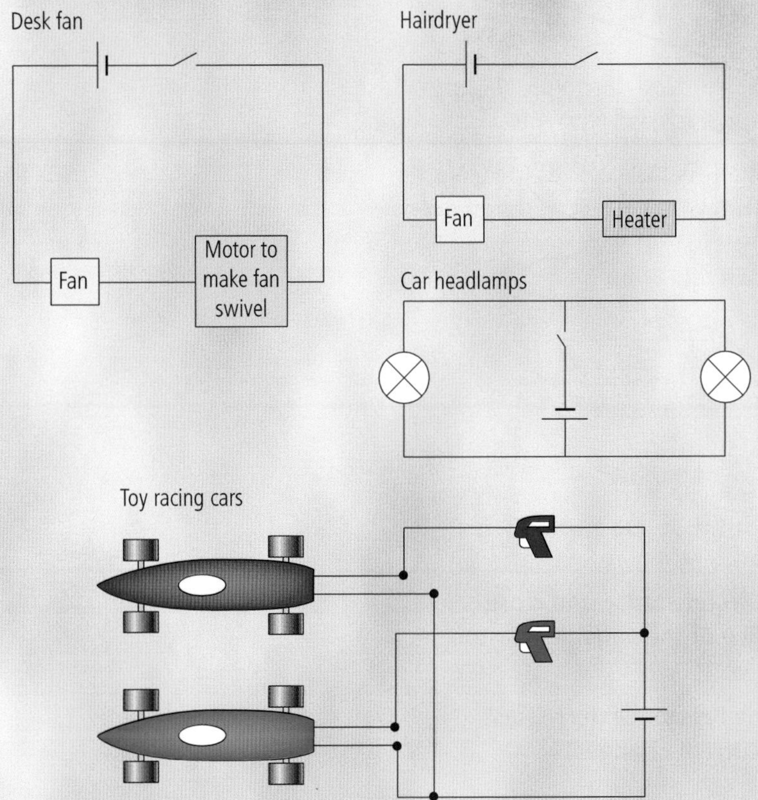

Some of these are series circuits, some are parallel. Can you work out why?

2 Designing a lighting circuit

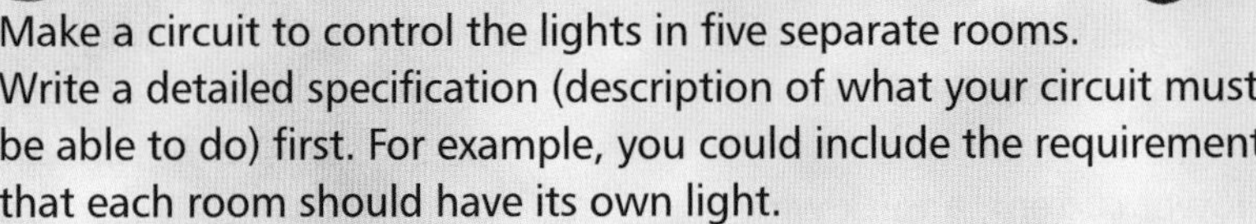

Make a circuit to control the lights in five separate rooms. Write a detailed specification (description of what your circuit must be able to do) first. For example, you could include the requirement that each room should have its own light.

Did you know

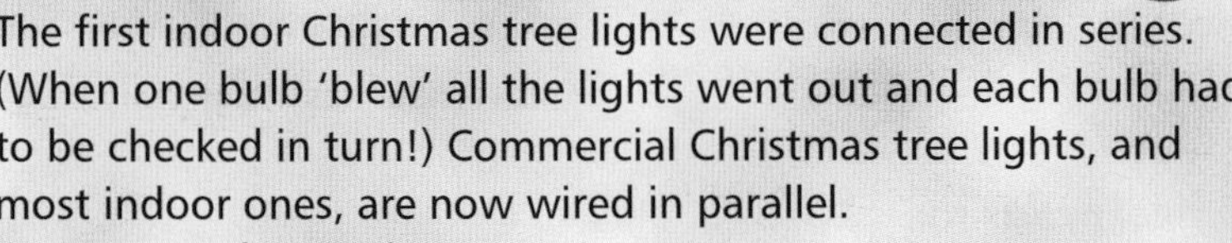

The first indoor Christmas tree lights were connected in series. (When one bulb 'blew' all the lights went out and each bulb had to be checked in turn!) Commercial Christmas tree lights, and most indoor ones, are now wired in parallel.
Can you work out why?

These Christmas lights are wired in parallel. Do you know why?

3 Electrical fuses

Set up the following circuit. (Your teacher may do this as a demonstration.)

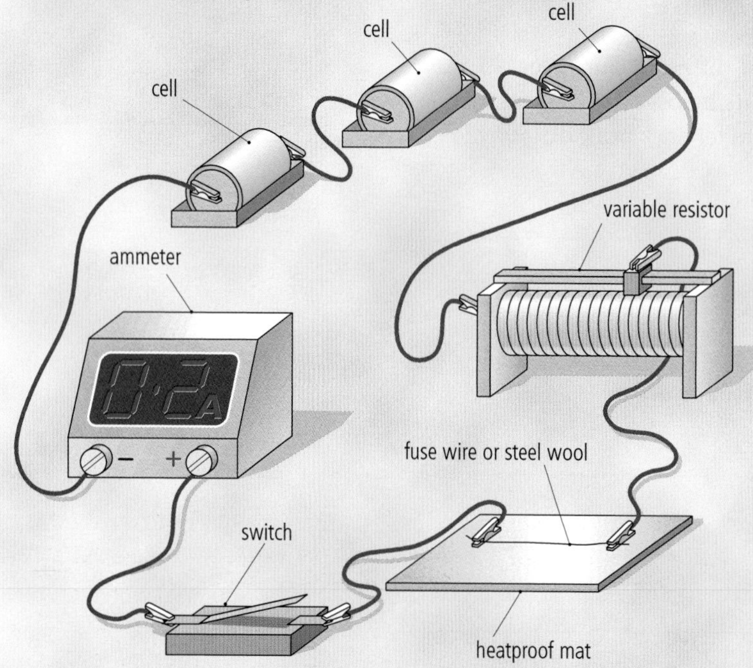

Always test fuse wire on a heatproof mat. Do not touch the fuse wire when the switch is on.

Set the variable resistor to its maximum resistance and close the switch. Slowly reduce the resistance of the variable resistor and observe the wire closely.

a What happens to the current as the resistance decreases?
b What happens to the wire as the current changes?

Points to discuss

Use a thought model to explain what happened to the fuse. Imagine the wire as a corridor with thin wooden walls.

1. What might happen if more and more people (current) try to squeeze through the corridor? Be imaginative!
2. Which is going to give way first, a wide corridor or a narrow corridor?
3. Which do you think will melt at a lower current, a thick wire or a thin wire?

This corridor has a high resistance!

4 Testing fuses

Fuse wires are given a **current rating** – the current that can flow through them before they melt. Design a circuit to test different fuse wires to find out their current rating.

Remember to test fuse wire on a heatproof mat. Fuse wire may be HOT.

Points to discuss

1 Why do you think fuses might be fitted in a circuit?

Sometimes circuits are fitted with 'trip switches' or 'circuit breakers' that stop the current but can be reset afterwards. (You will find out in detail how these work at Key Stage 4.)

2 Discuss where you might use these and the advantages they have over simple fuses.

Mains electricity is DANGEROUS

You all know mains electricity is dangerous. It can kill. But do you know why? Discuss in your group and jot down your ideas.

Mains electricity is dangerous because it has a lot of energy. (Imagine how much energy a trolley would have if you pushed it very hard, compared with one that you pushed gently.)

It is not easy for electricity to flow through you. You have a high resistance. If mains electricity flowed through you, you would act like a fuse. Your body tissues would get very hot, which would kill them. If you were lucky, you would receive serious burns. Most likely, something vital would be damaged and you would die.

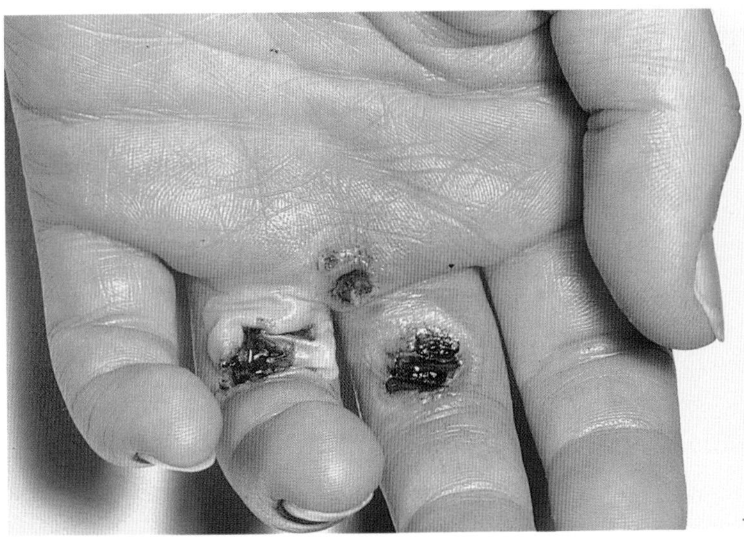

Electrocution can cause very serious burns

5 Electrical safety

Design a leaflet/poster to describe the danger of mains electricity. Be gory!

6 Electrical discoveries

Find out about some famous electrical discoveries. Present your findings on a time-line.

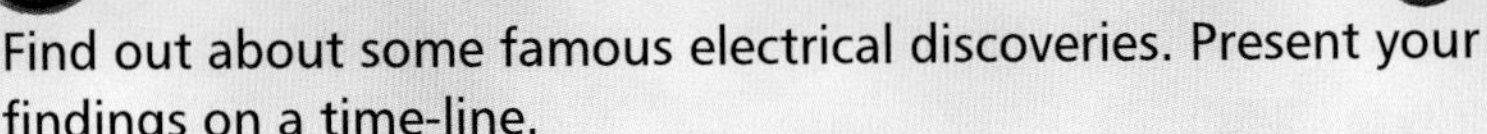

Mains electricity is dangerous

Did you know

Birds can sit safely on overhead mains power cables. This is because they are not touching anything else. The electricity does not flow through them because there is nowhere for the electricity to flow to. If they were to touch two cables, the electricity would flow through them and they would be killed instantly.

Did you know

The mains electricity in our homes has a voltage of 230 V (that's more than 150 'ordinary' cells!), but it comes to us at an even higher voltage. Power stations in the UK distribute electricity over long distances at a voltage of 400 kV (400 000 V). In some countries it is as high as 1000 kV. You can see why overhead power cables are so dangerous!

Electricity in nature

Your body runs on electricity! This isn't quite true, but your nerves are better electrical conductors than the rest of your body. Many life processes of your body are controlled by messages from your brain that travel as tiny electrical signals along your nerves.

7 Electricity in nature

Below are brief details about electricity occurring naturally. Choose one topic. Find out more about it. Present a short talk (2 or 3 minutes) explaining it to the rest of your class.

Hammerhead sharks have sensory organs that can detect tiny electrical currents. They use these to find prey.

New rocks similar to those formed in volcanoes have been found at places where lightning has struck the ground.

Electric rays have chemical 'batteries' inside capable of producing pulses of high voltage electricity. They use these for hunting.

Aeroplanes flying through storms can be struck by lightning without the passengers on board being electrocuted.

Did you know

Currents as small as 20 mA (20 thousandths of an amp) can interfere with signals from the brain that keep the heart beating regularly. This can be fatal.

Did you know

A man in Kiev, Ukraine, used a similar method to the electric ray to go fishing. He connected cables from the mains electricity supply in his house to the river. When the dead fish floated to the surface he waded into the river to collect them. The result?

Electric rays use pulses of high voltage electricity to kill fish

Summary

Current in a **circuit** is measured using an **ammeter** connected in **series**.

The current in any given circuit can be **increased** either by **increasing the voltage** or by **decreasing the resistance**.

In a **series circuit**, the size of the current is the same at all points around the circuit. In a **parallel circuit** the current splits up, some of it going along each available path.

Current and **voltage** can be imagined using a 'people in corridors' model.

Current flow around a circuit **transfers energy** from the **cell battery** or **power supply** to the **components** in the circuit.

Increasing the **voltage** in any given circuit **increases** the **energy** being **transferred** around that circuit.

Electricity can be dangerous because the energy it carries can cause serious or fatal burns. Electrical safety devices work by breaking the circuit, switching off the electric current.

Key words

ammeter
cell
circuit
component
conductor
current
current rating
energy transfer diagram
fuse
parallel
resistor
series
voltage

Did you know

Televisions, radios, music centres and so on all use variable resistors to make the volume louder or quieter.

Summary Questions

1 Make your own glossary (list of meanings) for the key words. Keep your definitions short.

2 List three things you would check in a circuit that didn't work.

3 Describe briefly (one sentence) the link between resistance and current. Can you explain this?

4 Which of the following statements are true for a parallel circuit?
- **a** The current is constant at all points.
- **b** The current flows equally between all possible paths.
- **c** All the current flows along the path of lowest resistance.
- **d** The current in each path depends on the resistance.

5 What is the purpose of a fuse? Be brief.

6
- **a** Explain what is meant by 'conductor' and 'insulator'.
- **b** What can you say about the electrical resistance of conductors and insulators?
- **c** What is a variable resistor?
- **d** What effect does a variable resistor have on the current in a circuit? Explain why.

7 Imagine you have been given four identical cells, each with a voltage of 1.5 V.
Draw diagrams to show how you would arrange all the cells to give a total voltage of
- **a** 0 V
- **b** 3 V
- **c** 6 V
- **d** Is it possible to arrange the cells to give a total voltage of 4.5 V?

8 Draw a circuit diagram to show how you could use one power supply to switch on a fan and a heater. It must be possible to switch on only the fan, or only the heater.

End of unit Questions

1 Gary uses the following circuit to operate the electric motor of his model crane.

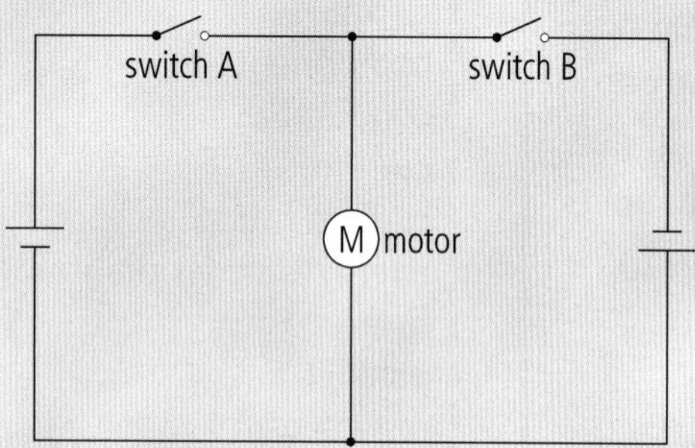

Look carefully at the way Gary has connected the two cells.
When he closes switch A the motor runs and the crane lifts a load.

a Gary opens switch A and closes switch B. Describe what happens to the motor. *1 mark*

b Gary closes both switches, A and B. Describe what happens to the motor. *1 mark*

c Both switches should **not** be closed at the same time. Explain why. *1 mark*

d Gary puts a resistor into his circuit as shown.

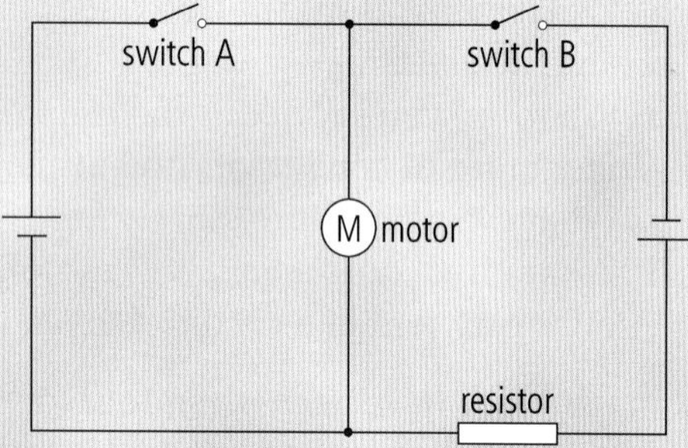

What difference does the resistor make to the motor:

i when switch A is closed and switch B is open? *1 mark*

ii when switch A is open and switch B is closed? *1 mark*

2 The drawing shows a hairdryer.

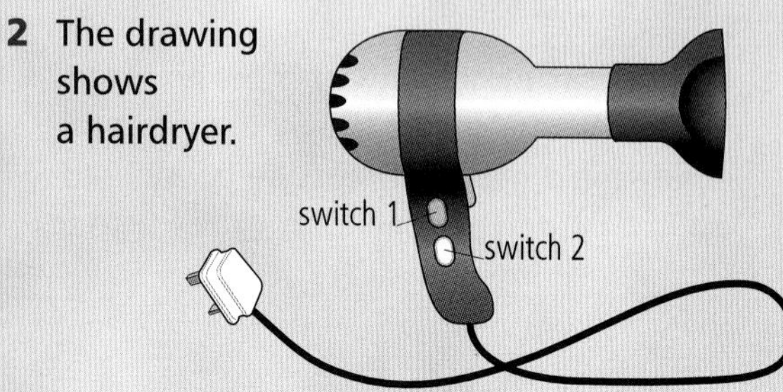

Ben drew the diagram below to show the circuit of the hairdryer.

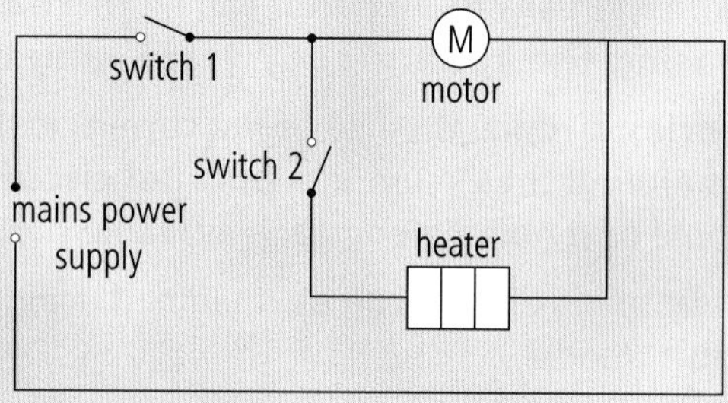

a Which of the switches must be closed for the heater to work? *1 mark*
switch 1 only switch 2 only
switches 1 and 2 neither switch 1 nor 2

b With this circuit, is it possible to have the heater on when the motor is switched off? *1 mark*
Explain your answer.

c The motor and the heater are both on. The motor blows air through the hairdryer. If the motor breaks, what will happen to the temperature of the hairdryer? *1 mark*

d The motor and the heater are both on. Suddenly the wire in the heater breaks. What effect, if any, will this have on the motor? *1 mark*

3 A two-way stair light circuit has a bulb at each end of the corridor.
They are connected as shown below.

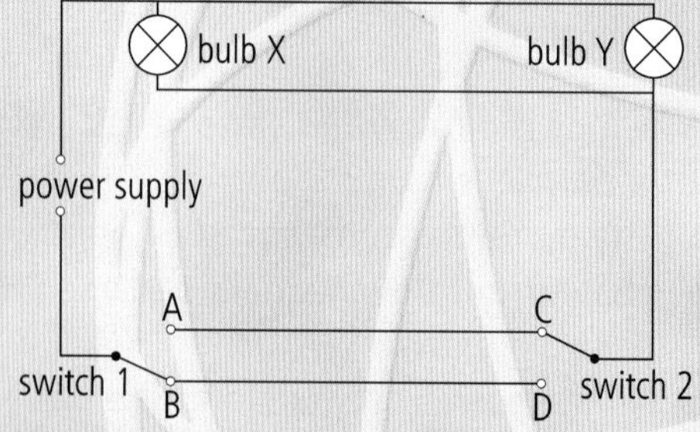

a In the diagram above, the switches are shown in positions B and C.
Which bulbs, if any, are on? *1 mark*

b The switches are arranged so that both bulbs are on. Bulb X breaks.
What, if anything, happens to bulb Y? *1 mark*

7K Forces and their effects

Introduction

Forces are all around us. We cannot see forces but we can often feel them, and we can see the effect they have. Sometimes you can tell forces exist because of what doesn't happen! In this unit you will learn about examples of forces in lots of different circumstances. You will also learn to apply 'forces thinking' to solve unfamiliar problems.

You already know

- that pushes and pulls change the speed, direction or shape of an object
- that the direction forces act in can be shown by drawing arrows
- how to use a force meter to measure the size of a force

In this topic you will learn

- the difference between mass and weight
- about the effect of balanced and unbalanced forces on an object
- how forces can be used to explain floating, air resistance and friction
- to relate changes in the motion of an object to the forces acting on the object

1 What can you remember?

Test your knowledge so far.

a Identify all the examples of forces below.

push	twist	gravity	pull	squash
friction	speed	distance	shape	

b What units would you use to measure force?

c Draw symbols to show forces acting

- upwards
- to the left
- downwards
- to the right

K1 What is weight?

YOU WILL LEARN!
- the difference between mass and weight
- why objects with a large mass have a large weight

What is mass?

The **mass** of something tells you how much matter there is in an object.

Look at a sponge and a block of metal the same size. Which has more 'stuff' in it? Which do you think has the bigger mass? That's right, the metal.

Look at a big block of wood and a little block of wood. Which has more 'stuff'? Which has the bigger mass? Right again, the big one.

Points to discuss

1 How can a little object have a big mass?
2 How can a big object have a little mass?

What is weight?

Weight is to do with gravity. The **gravity** (gravitational force) from Earth pulls downwards equally hard on every bit of matter. If an object has a large mass (a lot of bits of matter), the gravity pulls down on every bit. All these little **forces** add up to make one big force. This big total force is called the weight of the object.

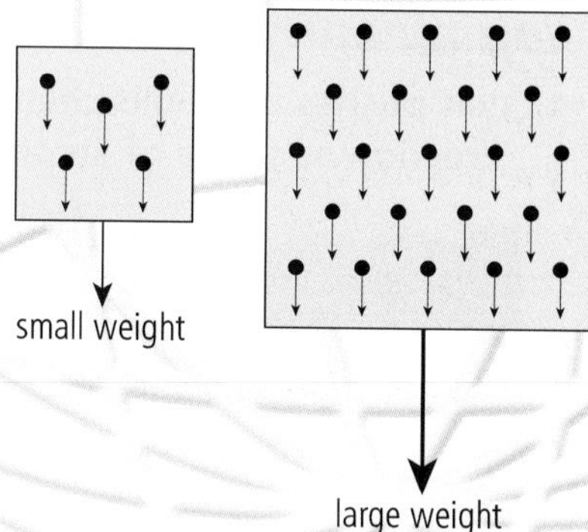

The total downward force on a mass is called its weight

1 Different weights

Take two different masses. Predict which will have the bigger weight. Test your prediction using a **force meter**.

Points to discuss

Discuss what would happen to your weight if you went to a planet with:

1 a force of gravity much bigger than Earth,
2 a force of gravity much smaller than Earth.

Astronauts found it easier to jump on the Moon than on Earth because the force of gravity pulling them down is less on the Moon

K2 Why do things float?

YOU WILL LEARN!

- what upthrust is and why it happens
- how displacement can be used to find density
- why objects float better in some liquids than in others

Look at the tray opposite floating on water:

What forces do you think are acting on the tray?

1 Floating trays

Float different size trays on water. Push down on each tray, being careful not to make the tray sink.

a What do you notice? **b** Which tray is hardest to push?

Can you work out why this tray does not sink?

Upthrust

When you push down on the tray, you are trying to push the tray through the water. Water has to move out of the way so the tray can go past. The water resists your efforts to make it move – it 'pushes back'. This is water resistance. (You have already met air resistance at Key Stage 2.) When you push downwards, the name given to the water pushing upwards is **upthrust**.

The upthrust (water resistance) on this tray is similar to the air resistance on this parachutist

Did you know ?

Boat designers have a problem. Boats are most stable – float best and are least likely to capsize if they are wide and flat. But then they are slow and use a lot of fuel. How do you think a keel helps them?

2 What shapes float?

A flat tray floats.

a What happens if you turn the tray on its side? (Check if you are not sure.)

b Explain this in terms of upthrust and water being 'pushed out of the way'.

Make a ball of plasticine about 4 cm in diameter. Put it in water. Can you make it float?

c Use forces to explain why sometimes the plasticine floats and sometimes it sinks.

3 Weight of floating objects

Look at a selection of (waterproof) objects.

a Predict which objects will float and which will sink.
b Use force meters to weigh the objects in air, then in water. Make a table like the one below.

Object	Force meter reading in air	Does it float?	Force meter reading in water

c What conclusion can you draw about objects that float?

Weigh your ball of plasticine from Activity 2. Change its shape and weigh it in water again. Repeat. Use the words 'upthrust' and 'weight' to explain what you notice.

Archimedes and his bath

Legend says that in about 200 BC the Greek scientist Archimedes got into his bath and it overflowed. He was so excited by this that he ran naked through the streets shouting 'Eureka!' – 'I've got it!'

EUREKA, I'VE SOLVED IT!

Legend says Archimedes made one of his most important discoveries in his bath

Baths had probably been overflowing for years but Archimedes knew why! He knew a lot more too – which you will find out in a moment.

When Archimedes got into his bath, he took up space that had been occupied by water. He pushed the water out of the way, which is why the bath overflowed. (You can check this by filling a see-through container with water, marking the level of the water, lowering an object into it and marking the new water level.) This 'pushing water out of the way' is called **displacement**.

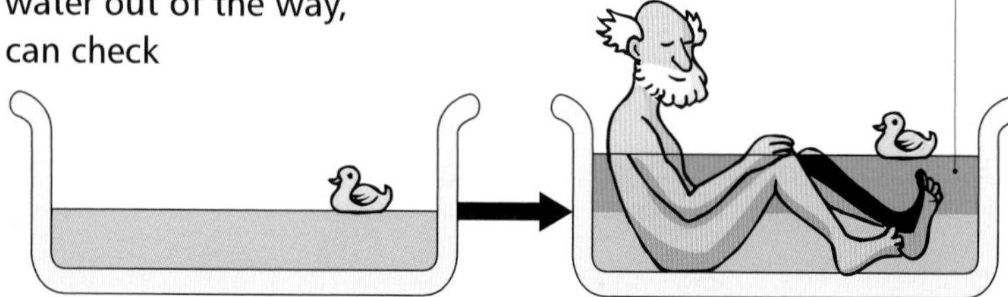
water displaced by Archimedes

Archimedes pushed water out of the way – he displaced it

Using displacement to find density

The King of Syracuse had a gold crown that he suspected might really be cheaper silver covered with gold. Archimedes reasoned like this:

- I can weigh the crown but I don't know exactly how big it is (its volume).
- If I put the crown in water, it will sink and push water out of the way.
- The volume of water displaced will be the same as the volume of the crown.
- I know how much space a gold crown of this weight should take up – so I can tell if it really is gold.

Archimedes was really finding the **density** of the crown – how much matter there is in a certain volume. All types of material have their own particular density, so the density of an object can be used to find what it is made from.
The equation for density is

$$\textbf{density} = \frac{\textbf{mass}}{\textbf{volume}}$$

Archimedes worked out what the crown was made of by measuring how much water it displaced to find its volume

4 Finding the density

Use displacement to find the density of solid objects made from different materials. (Use a pencil to immerse – push under – objects that naturally float.)

a Calculate the density of water, using the weight of 100 cm^3.

b What do the densities of floating objects have in common?

c Could you use this displacement method to find the density of air? Discuss with your group how you might do it.

Finding the volume using the displacement method

Why do some objects float?

Floating depends on balanced forces. The weight of an object is a downward force, displacing some water. The displaced water exerts a force as it tries to return to its original position. Imagine it like a see-saw.

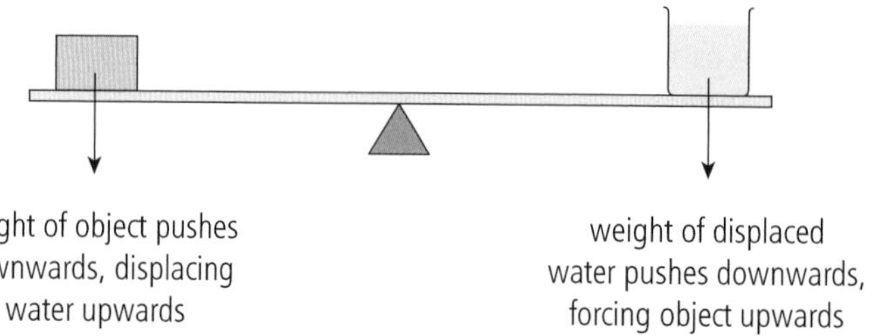
weight of object pushes downwards, displacing water upwards
weight of displaced water pushes downwards, forcing object upwards

An object sinks downwards through the water until the two forces are balanced. That is until:

weight of object = weight of displaced water

When this happens the upward and downward forces on the object are balanced. If hung on a force meter, the floating object will appear to have a zero weight.

Points to discuss

1. Why would a solid metal boat sink but an empty boat, and even a boat full of cargo, float? Think about the weights of the three boats and the amount of water they displace.
2. Use the see-saw idea, and your knowledge of the forces acting, to explain why a golf ball sinks but a table-tennis ball floats.
3. A wooden ball was accidentally hit into a pond. It floated but the following day it had sunk. Use ideas of density to explain why.
4. Explain how armbands and swimming rings help beginner swimmers. Use correct scientific terminology.

КАЛИНИНГРАД

The plimsoll line tells how much weight the ship can safely carry

Floating in different liquids

People often claim it is easier to float in the sea than in fresh water. This person is certainly finding it easy to float in the Dead Sea, the saltiest sea on Earth:

Floating in the Dead Sea is easy

5 Comparing how easy it is to float in different liquids

Method 1: Attach plasticine to the open end of a pen top to make a pen-top diver. Adjust the amount of plasticine so the diver **just** floats in tap water. Use your diver to compare how easy it is to float in different liquids.

Method 2: Use a 'boat' or container that can be loaded with different weights, with markings on the side to show how far into the liquid it has 'sunk'.

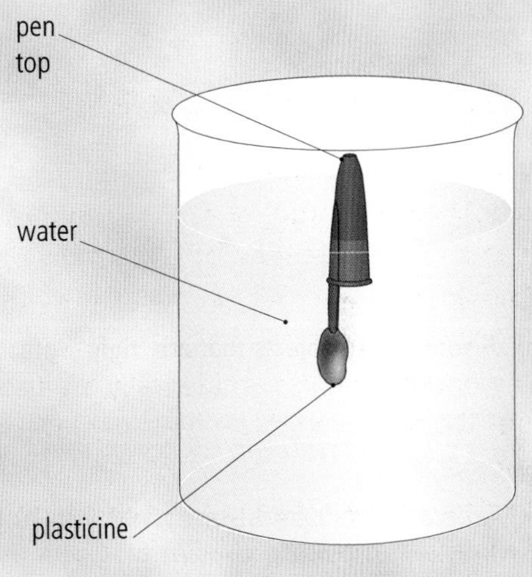

A pen-top diver

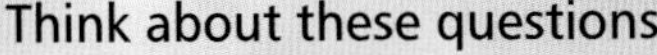

Think about these questions

a Which is easier to float in, fresh water or salt water?

b Which is denser, fresh water or salt water? (Which is heavier for a particular volume?)

Points to discuss

Use your knowledge about weight of displaced liquid and upthrust to explain why it is easier to float in some liquids than others.

How do different materials stretch?

YOU WILL LEARN!

- how stretchy materials behave when forces act on them
- why some materials are more stretchy than others

Pulling things

Imagine you fasten one end of a piece of material so that it cannot move, then pull on the other end. The material might behave in one of three ways. It might:

- remain unchanged. These are 'rigid' materials.
- change shape and stay in its new shape when you stop pulling. These are 'plastic' materials.
- change shape but return to its original shape when you stop pulling. These are '**elastic**' materials.

All these different types of materials will break if you pull them hard enough.

Can you think of some examples of rigid, plastic and elastic materials?

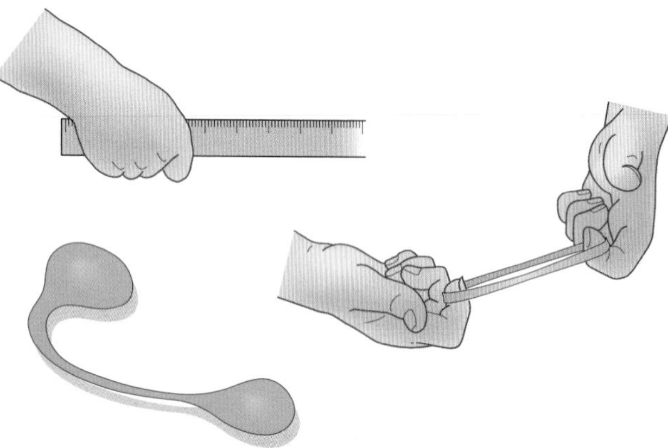

Think of some more objects that are 'rigid', 'plastic' and 'elastic'

1 Extending a spring

a Make a prediction about what will happen if you hang weights on a spring. Try to be more precise than just 'It will stretch.' Sketch the shape of the graph you would expect.

Design an investigation to find out what happens to the **extension** of a spring when different forces are applied to it. Your teacher may set a maximum force you may use.

Your investigation should include:

- a way of increasing the force by regular amounts,
- an accurate way of measuring or calculating the extension,
- ways to improve the accuracy and reliability of readings.

Investigating the extension of a spring

b Plot a graph of extension (*y*-axis) against force (*x*-axis) for the spring.

c Use your results and your graph to write a conclusion.

2 Extending an elastic band

Investigate how the extension of an elastic band varies when different forces are applied to it.

Elastic bands may break. You must include ways to protect yourself from snapping elastic bands, and to protect your feet from dropping weights. Ask your teacher to check your safety precautions before carrying out your investigation.

Plot a graph of extension against force for the elastic band.

How does the extension of the elastic band differ from the extension of a spring?

Repeat the activity for elastic bands of different thickness (but the same original length). Plot the values of extension against force on your original graph, using a different colour for each elastic band. Use ideas of force to explain why the lines are different.

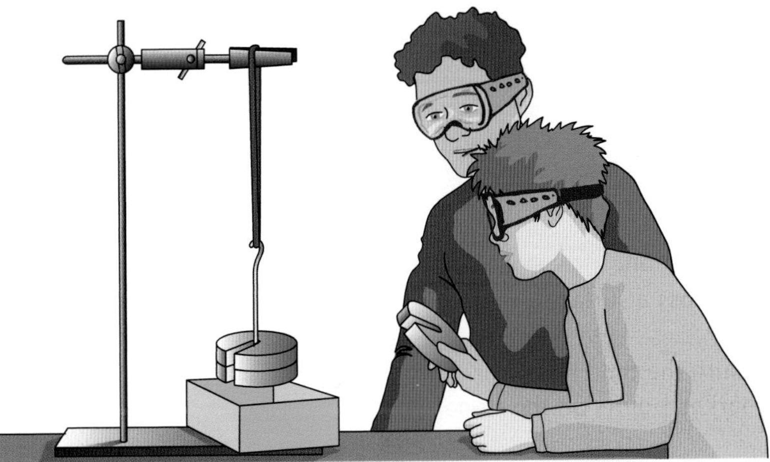

These students are taking sensible safety precautions

Why some materials are stretchy

You already know that all materials are made up of tiny particles. Forces hold the particles together. You might find it helpful to imagine the forces like bits of string between the particles. Without these forces, all materials would just fall apart.

Points to discuss

1 Why do some materials stretch and others don't? (Guess what the forces – 'bits of string' – between particles might be like.)

Use ideas of balanced and unbalanced forces to explain:

2 why elastic materials return to their original shape when you stop pulling,

3 why a certain size force stretches an elastic material by only a certain amount.

Did you know

Spiders make their webs using natural silk made from molecules (particles) that are very long, thin strands. Spiders' silk is very stretchy, so the web doesn't break when a fly struggles in it. It is also stronger than the same thickness of steel wire. Chemists have not yet succeeded in making artificial materials that are as strong for their weight as spiders' silk.

K4 What does friction do?

YOU WILL LEARN!

- some of the factors that affect friction between surfaces
- some situations where friction is useful

Some things slide easily over each other, some don't. **Friction** is the name given to the force that acts to prevent surfaces sliding past each other.

Points to discuss

1 Can you explain the effects of friction in these circumstances?
- Knots in natural fibre string stay tied.
- Knots in plastic thread often come undone.
- Oiled bike wheels turn more freely than non-lubricated wheels.
- Sledges are easier to pull on ice than on tarmac.
- Tiled floors are more slippery than carpets.

2 Think of a general statement to describe the direction in which the force of friction acts.

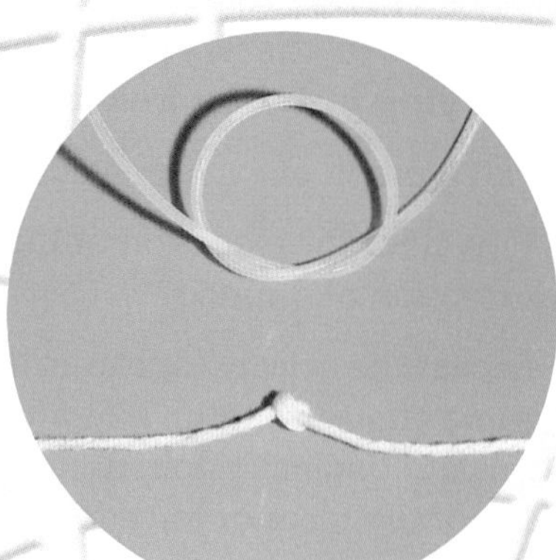

Smooth plastic thread comes undone easily

1 Investigating friction

a List the factors that might affect the friction between an object and a surface.

Here are two different ways to measure friction:
- Use a force meter to pull an object across a surface. Measure how much force is needed.
- Slide an object down a slope. Measure the time taken for the object to slide between two marked points on the slope.

Investigating friction

Did you know?

Friction can make things hot. If you rub your hands together hard you will feel them warm up. When a space shuttle returns to Earth it is moving so fast that the friction between the space shuttle and the air would make it burn up, if it was not coated with special tiles. The non-stick coating used on many saucepans was originally invented to use on spacecraft!

1 *continued*

Choose one of the methods. Investigate how friction is affected by changing one of the factors in your list.
(If you investigated the effect of changing the type of surface at Key Stage 2, choose a different factor here.)
You should include ways to:

- ensure a fair test (what will you change and what will you keep the same?)
- ensure results are reliable and repeatable (how many readings will you take? What will you do to make them as accurate as possible?)

b Plot a graph to show how the friction you recorded varies with the factor you changed.
c Can you predict other values of friction from your graph?
d What have you found out from this investigation?

Friction – good or bad?

Friction can be useful, for example shoe treads 'gripping' the ground, or a nuisance, such as rusty bolts sticking instead of turning.

Points to discuss

1 Think of as many examples of friction as you can, and state whether it is helpful or unhelpful.
2 For each example, think of a way to increase or decrease friction to improve the situation.

What are the advantages of keeping this steam locomotive well lubricated?

Did you know

It has been suggested that the phrase 'the real McCoy' (meaning something is very good or 'the real thing') comes from the 19th century, when an American, Elijah McCoy, invented a very good system of lubrication for steam locomotives.

K5 Stopping distances

YOU WILL LEARN!

- the main forces acting on a moving car
- some of the factors affecting the stopping distance of a moving car

How quickly a car can stop depends on the size of the forces acting on it.

1 Forces on a car

The diagram opposite shows the main forces acting on a moving car.

a List the main things that affect the size of each of the forces shown.

b What can you say about the relative size of the forces when the car is:

- speeding up,
- slowing down,
- moving at constant speed.

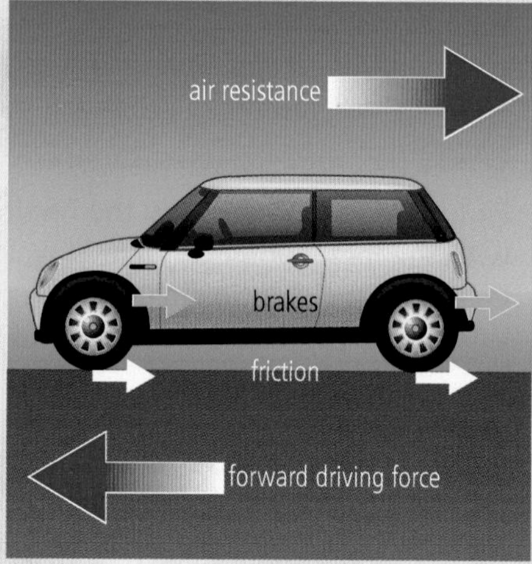

The main forces acting on a car

The Highway Code gives details of the shortest **stopping distance** for cars travelling at different speeds. The stopping distance is measured from the point where the driver spotted a hazard to the point where the car stopped. It includes the distance the car travels in the driver's reaction time and the distance the car travels while braking. The figures (in the Highway Code) are calculated for an alert driver in a well maintained Ford Anglia (a popular car in the 1960s).

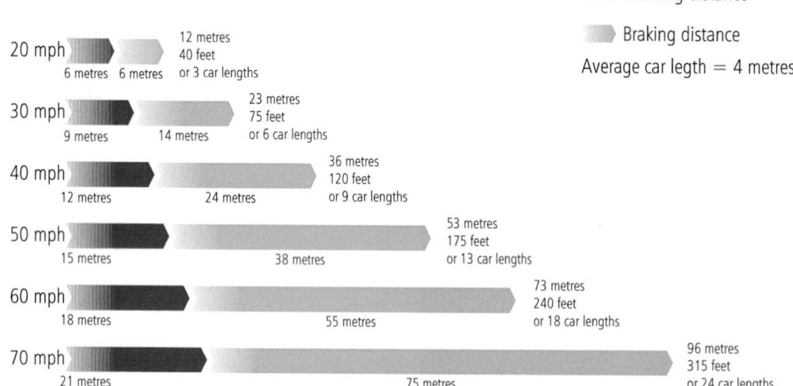

Stopping distances change as speed changes

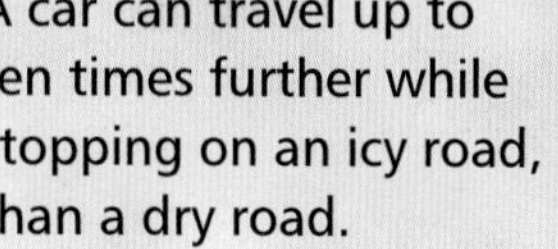

A car can travel up to ten times further while stopping on an icy road, than a dry road.

2 Stopping distances

a Plot a graph of stopping distance against speed.
b What does the graph tell you?

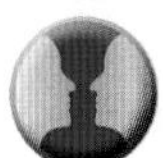

Points to discuss

1 How do you think stopping distances of modern cars compare with those given in the Highway Code?
2 What factors might increase the stopping distance? (Think about the driver and the car.)
3 Typically, sports cars have the shortest stopping distances and 'people carriers' the longest. How should this affect drivers' behaviour?

3 Racing car tyres

The tyres for an 'ordinary family car' and a racing car are very different. This is because the friction on wet and dry roads is very different. Which do you think has the lower friction, a wet road or a dry road? Can you explain why?

Look at the photographs of car tyres:

The 'dry weather' racing car tyres are wide and smooth to increase the area of tyre in contact with the road. Decide what effect this will have on the friction between tyre and road, and how this will affect the way the car behaves.

The 'wet weather' tyre has a tread that forces water into the gaps in the tread, preventing a layer of water collecting between the tyre surface and the road. Why would a layer of water be extremely dangerous?

a Why do you think it is illegal to drive cars with insufficient depth of tread on their tyres?

b Design an advertisement for a tyre for either a racing car or a 'family car'. State what conditions your tyre is designed for, and use ideas of friction to explain your tyre's advantages.

Family car tyre

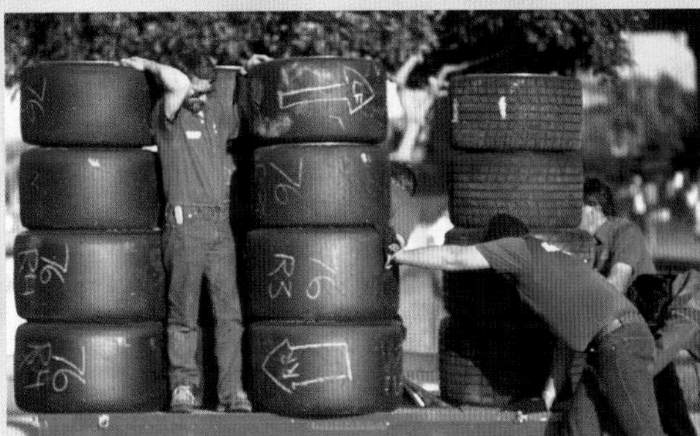

Cart loaded with race car tyres (wet and dry)

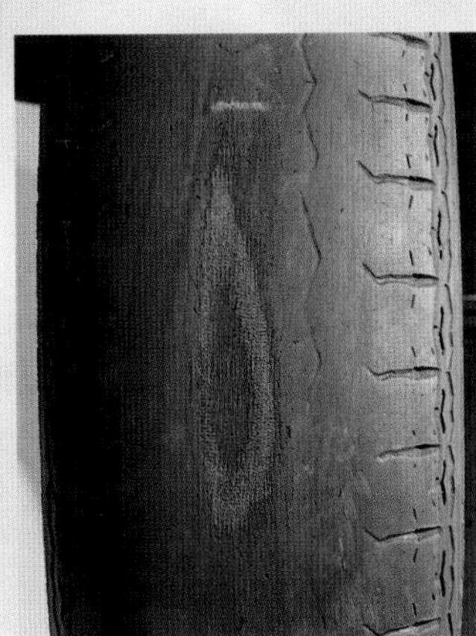

All these tyres are illegal because they are dangerous

K6 Graphs to represent motion

- how to show fast and slow speeds on a distance–time graph

Graphs are sometimes a very quick way to show how something is moving.

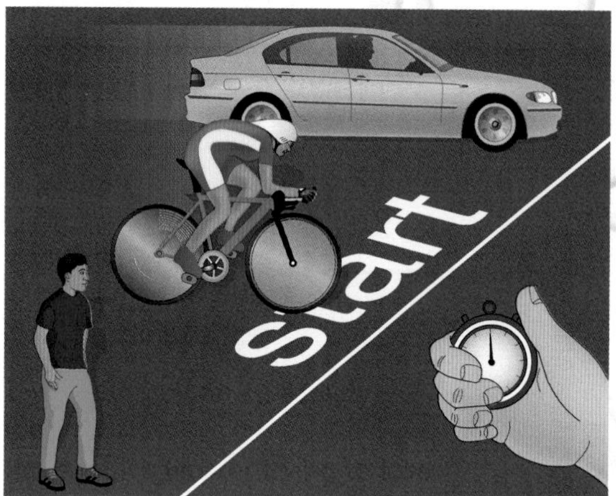

In 1 second, which of these would travel furthest?

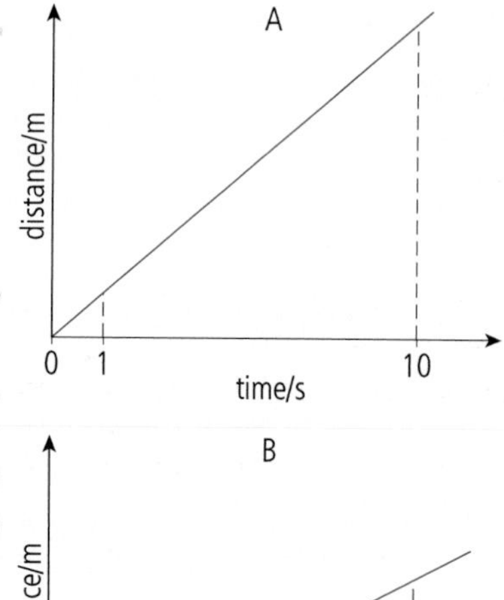

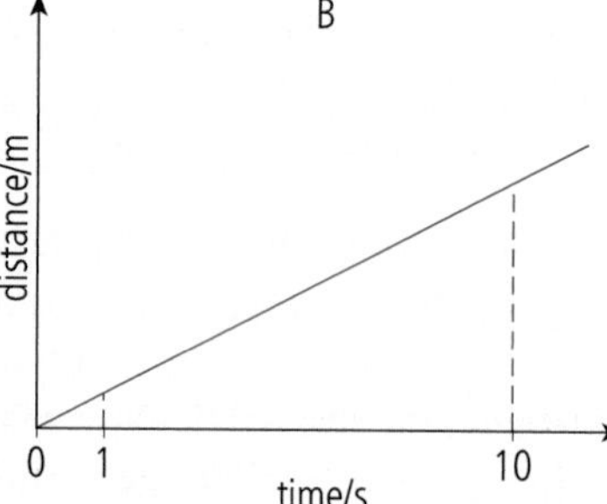

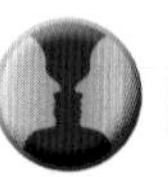

Points to discuss

The graphs opposite show how far the car and the bicycle travelled in certain times.

1. 1 s after they started, which had travelled further, A or B?
2. 10 s after they started, which had travelled further, A or B?
3. Which do you think is travelling faster, A or B?
4. Decide which graph belongs to the car. Which belongs to the bicycle?

Could you draw the graph of distance against time for the person walking? How steep would the line be?

1 Graphs of motion

The graph opposite shows somebody driving to work.

- **a** When were they driving slowly?
- **b** When were they going fast on the main road?
- **c** When were they stuck in a traffic jam?
- **d** Draw a distance–time graph for someone who walks to the bus stop, rides on the bus to school, then stops.

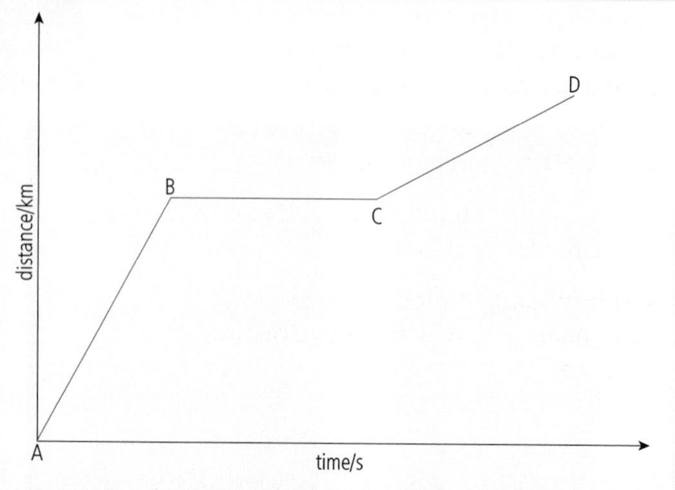

Distance–time graph for a journey to work

Summary

The **mass** of an object tells us how much matter there is in the object.

The **weight** of an object tells us how hard it is being pulled downwards by **gravity**. Weight is a **force**, measured in **newtons**.

Unbalanced forces change the shape of an object, make it move, or change its movement.

Floating objects have two **balanced forces** acting on them: weight acting downwards and **upthrust** acting upwards.

Denser liquids are easier to float in.

Elastic materials stretch until the force pulling them is exactly balanced by the internal forces trying to pull them back to their original shape.

Friction is a force that acts to slow down the movement of surfaces sliding over each other. Friction is less between surfaces that are smooth or lubricated. Friction is very important in car brakes and tyres to slow cars down and stop them skidding.

Graphs of distance against time can be drawn to show how quickly an object is moving.

Key words

density
displacement
elastic
extension
force
force meter
friction
gravity
mass
stopping distance
upthrust
weight

Did you know 

Early brake blocks on horse-drawn carriages were made of wood. Braking too hard or too long would make the wood so hot it caught alight.

Summary Questions

1 Make your own glossary (list of meanings) for the key words. Keep your definitions short.

2 Name the two forces acting on an object in water. What can you say about the size of these forces if the object sinks?

3 If a weight is hung from a piece of elastic material, which of the following describe what might happen?
A: nothing
B: the elastic material will get longer
C: the elastic material will get shorter
D: the elastic material will break

4 What happens to the stopping distance for a car as the car travels faster?

5 Will increasing the friction between car and road increase or decrease the stopping distance?

6 What type of graph is used to show how fast an object is moving?

7 **a** A submarine has special tanks, called ballast tanks, that can be pumped full of either sea water or air. Explain what the submarine would use these tanks for.
b Most fish have similar 'tanks' called swim bladders. Special muscles make the swim bladder expand or contract. Suggest what the fish use their swim bladders for.

8 Describe one situation where friction is useful, and one situation where friction needs to be as low as possible.

Imagine you have somehow become stranded in the middle of some ice with zero friction. Will you be able to reach the edge of the ice? Explain your answer.

End of unit Questions

1 When a car is being driven along, two horizontal forces affect its motion. One is air resistance and the other is the forward force.

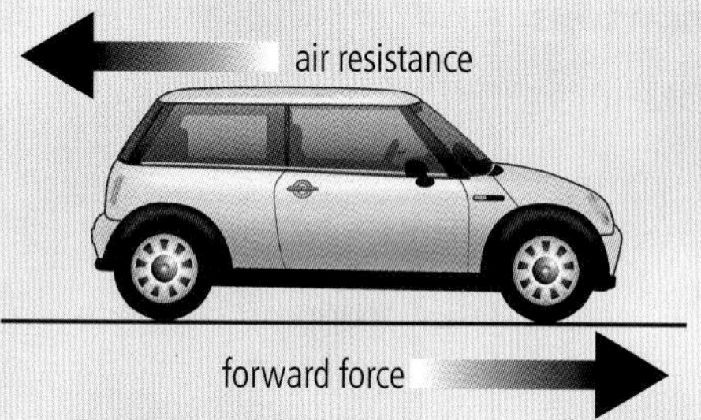

a **i** Explain how molecules in the air cause air resistance. *1 mark*

ii Explain why air resistance is larger when the car is travelling faster. *1 mark*

b **i** Compare the sizes of the forward force and the air resistance when the car is speeding up. *1 mark*

ii Compare the sizes of the two forces while the car is moving at a steady 30 miles per hour. *1 mark*

c The forward force has to be larger when the car is travelling at a steady 60 mph than when it is travelling at a steady 30 mph. Why is this? *1 mark*

d The forward force is the result of the tyres not being able to spin on the road surface. What is the name of the force that stops the tyres spinning? *1 mark*

2 The drawing shows a boy with a bow and arrow. He is holding the arrow and pulling it back.

a Two horizontal forces act on the arrow. These are the force exerted by the boy's hand and the force exerted by the string. The arrow is **not** moving.

The boy pulls the arrow with a force of 150 N. What is the size of the force exerted by the string on the arrow? *1 mark*

b When the boy lets go of the arrow, it starts to move forward.
Explain why it starts to move. *1 mark*

c The arrow flies across a field and hits a target.
Two forces act on the arrow while it is in the air. Air resistance acts in the opposite direction to the movement, and gravity acts downwards. These two forces cannot balance each other, even when they are the same size. Why is this? *1 mark*

3 The diagram shows a chain hanging down over the edge of a table.

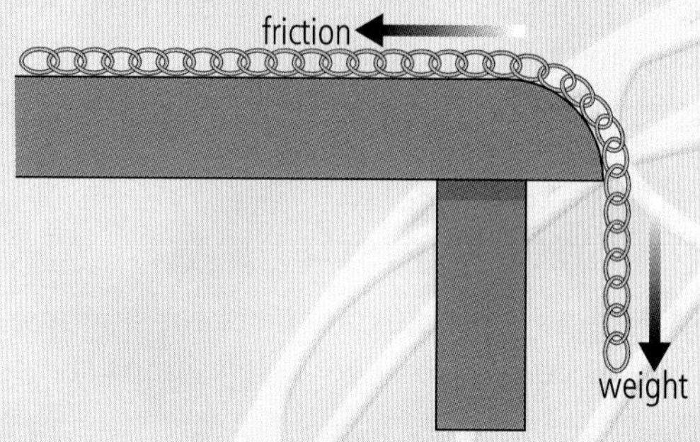

Two of the forces on the chain are:
the weight of the part of the chain which is hanging over the edge;
friction between the chain and the table.

a The chain is **not** moving. What does this tell you about these two forces acting on the chain? *1 mark*

b The chain is moved slightly to the right. It begins to slide off the table.

i What does this tell you about these two forces now? *1 mark*

ii Describe how the size of each force changes as the chain slides off the table. *2 marks*

iii How does the speed of the chain change as it slides off the table? *1 mark*

7L The solar system and beyond

Introduction

Our planet Earth is just a tiny part of the vast solar system with our Sun at its centre.
In this unit you will find out more about how the solar system affects us on Earth, just how big the solar system really is, and what lies beyond it.

You already know

- the Sun, the Earth and the Moon are roughly spherical
- the Earth orbits the Sun once each year and the Moon orbits the Earth once each 28 days
- the rotation of the Earth causes night and day, causes shadows to change, and causes the Sun to appear to move across the sky

In this topic you will learn

- why we sometimes see eclipses of the Moon and Sun
- what causes the seasons and why they are different in different places
- what different planets are like, and whether there is life on other planets
- what is beyond the solar system

1 Can you put these events in the right order?

- man thinks the Earth is flat
- man walks on the Moon
- the telescope is invented
- the discovery that planets and stars are not the same thing
- manned spacecraft travel beyond the solar system

Which is the odd one out? Can you guess why?

L1 Time zones

YOU WILL LEARN!

- why there are different time zones around the world

Points to discuss

Use the shape and movement of the Earth and Moon to explain these things:

1 Boats always seem to sink below the horizon as they sail away from land.

2 We have night and day on Earth.

3 The connection between a month and the Moon. How long is a lunar month?

Did you know

A freely swinging pendulum can be used to show the spinning of the Earth. Throughout the day, the direction of swing of the pendulum seems to change. Actually, the pendulum swings in the same direction, but the Earth turns underneath it.

Time zones

For thousands of years people defined noon (midday) as the time when the Sun was highest in the sky. As the Earth rotates, this happens at different times in different places. Clocks in Bristol were about 10 minutes behind clocks in London, so when rail travel first started no one could agree whether or not the trains were on time. So in 1883 Standard Time was introduced. The Earth was divided into 24 sections (time zones) running north to south. All places in one time zone use the same time. The time zone to the east is 1 hour ahead; the time zone to the west is 1 hour behind. This is why you often have to change the time on your watch if you fly abroad.

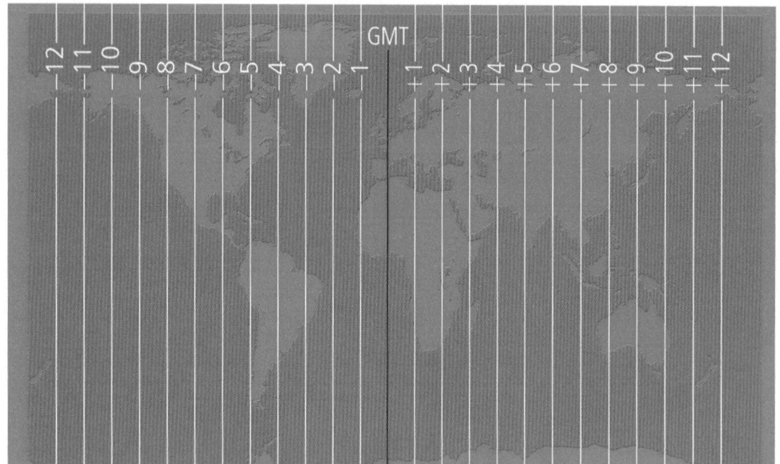

The world is divided into 24 time zones, 1 hour apart

1 The Date Line

a Find out what the International **Date Line** is and why it is necessary.

b Find out how John Harrison used an accurate clock to make travelling safer.

John Harrison's chronometer, the most accurate clock of its time

L2 How do we see the Sun and Moon?

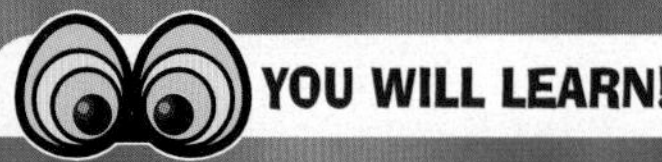

- the difference between luminous and reflective objects
- why we see different phases of the Moon
- why the Moon is visible in the sky at different times

Our Sun is a **star**. It is **luminous**; it gives off light. The Sun also radiates (gives off) lots of energy in forms we can't see, such as heat, ultraviolet radiation and X-rays. All other 'heavenly bodies' in the solar system are reflective; they just reflect light from the Sun.

Points to discuss

1 How can we see the Moon and the **planets** if they do not give off light?

2 Why can't we see the planets in the daytime sky? Are they still there?

Phases of the Moon

You can demonstrate the **phases of the Moon** with a model like this.

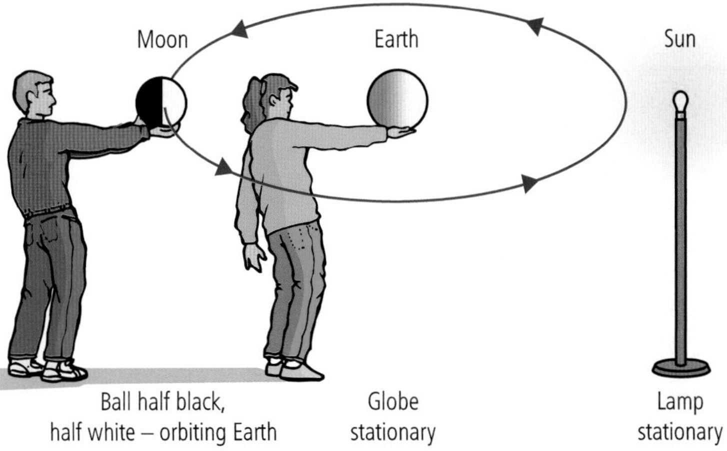

Using a black and white ball to model the phases of the moon

1 Phases of the Moon

Use the model to demonstrate the phases of the Moon.

a Why is the 'Moon' half black and half white?

b Which half must always face the Sun? Why?

c Copy the diagram of the model. Miss out the Moon.

Use your model to work out what phase we see when the Moon is in different positions.

d Draw the phases of the Moon on your diagram.

e Would a person on the Moon see 'phases of the Earth'? Explain, or use a model to demonstrate your answer.

Moon rise and Moon set

Daily papers give information on the time the Moon 'rises' and 'sets'. These times vary as the Moon **orbits** the Earth. The Moon 'rises' when it becomes visible in the sky, and 'sets' when we can no longer see it.

2 Moon rise and Moon set

Replace the 'Earth' in your model with a globe. Mark the position of your country clearly. Place the 'Moon' in its 'full moon' position. Turn the 'Earth' slowly to show day and night.

As the Earth turns on its own axis (day and night), sometimes people in your country won't be able to see the Moon because your country is facing the wrong way. Decide when people in your country would be able to see the Moon (all night, the second half of the night, all day, etc.). Repeat with different positions of the Moon.

Did you know

Because the Moon orbits around the Earth it does not 'rise' at the same time each night. Each night it first becomes visible about 40 minutes later than the previous night.

Lunar eclipses

Every opaque object in sunlight casts a shadow. The Earth casts a shadow. So does the Moon. If the Moon passes into the Earth's shadow, it appears a dull red colour and is much harder to see. This is a **lunar eclipse**.

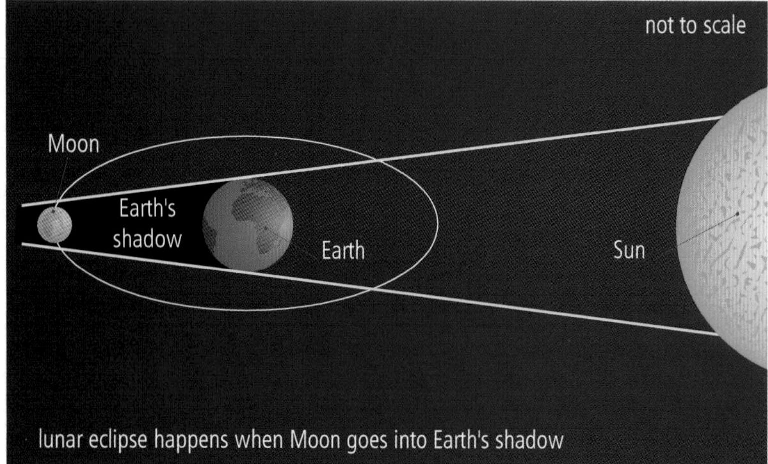

A lunar eclipse occurs when the Moon passes through the Earth's shadow

So why don't we see a lunar eclipse every month? The Moon doesn't orbit the Earth in a smooth, flat circle. The diagram shows how its orbit moves up and down. Most of the time it passes behind the Earth without going into the shadow, like this.

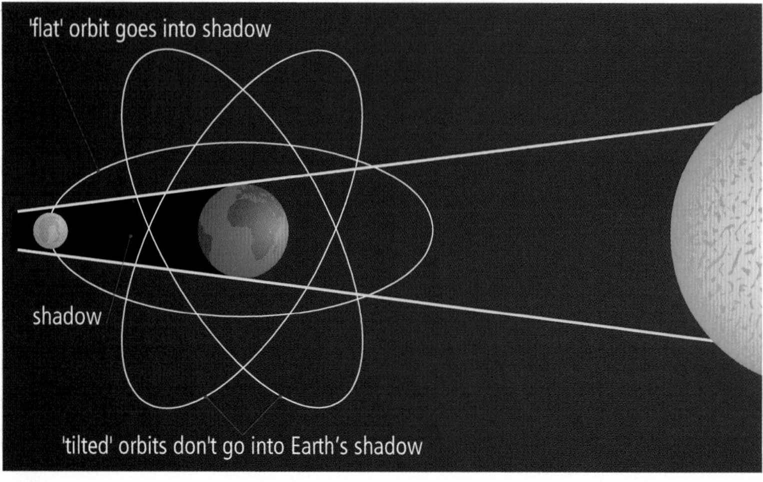

A lunar eclipse does not occur every month because sometimes the Moon misses the Earth's shadow

Points to discuss

- What phase of the Moon will it be during a lunar eclipse?

Solar eclipses

A total eclipse of the Sun is visible from somewhere on Earth about once every 18 months.

A **solar eclipse** happens when the Moon passes exactly between the Earth and the Sun. This is rare because the orbits of the Earth and Moon are not flat and smooth – the orbit of the Earth around the Sun tilts, just as the orbit of the Moon around Earth does.

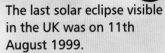

Did you know

The last solar eclipse visible in the UK was on 11th August 1999.

The next solar eclipse visible in the UK will be in 2090.

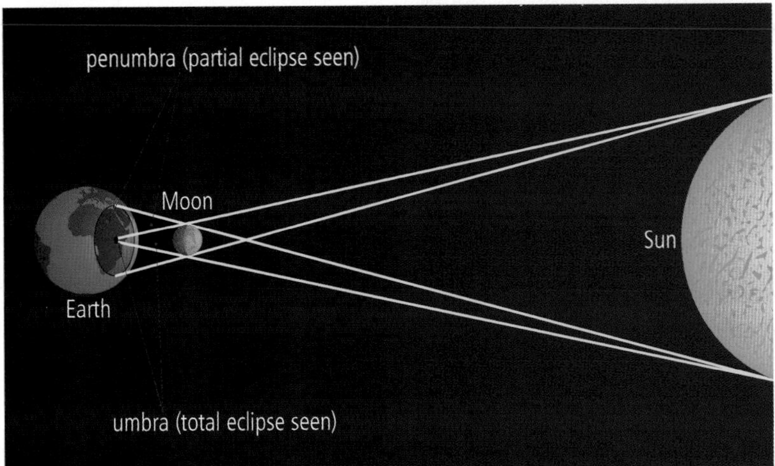

A solar eclipse occurs when the Moon's shadow falls on Earth

In some areas the Moon exactly covers the Sun. This is a total eclipse. In other areas the Moon partly covers the Sun. This is a partial eclipse.

Did you know

Birds go to roost during a total eclipse because they think it is night time.

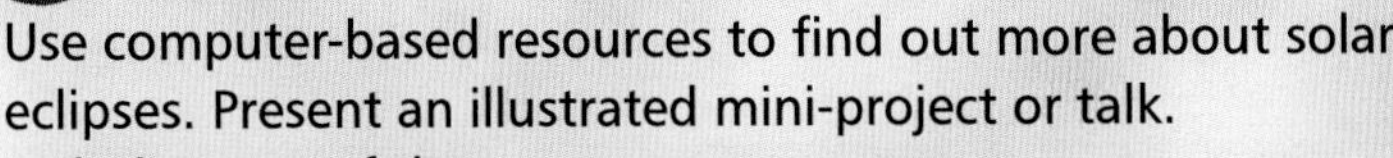

3 Solar eclipses

Use computer-based resources to find out more about solar eclipses. Present an illustrated mini-project or talk.
Include some of these:

- Why eclipses happen.
- What they are like.
- How to view eclipses safely.
- Myths about eclipses

Points to discuss

In a total eclipse the Moon covers the Sun exactly. This is because the Sun is 400 times as large as the Moon but also 400 times further away!

1 What would an eclipse look like if the relative distances or sizes were different?
2 How old will you be when the next solar eclipse is visible in the UK?

L3 What causes the seasons on Earth?

YOU WILL LEARN!

- how the temperature on Earth is related to the position on the Earth's surface
- how the tilt of the Earth and its rotation about the Sun causes the seasons

Near the equator radiation from the Sun is concentrated on a small area. At the poles the radiation is much more spread out. You can show this with a globe and a narrow beam torch.

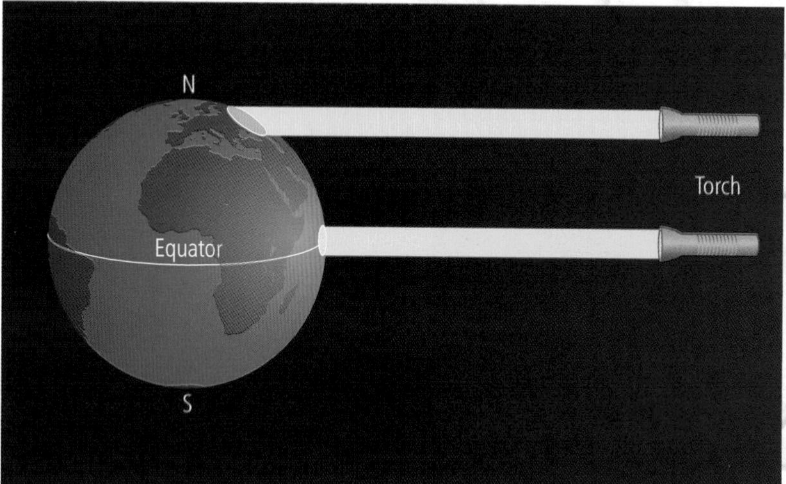

Radiation is spread out at the poles and concentrated at the equator

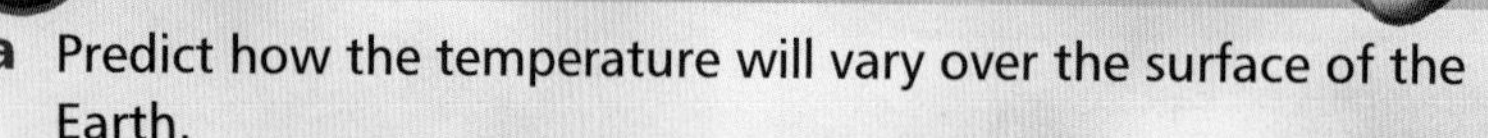

1 Hot or cold?

a Predict how the temperature will vary over the surface of the Earth.

Place a large globe near to a small bright lamp, to represent the Sun. Use a temperature sensor and a datalogger to record how the temperature changes at different points on your globe. Plot a graph of temperature against distance from the equator.

b Do the results match your prediction?

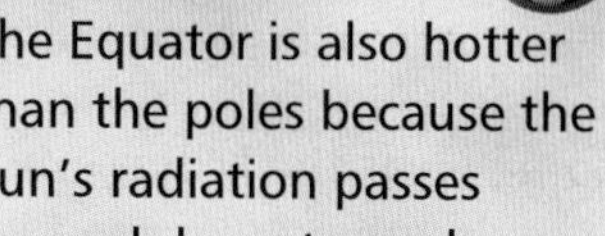

The Equator is also hotter than the poles because the Sun's radiation passes through less atmosphere.

Different climates happen because different parts of the world have different average temperatures

The tilted Earth

The **axis of rotation** of the Earth is the line through the middle of the Earth from the North Pole to the South Pole. The axis is tilted with respect to the Sun's radiation.

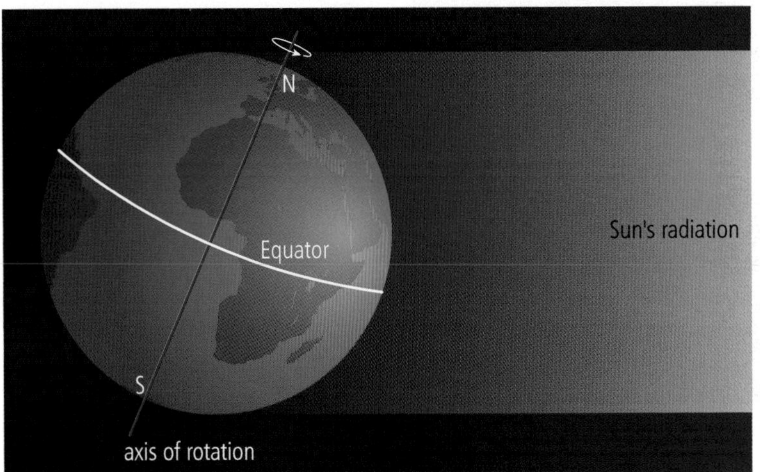

The Earth's axis of rotation is tilted with respect to the Sun's radiation

Did you know

The poles are in darkness for six months of every year. This causes the temperature to fall very low. The lowest temperature ever recorded was –89.6 °C in Antarctica in August 1960.

Did you know

The Earth is tilted at an angle of $23\frac{1}{2}°$ to the 'upright' position.

Points to discuss

Look at a globe. Imagine where the Sun is and tilt the top of the axis towards the Sun.

1 Will the temperature in Britain be warmer or colder than in the 'upright' position?
2 Can you explain why?

Tilt the top of the axis away from the Sun.
3 What will happen to the temperature in Britain now?

2 Tilted Earth

Set up a globe and bright lamp to represent Earth and the Sun. Use a temperature sensor on your model to record the average temperature in Britain when the axis is tilted towards and away from the Sun. Don't forget to rotate the globe to model day and night time.

Were your ideas in *Points to discuss* correct?

3 Day length

Replace the temperature sensor in Activity 2 with a light sensor. Rotate the globe slowly and steadily and record when it is lighter (day) and darker (night).

a Which way does the globe have to tilt for maximum day length?
b When is the day length shortest?

The Earth orbits around the Sun but the tilt of the Earth stays the same.

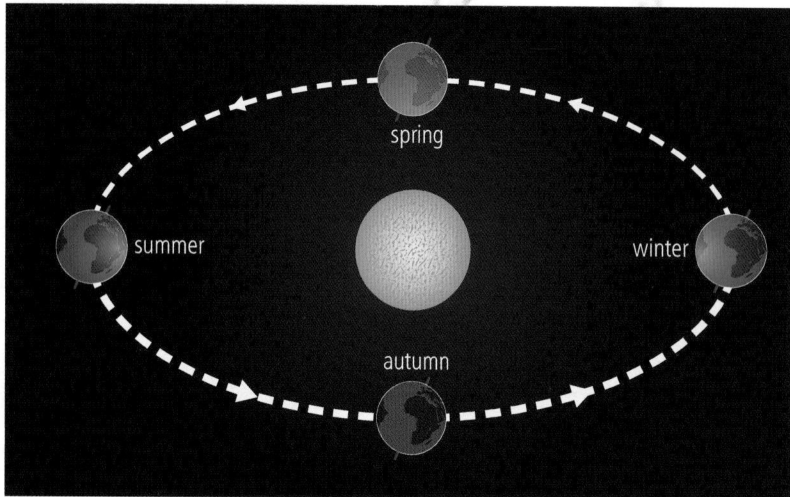

As the Earth orbits the Sun, its tilt stays the same

Points to discuss

Use your knowledge of the Earth's orbit around the Sun to explain:

1 the Earth's orientation (amount and direction of tilt) in its orbit when it is summer, winter, spring or autumn,
2 why temperature varies in the different seasons,
3 why day length varies in the different seasons,
4 why the highest point of the Sun in the sky is different in summer and winter.

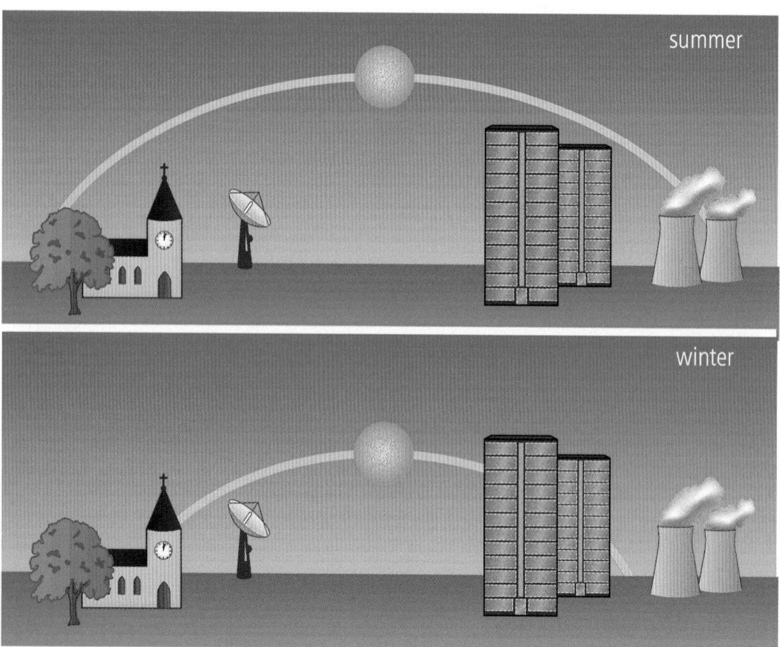

The Sun appears to climb higher in the sky in summer because we are tilted towards the Sun

Did you know 

On the 21st March and 21st September, day and night are equal lengths. These dates are called 'equinoxes'. The Southern Hemisphere and the Northern Hemisphere have equal amounts of daylight.

Did you know 

Many plants and animals have their behaviour controlled by the day length in different seasons. Migrating birds can be made to migrate the wrong way by giving them artificial days of the wrong length.

Seasons in different places

The seasons on Earth are different in different places.

When a country is tilted towards the Sun, the Sun's radiation is spread over a smaller area, and the country is hotter. When a country tilts away from the Sun, the Sun's radiation spreads over a larger area and the country is cooler. Whether a country tilts towards the Sun or away from the Sun depends on the Earth's position in its orbit around the Sun.

4 Seasons

Find out about the seasons for countries close to the equator and those close to the poles. Write a paragraph for each to describe what the seasons are like and to explain them. Use your ideas of the Earth's tilt and orbit around the Sun in your answers.

Did you know

If you look at a globe you will find two lines, the Tropic of Cancer and the Tropic of Capricorn, one each side of the equator. For countries between these two lines, the Sun will be directly overhead at some time during the year. Outside these two lines the Sun is never directly overhead at any time of year.

Look at these imaginary planets orbiting around our Sun.

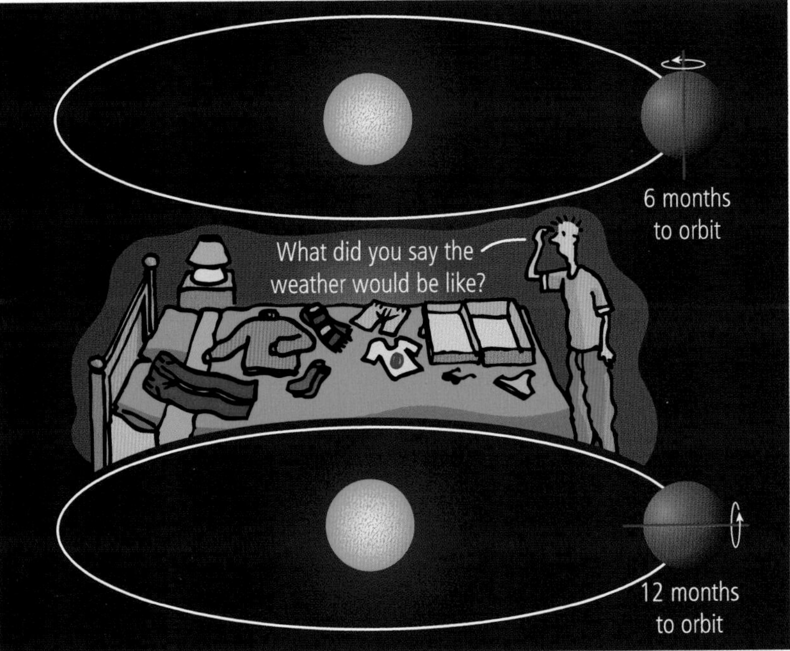

Seasons are caused by the tilt of the Earth

Points to discuss

For each of the planets shown, answer these questions.

1 How will the day length change throughout the 'year'?

2 What path would the Sun appear to take through the sky?

3 What would the seasons be like in different places?

L4 What does the solar system consist of?

YOU WILL LEARN!

- the main bodies in the solar system
- how to use planetary information to compare different planets
- some relative sizes and distances between bodies in the solar system

There are nine planets orbiting around the Sun in **elliptical orbits** (squashed circles). Starting from the Sun and going outwards these are:

Try this mnemonic to remember them.

My Very Easy Method Just Speeds Up Naming Planets

Can you make up your own mnemonic?

1 Planetary survey

Use library or computer-based resources to find out about a planet of your choice. How big is it? How far is it from the Sun? What is it made from? Does it spin? When was it discovered? Who by?

a Write a short leaflet called 'Things you need to know before moving to ...'

or

b Prepare a short talk to describe the important points about your planet.

The Sun and the planets in the solar system all affect each other. There are often patterns in the way the planets move.

2 Patterns in the solar system

Write a list of questions you could investigate to find out more about the solar system. One example has been done for you.

- Does the mass of a planet affect its time to orbit the Sun (the length of its planetary 'year')?

3 Using a planetary database

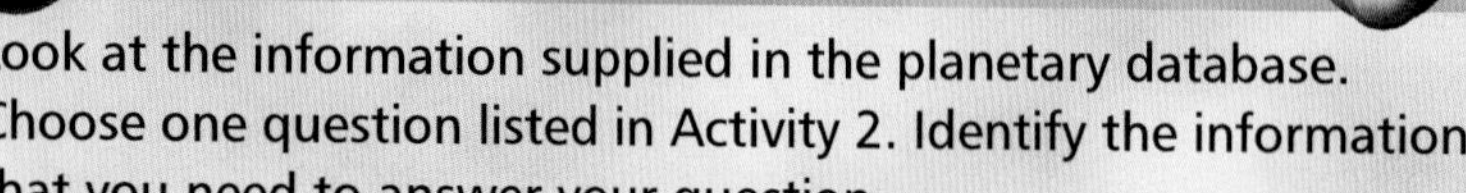

Look at the information supplied in the planetary database. Choose one question listed in Activity 2. Identify the information that you need to answer your question.

a If appropriate, plot a graph to display this information.
b Use information from your graph or the database to write a conclusion containing the answer to your question.
c Explain how you reached your conclusion.

Did you know

Clyde Tombaugh discovered Pluto in February 1930. The name was suggested by an 11-year-old English girl, Venetia Burney. A few months later the Walt Disney dog Pluto made his first appearance.

How have astronomers found out about the solar system?

Early astronomers made careful observations, then built 'thought models' that fitted what they saw. Later they used telescopes and other instruments to look in greater detail. Modern astronomers still rely on 'thought models' and computer models to help them picture what the solar system is really like.

Did you know

When the Hubble space telescope was first launched in 1990 scientists found that the main mirror wasn't quite the right shape and the pictures were distorted. In an 11 day repair mission in December 1993, astronauts did a record five space walks to put in a special lens to make the pictures clear again.

Very early telescope

Did you know

Many modern telescopes do not look for light from distant stars. Instead they detect radio waves. They can work in all weathers. Cloud does not stop radio signals reaching Earth.

Hubble telescope

The ancient Greeks noticed that the planets (from the Greek word 'planetes' meaning 'wanderers') moved about among the fixed stars.

Points to discuss

- Compare a very close moving object with a very distant one moving at the same speed. Which seems to move faster?

Ancient Greeks used the apparent speed of the planets across the sky to put them in order of distance away.

Kepler (16th century) described the relative positions of the Sun and planets accurately but he didn't know the distances.

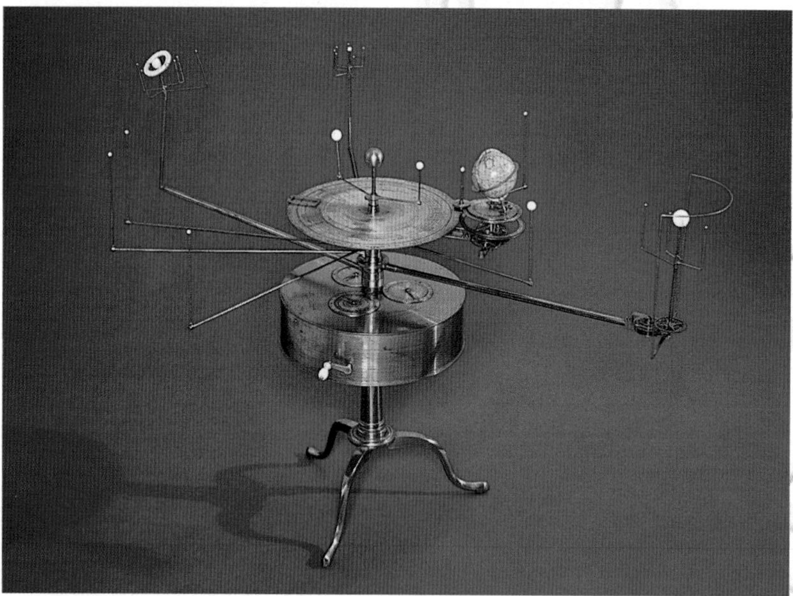

An orrery is a model to show how the planets move around the Sun

Modern astronomers use telescopes that detect light and radio waves, and telescopes that orbit around Earth. They have measured the position and distance of millions of stars. They are even able to use the type of light given off by stars to work out what the star is made of and how hot it is.

Did you know?

In 1967 astronomers were excited to find a star that blinked at them. They thought they had discovered life on another planet. It turned out to be a pulsar, a spinning **star** sending out a beam like a lighthouse. Astronomers were seeing the beam once every revolution, as it pointed in our direction.

4 Parallax

Hold your finger upright at arm's length. Shut one eye. Line up your finger with a distant object. Now look with the other eye instead.

a What happens?

b Move your eye from side to side a little bit, then much more. When does your finger seem to move more?

c Keep your head still. Look with first one eye, then the other. When does your finger seem to move more, when it is close or distant?

Points to discuss

- Astronomers used the **parallax** method to work out how far away the planets were. Suggest how.

When astronomers knew the distances, they worked out how big the planets are from how big they look.

- the conditions necessary for life forms to survive
- whether these conditions exist on any other planets

L5 Life on other planets

Points to discuss

1 Do you think any other life forms exist in our solar system?
2 If you do, what do you think they are like?
3 Might life exist elsewhere in the **Universe**?

Some of the radio and television signals, light, X-rays and microwaves that we use on Earth leak out into space. These signals could cross the solar system in about 11 hours. No such signals have been spotted from any other planets.

Points to discuss

- Think about all the different life forms you know on Earth. What do they all have in common? What do they all need to survive?

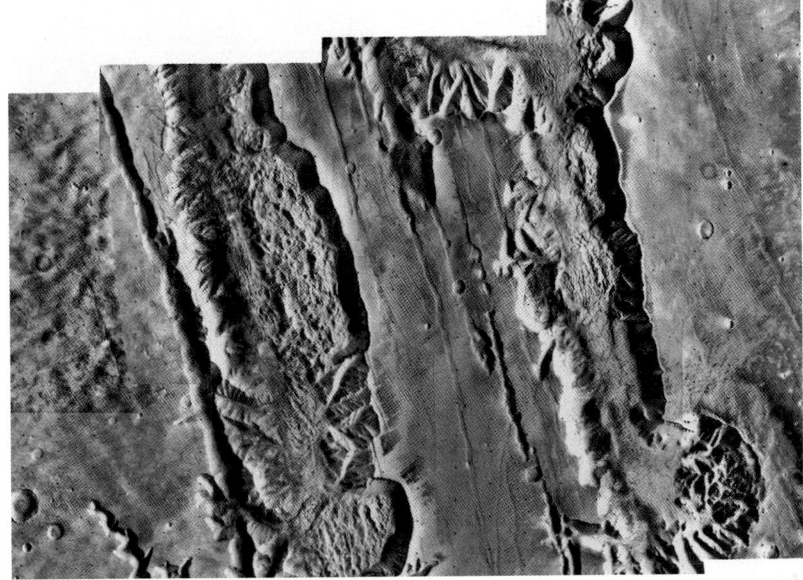

Some scientists believe this landscape may have been made by water, and there may once have been life on Mars. Other scientists disagree

1 Life on other planets

For each of the planets, except Earth, look at temperature and chemical composition. Do you think life is possible/likely? Write a sentence or two for each planet, explaining your conclusion.

Did you know

The Search for Extra Terrestrial Intelligence is an organisation that searches for life forms in the solar system and elsewhere in the universe. They have a website you can visit: www.seti.org

L6 Beyond the solar system

YOU WILL LEARN!

- why our Sun looks so much brighter than other stars
- why the stars seem to move, and how people have used this apparent movement

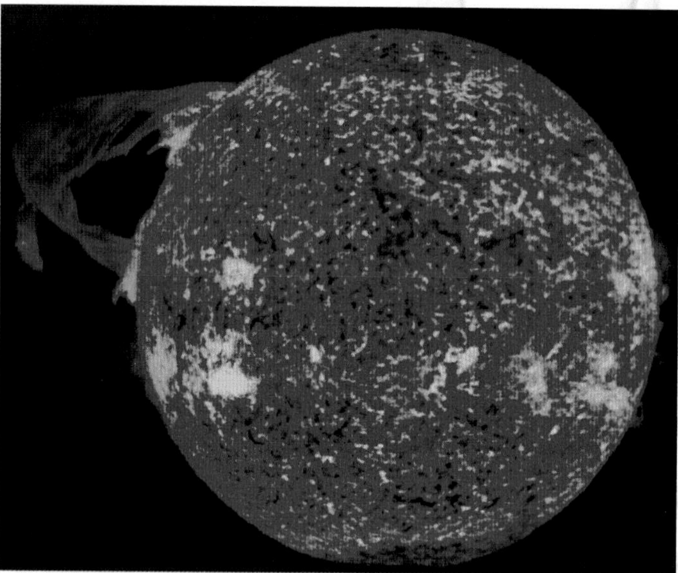

Solar flares are very active regions of our Sun; sunspots are cooler regions

Did you know

Our Sun is a very ordinary star, giving out a very ordinary amount of light. It is just like billions of other stars in the universe. Our Sun is almost 150 million kilometres away from Earth. It takes light 8 minutes to travel to us from the Sun. The next nearest star is 4 light years away – it takes the light 4 years to reach us.

Points to discuss

1 Think how bright other stars seem compared with our Sun. If they are like our Sun, how far away do you think they are?
2 If there are billions of stars in the universe, why can't we see billions of stars in the night sky?

The stars that are visible in the sky depend on:

- whether you are in the northern hemisphere or the southern hemisphere,
- the time of year.

Throughout the night the stars seem to move across the sky.

1 Star charts

a Explain why the stars seem to move across the sky. (Hint: think about the Sun.)
b Find out how sailors and desert travellers used the visible stars to work out where they were.

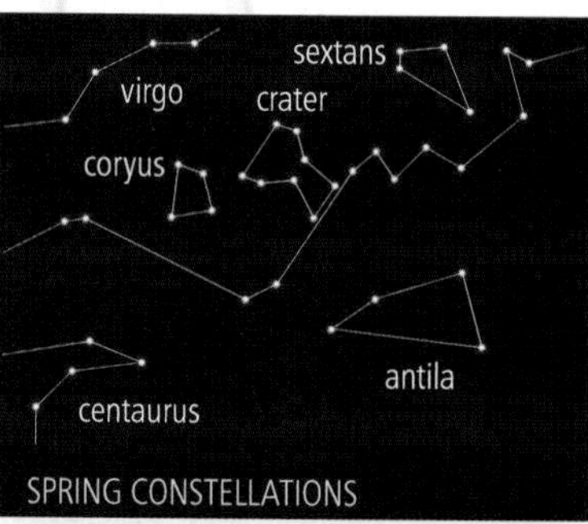

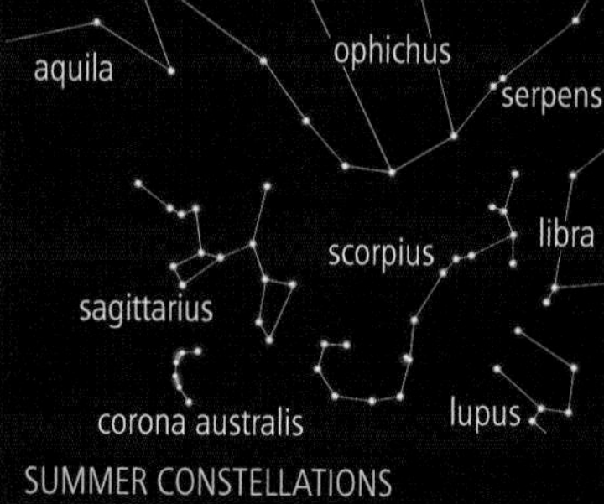

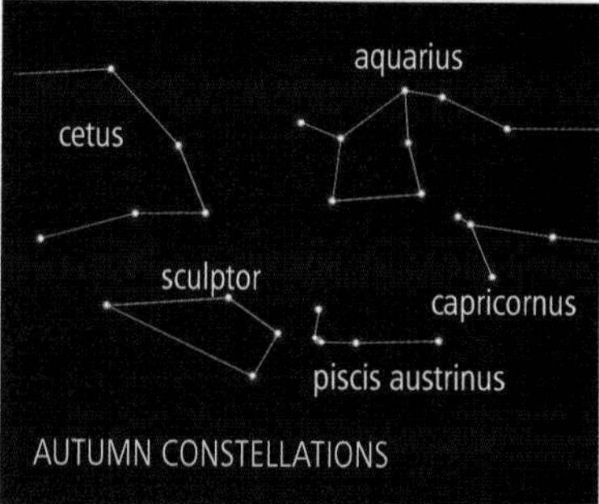

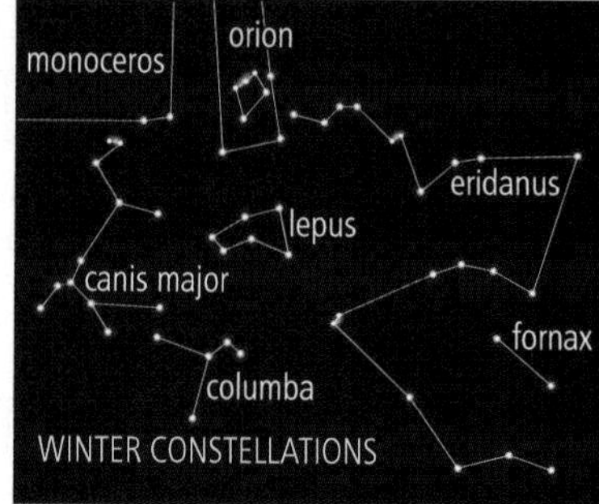

Different stars are visible at different times of year, and from the Northern and Southern Hemispheres

Summary

The Earth takes **24 hours** to turn once on its own axis, causing **day** and **night**, and 1 **year** to **orbit** the Sun. The Moon takes **28 days** to orbit the Earth, causing the **phases of the Moon**.

The Sun is **luminous**; it gives off light. All other bodies in the solar system are visible because they reflect the Sun's light.

Lunar eclipses happen when the Earth's shadow falls on the Moon. **Solar eclipses** happen when the Moon passes between the Earth and the Sun.

The **seasons** occur because the Earth's axis is **tilted** relative to its **orbit** around the Sun.

There are nine known **planets** in the solar system. Going outwards from the Sun they are Mercury, Venus, Earth, Mars, Jupiter, Saturn, Uranus, Neptune and Pluto.

The Earth is the only planet we know to support life.

There are billions of other stars in the **Universe** similar to our Sun.

Key words

axis of rotation
date line
elliptical orbit
luminous
lunar eclipse
orbit
parallax
phases of the Moon
planet
solar eclipse
star
Universe

Did you know ?

Astronomers think there may be a tenth planet, beyond Pluto, but no one has found it yet.

Summary Questions

1 Make your own glossary (list of meanings) for the key words. Keep your definitions short.

2 The circumference of the Earth at the equator is approximately 40 000 km. Two places on the equator are separated by six time zones. Approximately how far apart are they?

3 Draw a diagram to show the positions of the Earth, Sun and Moon during
- **a** a solar eclipse,
- **b** a lunar eclipse.

4 If the tilt of the axis of the Earth were to increase, describe the effect this would have on the seasons in Britain.

5 Explain the effect that distance from the Sun has on the surface temperature of a planet.

6 An amateur astronomer points her telescope at the star Sirius B early in the evening. Explain why she can't find the star when she returns to her telescope just before dawn.

7 The time zones were introduced so that people all around the world could agree on the time. If you were half way across one time zone and you compared your watch with the time when the Sun was at its highest position in the sky, what would you expect to find and why?

8 Draw a diagram to show the relative positions of the Earth, Moon and Sun when a half moon is seen. How long would you have to wait before seeing a half moon again?

9 Each of the statements below is **incorrect**. Say what is wrong with each statement and write a corrected statement:
- **a** The phases of the Moon are caused by the Earth's shadow covering part of the Moon.
- **b** Solar eclipses happen when the Sun passes between the Earth and the Moon.
- **c** The Equator is hotter than the poles because it is nearer to the Sun.
- **d** If the axis of the Earth was tilted the other way there would not be any seasons.
- **e** The planets are all the same size. The only way scientists can work out how far away they are is to compare how big they look.

End of unit Questions

1 On 11th August 1999 there was an eclipse. The shadow of the Moon passed over part of the Earth.

a The diagram below shows the Moon, the Moon's shadow and the Earth.

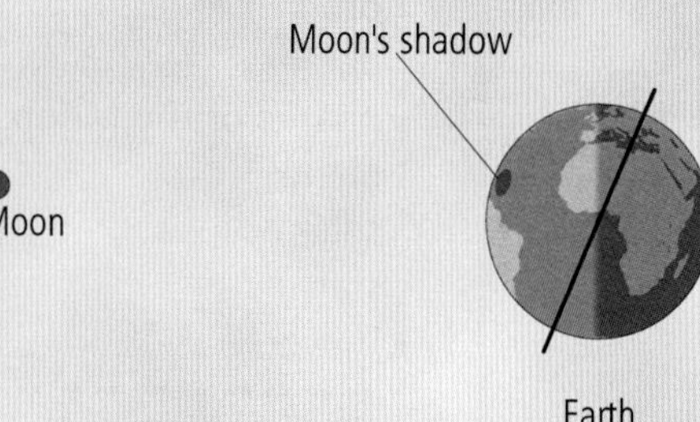

On the diagram, draw an arrow pointing towards where the Sun must be. *1 mark*

b At about midday the Moon's shadow passed over Cornwall in England. Where, in the sky, is the Sun at midday? Choose from the list below: *1 mark*

towards the North

towards the West

towards the East

towards the South

The map shows the shape of the Moon's shadow and the path it took across Cornwall.

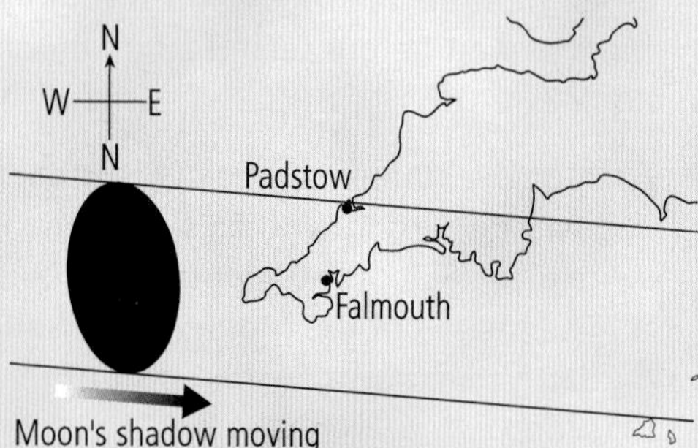

c The Moon's shadow took about 2 minutes to move across a house in Falmouth. It took less than 2 minutes to move across a house in Padstow. Explain why it took less time for the Moon's shadow to move across a house in Padstow than to move across one in Falmouth. *1 mark*

d Why does the Moon's shadow move over the surface of the Earth? *1 mark*

2 The diagram shows the orbits of the Earth, Mars and Venus. The position of the Earth is shown.

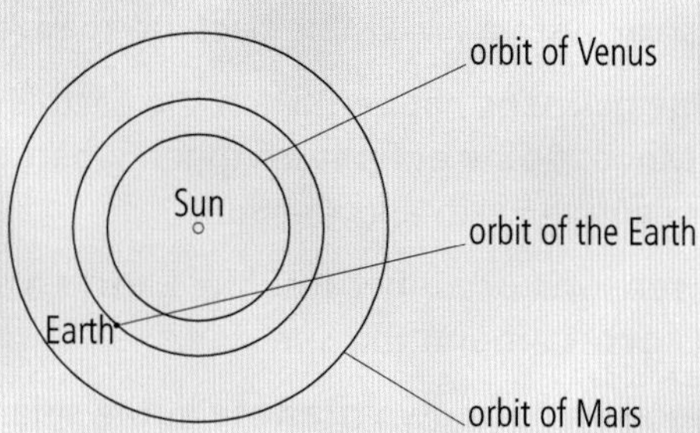

A person on the Earth observes Mars and Venus.

a i On the diagram above, draw **two** more dots to show the positions of Mars and Venus when they are closest to the Earth. Label the dot for Mars with a letter M and the dot for Venus with a letter V. *1 mark*

ii Why is it easiest to see Mars when it is closest to the Earth? *1 mark*

b What force keeps the Earth in its orbit and stops it flying off into space? *1 mark*

c From the Earth, the Moon always looks approximately the same size. What can you conclude from this about the orbit of the moon around the Earth? *1 mark*

d The diagram shows the Earth in its orbit around the Sun.

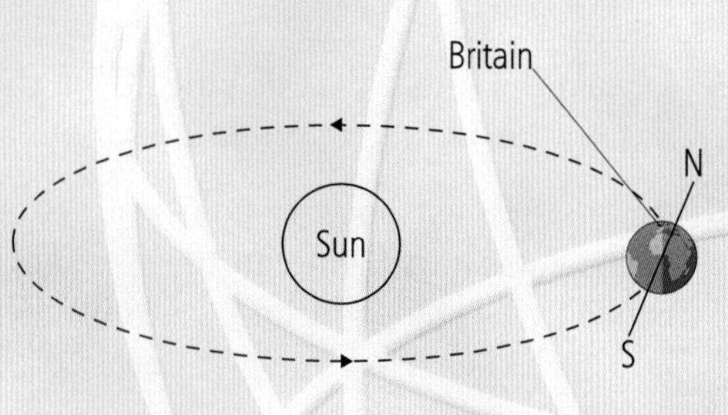

What season is it in Britain? Explain your answer. *2 marks*

Index

All page numbers in **bold** type show places where information is contained in a table or an illustration.

A

B

C

D

E

I

J

K

L

M

N

T

U

Acknowledgements

Bernard/Oxford Scientific Films **3a**; DIGITAL VISION Ltd. **3b**, **3c**, **3d**; Petit Format/Nestle/Science Photo Library **3e**; Martyn F. Chillmaid **3f**; DIGITAL VISION Ltd. **3g**; Corel **3h**; Corel **3I**; Martyn F. Chillmaid **4a**; Rex Features **4b**; Rod Leach/Collections **4c**; Corel 550 (NT) **4d**; DIGITAL VISION Ltd. **4e**; Zooid Pictures **4f**; Science Photo Library **7t**, **7c**; Biophoto Associates **7b**, **11t**; Mike Delvin/Science Photo Library **11b**; CNRI/Science Photo Library **12cl**, **12l**, **12cr**, **12r**; G.I. Bernard/Oxford Scientific Films **13t**; PhotoDisc **13b**; Chris J. R. Thomas **14**; Oxford Scientific Films **20tl**; Alistair MacEwen/Oxford Scientific Films **20tc**; DIGITAL VISION Ltd. **20tr**; Brian Kenney/Oxford Scientific Films **20b**; Corel **21l**, **21c**; Oxford Scientific Films **21r**; PhotoDisc **24t**; Petit Format/ Nestle/Science Photo Library **24b**; Corel **25t**; PhotoDisc **25c**; Rex Features **25b**; Edelmann/Science Photo Library **26l**; Petit Format/ Nestle/Science Photo Library **26c**; Corel **26r**; Alan Towse; Ecoscene/Corbis UK Ltd. **28l**; Science Photo Library **28r**; Corel **31**; Angela Hampton; Ecoscene/Corbis UK Ltd. **32tl**; Nils Jorgensen/Rex Features **32bl**; Richard Hamilton Smith/Corbis UK Ltd. **32tc**; Fotografia, Inc./Corbis UK Ltd. **32tr**; Oscar Burriel/Science Photo Library **32br**; Bettmann/Corbis UK Ltd. **33**; Corel **40tl**, **40bl**; PhotoDisc **40bc**; Mike Birkhead/Oxford Scientific Films **40tr**; Corel **40br**, **40c**; Andrew Brown; Ecoscene/Corbis UK Ltd. **41tl**; Paulo De Oliviera/Oxford Scientific Films **41cl**; Corel **41bl**, **41tc**, **41tr**, **41cr**; Colin Milkins/Oxford Scientific Films **41br**; William Gray/Oxford Scientific Films **43t**; Corel **43b**; Hermann Eisenbeiss/Science Photo Library **44tl**, **44bl**, **44tr**, **44br**; Peggy Heard; Frank Lane Picture Agency/Corbis UK Ltd. **45tl**; George Lepp/Corbis UK Ltd. **45cl**; PhotoDisc **45bl**; **45tr**; Corel **45br**, **46tl**; Pat & Tom Leeson/Science Photo Library **46tr**; Corel **46b**; PhotoDisc **48tl**; Corel **48bl**; DIGITAL VISION Ltd. **48bc**; Corel **48tr**; DIGITAL VISION Ltd. **48br**; PhotoDisc **48c**; Corel **54tl**, **54tc**, **54tr**, **54b**; PhotoDisc **55c**, **55b**, **55a**, **55d**, **55e**, **55f**, **55g**; Martyn F. Chillmaid **70**; Rex Features **71**; Martyn F. Chillmaid **72l**; Zooid Pictures **72r**, **73t**; Martyn F. Chillmaid **73b**, **74t**, **74b**, **75**, **78**, **79**, **80l**; Robert Stevens/Corbis UK Ltd. **80r**; Martyn F. Chillmaid **84t**, **84b**, **85t**, **85b**; Zooid Pictures **86t**; Corel **86b**, **88t**; Martyn F. Chillmaid **88b**; Trip & Art Directors Photo Library **89**; London Fire Brigade **90tl**; Martyn F. Chillmaid **90bl**; Rex Features **90r**; Science Photo Library **94**; Dave Bartruff/Corbis UK Ltd. **98**; Martyn F. Chillmaid **99**; Archivo Iconografico, S.A./Corbis UK Ltd. **102**; Martyn F. Chillmaid **104**; Staffan Widstrand/Corbis UK Ltd. **110t**; Rod Leach/Collections **110b**; Andrew Lambert Photography **116**; DIGITAL VISION Ltd. **126**; Biophoto Associates **127**; PhotoDisc **128**; Corel **131**; Rex Features **132**; Lakeview Cafe, Redditch/Martyn F. Chillmaid **134**; John Cleare Mountain Camera **135t**; Anthony Bannister; Gallo Images/Corbis UK Ltd. **135b**; Corel 550 (NT) **136**; Zooid Pictures **140**, **143**; Archivo Iconografico, S.A./Corbis UK Ltd. **145t**; Zooid Pictures **145b**; Corel **147**; St. Stephen's Hospital/Science Photo Library **149**; Stephen Frink/Corbis UK Ltd. **150**; NASA/Rex Features **154**; Alan Sparrow/Collections **158t**; Alan Barnes/Collections **158b**; Rex Features **159**; Zooid Pictures **162**; Corel **163**; Dunlop Tyres Ltd. **165bl**, **165bc**, **165br**; Andrew Lambert Photography **165t**; JosephSohm; ChromoSohm Inc./Corbis UK Ltd. **165c**; Science Museum/Science & Society Picture Library **170**; Corel **174l**, **174r**; Bettmann/Corbis UK Ltd. **179t**; DIGITAL VISION Ltd. **179b**; Science Museum/Science & Society Picture Library **180**; www.corbis.com/Corbis UK Ltd. **181**; DIGITAL VISION Ltd. **182**

Picture research by Zooid Pictures Limited and Stuart Sweatmore.

Every effort has been made to trace all the copyright holders, but if any have been overlooked the publisher will be pleased to make the necessary arrangements at the first opportunity.